Resumes

FOR

DUMMIES®

6TH EDITION

Resumes FOR DUMMIES®

6TH EDITION

by Joyce Lain Kennedy

WILEY

Wiley Publishing, Inc.

Resumes For Dummies® 6th Edition

Published by
Wiley Publishing, Inc.
111 River St.
Hoboken, NJ 07030-5774
www.wiley.com

WILEY

About the Author

Joyce Lain Kennedy is America's first nationally syndicated careers columnist. Her twice-weekly column, CAREERS NOW, appears in newspapers and Web sites across the land. In her four decades of advising readers — young, senior, and in-between — Joyce has received millions of letters inquiring about career moves and job search and has answered countless numbers of them in print.

Joyce is the author of seven career books, including *Joyce Lain Kennedy's Career Book* (McGraw-Hill), and *Electronic Job Search Revolution, Electronic Resume Revolution,* and *Hook Up, Get Hired! The Internet Job Search Revolution* (the last three published by Wiley Publishing, Inc).

Resumes For Dummies is one of a trio of job market books published under Wiley's wildly popular *For Dummies* branded imprint. *Job Interviews For Dummies,* 3rd Edition, won the coveted Benjamin Franklin Award for best career book of the year, as it did for its first edition. The other book in the suite is *Cover Letters For Dummies,* 3rd Edition, which also received the Benjamin Franklin Award for best career book of the year.

Writing from a San Diego suburb, the country's best-known careers columnist is a graduate of Washington University in St. Louis. Contact Joyce at `jlk@ sunfeatures.com`.

About the Technical Reviewer

James M. Lemke has earned a reputation as a leader in talent strategies and processes. He is director of organizational development for Opportunity International. Previously, Jim spent 15 years as a human resources consultant. His client list included: Real Networks, Southern California Metropolitan Water District, Northrop Grumman, Southwest Airlines, Jet Propulsion Laboratory, United Arab Emirates University, and the White House. Jim has held executive positions with Wachovia Bank, TRW, UCLA, Walt Disney Imagineering, and Raytheon. He resides in Buckeye, Arizona. Contact Jim at `jamesmlemke@gmail.com`.

Author's Acknowledgments

Traci Brink Cumbay, project editor, who enormously improved this book. I appreciate Traci's strong editorial skills, analytic mind, and frank calls for more clarity when I wasn't getting the mush out of my mouth, er . . . computer. Traci's an authentic author's delight.

James M. Lemke, technical editor and reviewer of this book, who cheerfully served his 12th hitch in the role. In addition to his expertise in employment technology, Jim also knows all that's worth knowing about company human resource operations. And what a sense of humor!

Yevgeniy "Yev" Churinov, college student and technical associate, who never met a computer he couldn't fix. His work on this guide was heroic in both writing and technical challenges. Yev is a talent for whom I have great expectations and even greater respect.

Gail Ross, literary agent-attorney and longtime friend, who continues to help me make the right publishing moves. I appreciate you.

Lindsay LeFevere, acquisitions editor for this book, who makes the glue stick and the pages turn in the publishing experience. Lindsay's way out in front in performance and awareness.

Kathryn Kramer Troutman, federal resume authority, who made an enormous contribution to this work with her amazingly quick technique to customize resumes. Good going, Kathryn.

Don Orlando, retired Air Force colonel, career coach, and resume writer, teaches job search skills to transitioning military veterans. I can't say enough good things about the value Don brought to the transition advice section of these pages.

Susan P. Joyce, the CEO of a popular job and career Web site, whom I award a year of gold stars for her immensely helpful coaching on a host of important issues addressed here.

Louise Kursmark, herself the author of acclaimed resume books, who suggested my inclusion of a strategic selection of sample documents that make it easy to distinguish the relationship between social networking online profiles, resumes, and bios.

And bowers of flowers to **Scott Swimley** and **Mark Sugalski,** stalwart sidekicks who assisted in the creation of *The Lemke Guide,* a chart that demystifies resume platforms in a digital age.

Publisher's Acknowledgments

We're proud of this book; please send us your comments at `http://dummies.custhelp.com`. For other comments, please contact our Customer Care Department within the U.S. at 877-762-2974, outside the U.S. at 317-572-3993, or fax 317-572-4002.

Some of the people who helped bring this book to market include the following:

Acquisitions, Editorial, and Media Development

Project Editor: Traci Cumbay

Acquisitions Editor: Lindsay Sandman Lefevere

Copy Editor: Traci Cumbay

Assistant Editor: David Lutton

Technical Editor: James M. Lemke

Editorial Supervisor and Reprint Editor: Carmen Krikorian

Editorial Assistant: Jennette ElNaggar

Art Coordinator: Alicia B. South

Cover Photo: ©istock.com/Andrew Johnson

Cartoons: Rich Tennant (`www.the5thwave.com`)

Composition Services

Project Coordinator: Sheree Montgomery

Layout and Graphics: Joyce Haughey, Julie Trippetti

Proofreaders: Melissa Cossell, Penny L. Stuart

Indexer: Estalita Slivoskey

Publishing and Editorial for Consumer Dummies

    Diane Graves Steele, Vice President and Publisher, Consumer Dummies

    Kristin Ferguson-Wagstaffe, Product Development Director, Consumer Dummies

    Ensley Eikenburg, Associate Publisher, Travel

    Kelly Regan, Editorial Director, Travel

Publishing for Technology Dummies

    Andy Cummings, Vice President and Publisher, Dummies Technology/General User

Composition Services

    Debbie Stailey, Director of Composition Services

Contents at a Glance

Table of Contents

Introduction

A short four years ago, I remember thinking, as I worked on the 5th edition of this guide, that its contents were a radical makeover from previous editions. Yikes! Putting that edition together was a frolic compared to this 6th edition, which contains about 75 percent new text.

My intense study of what's happening on the current recruitment scene reveals a job-search process being reset. In fact, I think of what's happening as a giant thumb pushing a big reset button as I report to you the mind-blowing burst of fresh digital ideas raining down on us — from social networking profiles to resume-capable mobile devices.

Much of what worked before for resume-writing job seekers still pays off handsomely. Eternal verities, you might say. But what you found in the 5th edition about moving along in job life is no longer enough. That's why you absolutely must have this edition right now.

Ready? Push the big reset button . . . *go!* Update your resume, catch up with a wave of new stuff, and find the job you need and want.

About This Book

Resumes For Dummies, 6th Edition, is a playbook showing you how to write powerful and targeted resumes, and how to use them with important new ideas and strategies in your search for a good job. The first seven chapters spotlight the latest resume technology and innovations; the remainder of the book covers timeless resume success factors, as well as samples of winning resumes.

Conventions Used in This Book

To help you navigate this book, I've established the following conventions:

- ✔ *Italic* is used for emphasis and to highlight new words or terms that are defined.
- ✔ Monofont is used for Web addresses.

✓ Sidebars, which are shaded boxes of text, consist of information that's interesting but not necessarily critical to your understanding of the topic.

Further, in the sample resumes throughout the book, I substitute a reminder to add the relevant dates in your resume with the word *dates* enclosed in editorial brackets — [dates] — instead of actual years to keep your attention focused on key resume concepts.

Watch out also for the numbering system I use in the sample resumes in Chapters 14 to 17. I put cross-matching numbers there to guide you through important aspects of each resume, but you don't want to stick numbers in yours.

Foolish Assumptions

I assume you picked up this book for one of the following reasons:

✓ You've never written a resume and want an experienced, friendly hand on your shoulder.

✓ You have written a resume — it got you where you are today — and you want to do better next time.

✓ You like where you are today but want more from life than blooming where you're planted. To move to the next level, your experience tells you that it's time for a resume makeover.

✓ You need a new resume for that great job you heard about but worry that too many competitors will submit virtually the same cookie-cutter document pirated from somewhere. To stop looking like a human photocopy machine, you want to understand resume writing from the ground up.

✓ You've heard about sweeping technology-based changes in the way people and jobs find each other. A realist, you know that technology can't be uninvented. You want to be sure your resume is in sync with the latest updates.

I further assume that you are someone who likes information that cuts to the chase, sometimes with a smile.

How This Book Is Organized

Getting through the job interview door depends on much more than just being a great candidate. This book takes you through everything you need to know about creating your best resumes, getting them into the right hands, and landing interviews. Here's where you find all the legs of the adventure.

Part I: Visiting the World of Resumes, Today and Tomorrow

This part features the latest innovations in Internet-based tools and services on the recruiting scene: social media, smart phones, tablets, and more. You can also refresh your memory of earlier and still popular resume-related technology, as well as discover how to protect or correct your online reputation and privacy.

Part II: Customizing Resumes: Your Many Faces in Many Places

Customized resumes directly aimed at a specific target are smartly replacing generic resumes in all but a few situations. Fortunately, you can customize quickly with new "Custom Lite" techniques explained here. You also find the first technical guide to presenting your resume correctly for new mobile devices. You get the memo on how to steer clear of resume black holes. A rundown of make-or-break resume content rounds out this part.

Part III: Resume Basics That Wow 'Em Every Time

Format, words, and design — all these factors impact the quality of your resume. Read special tips for new graduates, over-50 job seekers, and transitioning military members. Consider answers to specific resume problems, such as work-history gaps or job-hopping. Discover here how best to highlight your good points while downplaying the not-so-good ones. And how to do it all with grace, clarity, and readable style.

Part IV: Bringing It All Together: Sample Resumes

What does an effective resume look like? Turn to this part to find out. Here you get to take a long look at resumes that make use of the strategies I describe in this book. Find resumes from new grads and baby boomers, from nurses and business analysts, and from people who've moved straight up in a career and those who've had a few stumbles. You also see some startling resume makeovers.

Part V: The Part of Tens

In these short chapters, discover quick bits of highly useful information on yet more resume topics. I offer guidance on proving your resume claims, choosing professional resume help, and, finally, using a resume checklist that won't take half a day to complete.

Icons Used in This Book

For Dummies signature icons are the little round pictures you see in the margins of the book. I use them to laser-guide your attention to key bits of information. Here's a list of the icons you find in this book and what they mean.

This icon directs your attention to techniques that cause readers to lavish praise and respect on your resume and then move it to the "you betcha" file.

Some points in these pages are so useful that I hope you keep them in mind as you read. I make a big deal out of these ideas with this icon.

Advice and information that can spark a difference in the outcome of your resume-led job search are flagged with this icon.

Watch out for deep waters filled with things that bite. This icon signals there may be trouble ahead if you don't make a good decision.

Where to Go from Here

Most *For Dummies* books are set up so that you can flip to the section of the book that meets your present needs. You can do that in this book, too. I tell you where to find the information you might need when I refer to a concept, and I define terms as they arise to enable you to feel at home no matter where you open the book.

But this book breaks new ground in resume creation and distribution. To get ahead and stay ahead, start by reading Chapters 1 through 7. In this era of tweeting and texting, they help you say hello to new ideas that offer more reach for your time investment.

P.S. Have you ever forgotten to push "send" on an e-mail and then wondered why your computer wasn't working? Me, too. The good news is that you need not be a techie to make sense out of the innovations described here. And, if by some wild, outside, totally unlikely chance, I didn't explain something clearly enough and you don't get it, grab the nearest teenager and ask for clarification. That's what I do.

Part I
Visiting the World of Resumes, Today and Tomorrow

The 5th Wave   By Rich Tennant

ON YOUR RESUME IT SAYS YOUR LAST WRITING ASSIGNMENT REALLY BROUGHT CUSTOMERS THROUGH THE DOOR.

PUSH   PUSH

In this part . . .

Changes aplenty make the current Web climate different from that of just a couple years ago, and this part
gets you up to date, especially on using the Internet and
social media to help — not hurt — your job-seeking cause.
I also show you how to sift through the myriad online job
boards and how to get your resume into the hands that
can get you the interview.

Chapter 1

Digital Age Changes Job Chase

. . . .

In This Chapter

▶ Growing your career with truly terrific resumes

▶ Blending human know-how with new technology

▶ Staying on the leading edge in job search

. . . .

*A*re resumes outdated? Every few years an employment expert excitedly announces a "new discovery" — that resumes are old hat and unnecessary. The expert advises job seekers to forgo resumes and talk their way into an interview. This advice rarely works in real life. Very few people are eloquent enough to carry the entire weight of an employment marketing presentation without a resume.

A newer resume attack turns not on oratorical talent but on technology. In one scenario, recruiting professionals encourage employers who've grown weary of hiking over mountains of resumes to do away with them, replacing resumes with rigid application forms on the Web — complete with screening questions and tests — to decide who gets offered a job interview.

Another recent scenario — also technology dependent — reflects the view that social networking online profiles are pinch hitting for resumes as self-marketing documents. As I point out in Chapter 2, online profiles are equivalent to generic resumes. Handle them with kid gloves for a very important reason: All-purpose online profiles are likely to be ignored for the vast majority of available jobs.

Resumes Are Here to Stay

At some point in a hunt for better employment, everyone needs effective career marketing communications. That is, everyone needs a resume — or something very much like a resume — that tells the employer why

✔ You're an excellent match for a specific job.

✔ The value you bring matters.

✔ Your skills are essential to the bottom line.

✔ You're worth the money you hope to earn.

✔ You're qualified to solve employer's problems.

✔ Your accomplishment claims can be believed.

Resumes that deliver on these decision points remain at the heart of the job-search ecosystem.

Keeping Up with Resume Times

The ongoing need for terrific resumes doesn't mean the job chase is frozen in time. Far from it. In this digital age — when one-third of women in the 18–34 age range check Facebook when they first wake up, even before they go to the bathroom or brush their teeth — every job seeker needs to embrace the entire fresh package of tools and strategies for getting a new job. The package contains new and traditional components:

✔ Digital tools that are rapidly altering the nature of how jobs are found and filled in America and across the globe.

✔ Timeless know-how and savvy developed by the best employment giants over decades.

New technological ideas standing on the shoulders of historically proven smarts are a winning combination. Technology changes in a decade; human nature doesn't.

Reset your concept of what you must know about resumes in the job chase. Writing great resumes is no longer enough. You must know how to distribute those resumes to people who can hire you, or at least can move you along in the process.

This book combines the details of how to create marvelous resumes, and also puts a microscope on various technological delivery options in the digital age. This chapter previews what's ahead in this comprehensive guide to resumes, and how to use resumes and other career marketing communications you need to reach your goal in the great job chase.

The targeted resume rules

Job seekers, brace yourselves: Trolling the job market is getting ever trickier and requires considerably more effort than the last time you baited your resume hook — even a short five years ago. The *generic resume* is at the top of the list of job search tools on the way out. (Read all about it in Chapter 6.)

Of friends and resumes

"The number one way to use your OnTarget resume is to find a friend to walk it into the hiring manager's office or recruiter's office with the friend's stamp of approval," advises Mark Mehler, cofounder and principal of CareerXroads and a long-time Internet job hunting expert. He says his firm's annual survey of how people get hired at major corporations shows that one out of three openings is filled this way.

You probably have an all-purpose resume lying around in a desk drawer somewhere. What legions of job seekers everywhere like about the all-purpose resume is that it casts a wide net to snag the attention of many employers — and it saves time for those of us who are too busy getting through the day to keep writing different resumes for different jobs. I appreciate that. But your one-size-fits-all work of art is obsolete, and it's getting lost in more and more recruiting sinkholes.

The generic resume has been replaced by the *targeted resume* (which I refer to in this book as OnTarget), a customized resume tailor-made for a specific employment opportunity.

An OnTarget resume is a valuable marketing tool to convince the reader your work will benefit a specific employer and that you should make the cut of candidates invited in for a closer look. An OnTarget resume

✔ Addresses a given opportunity, showing clearly how your qualifications are a close match to a job's requirements.

✔ Uses powerful words to persuade and clean design to attract interest.

✔ Plays up strengths and downplays any factor that undermines your bid for an interview.

Unfit resumes are zapped

The word got out, slowly at first. And then — *whoosh!* — millions of job seekers found out how easy it is to instantly put an online resume in the hands of employers across the country as well as across town.

Post and pray became the job seeker's mantra as everyone figured out how to manipulate online resumes and click them into the online world as quickly as fast-shuffling dealers lay down cards at casino tables.

Resume overload began in the first phase of the World Wide Web, a time frame of about 1994 to 2005. It became exponentially larger and more frustrating as commercial resume-blasting services appeared on the scene. Almost overnight, it seemed, anyone willing to pay the price could splatter resume confetti everywhere an online address could be found.

The consequences of resume spamming for employers were staggering: Despite their use of the era's best recruiting selection software, employers were overrun with unsolicited, disorganized generic resumes containing everything but the kitchen sink.

And what about the job seekers who sent all those generic, unstructured resumes? They were left to wonder in disappointment why they never heard a peep from the recipient employer.

The answer's in the numbers: A job advertised online by a major company creates a feeding frenzy of many thousands of resumes. Employment databases are hammered with such mismatches as sales clerks and sports trainers applying for jobs as scientists and senior managers, and vice versa.

Tried-and-true techniques remain

A resume that doesn't show off the great goods you're selling isn't worth much. Show off your assets in effective style by making sure that you follow the suggestions in this book. I show you how to

- ✔ Choose the resume format that fits your goals and situation. What goes where in a resume isn't a one-size-fits-all consideration. An example: Whether you lead with your education or the qualifications that suit you for the job depends on which job you want. Chapter 9 tells you about formatting your resume and provides templates for popular resume designs.

- ✔ Get your points across in powerful language. Make your strengths stronger by describing them in vibrant language that stands tall. I give you examples in Chapter 10.

- ✔ Use design techniques effectively. Big chunks of text cause eye strain (and boredom). Present your information in a way that enables readers instead of inhibiting them. Chapter 11 shows you how.

- ✔ Overcome hurdles. Getting attention from potential employers is harder in certain situations. If you're just getting out of school, for example, you have to overcome some less-than-ideal perceptions. Chapter 12 gives you suggestions for easing your transition into a new phase of life. Chapter 13 helps you manage any bits of your background that may turn off employers.

Web code ups privacy fears

In the next few years, a new heavy-duty technology for computers and mobile devices will become available to Web developers and may give marketers and advertisers a clear shot at who you are and what you've been up to.

The new technology is a Web language called HTML5. It buries "supercookies" in your computer that are difficult to ditch. The supercookies track your data — including e-mail and site visits — and hide the data in at least ten places on your computer where third parties can access it. Already in limited use, HTML5

has an upside: It makes your browsing easier (and faster — no retyping of usernames and passwords, for instance).

As with any feature of this magnitude, problems will inevitably surface. Who knows what damage supercookie snooping will do to your online reputation? As Pam Dixon, executive director of the World Privacy Forum in California, told a newspaper reporter: "HTML5 opens Pandora's box of tracking on the Internet."

Send your resume off to job market battle by leading with strength: Feature your most impressive career accomplishments and honors at the top of page one, not tucked in as afterthoughts on page two. This simple strategy encourages employers to read the whole thing.

Technologies Facilitate Job Search

After the Internet caught job-search fire in the mid-1990s — instantly whisking resumes to and fro — little new technology changed the picture until the social Web groundswell burst upon us in the mid-2000s. Now job seekers have the tools to

- ✔ Use social networks to dramatically enlarge personal networks
- ✔ Tap their networks to identify jobs and for recommendations
- ✔ Go directly to hiring authorities
- ✔ Market accomplishments in professional profiles
- ✔ Pinpoint employment targets with position-mapping

Continue to apply for jobs with a customized resume and cover letter, just as you've done so far. Classic job searching methods continue to pay off, but they're not enough in an economy where jobs have gone missing.

Work every day on a well-rounded approach that includes the whole enchi-lada — from face-to-face networking, job boards, print ads, and professional associations, to the dazzling array of new social Web tools.

Social networking scoops jobs

Enormously popular social networking sites and social media are poised to gain even more fans in the employment process. Chapter 2 reports on the state of the industry and suggests how you can "go social."

I expect a never-ending stream of new technical bells and whistles in going social. Location awareness is one example of what's new. When Facebook launched its Places feature in late 2010, social media expert Charlene Li explained: "Until now, Facebook knew who you were, what you are doing, and when you did it. Now they add an even richer dimension — where you are — that completes the picture." Facebook added Places to its posts, a smart phone app, and a mobile site.

How can a location-aware feature facilitate a job chase? Suppose you're look-ing for a retail or restaurant job in a given locale. The activity stream of a location feature indicates which restaurants and retail stores are the most popular — and, thus, good prospects for employment.

For breaking news about social networking, become acquainted with the fol-lowing two Web sites:

- **Mashable** (www.mashable.com) is a top guide to social media and a hub for those looking to make sense of the online ream.

- **Altimeter Group** (www.altimetergroup.com) focuses on all things social, including the new field of social commerce. Be sure to read the Group's admirable disclosure policy.

Chapter 5 discusses ways to keep your online reputation in good shape for the job search.

Mobile's on the move

Smart phones came on fast. Tablet computers are picking up steam. Mobile communication is what's new and it's already happening. Even when you're not rooted to a desktop computer, you can send and receive e-mails, network online, and download apps. Chapter 3 examines the latest in mobile job chasing.

Quick-change process customizes content

In this employers' market, you may have to apply for 100 times as many jobs as you would in a candidates' market. As Chapter 6 details, the generic resume has become a nonstarter, and successful seekers are writing customized resumes.

Time is the problem: How can you whip out effective customized resumes and still get three hours of sleep at night? Expert Kathryn Troutman answers that perplexing question in Chapter 6 as she steps you through an eye-opening "Custom Lite" resume process.

Resumes find digital docks

Here's a digital definition of frustration: Craft a perfect resume that looks and markets like a jewel only to discover that your intended digital dock, or *platform* — job board, Web site, recruiting firm, smart phone, and so on — won't accept anything but plain text. There is a solution, and Jim Lemke, this book's technical editor, neatly packed the answers into chart form; find the Lemke Guide in Chapter 7.

Bios gain new importance

The short professional bio (see the Sarah Tobin bio in Chapter 2) is positioned for immense popularity, thanks to social media. The short bio helps when you want to apply for a job, network, post on a guest blog, and so on. It tells people quickly who you are, what you do, and why they should care.

Plan on writing a bio in three lengths — a micro bio, a short bio, and a longer bio. A micro bio is a sentence you can use on your Twitter profile (140 characters). A short bio is a paragraph (about 100 words). A long bio can be up to a page.

"YourName.com" becomes vital

More people are living their lives on the Internet, and episodes of name high-jacking are rising. Realization is mushrooming that controlling the exclusive online rights to your own name makes sense, even if you're not a business owner.

When technology fails: The human antidote

The job market is made up of A-list candidates and B-list candidates (and many candidates who are perceived to be farther down the alphabetic scale).

If you're a seasoned worker, have you ever noticed that A-list candidates are typically younger than you and have recently done the very job the employer is trying to fill?

On the other hand, when you're a rookie, does it seem as though those on the A-list are typically older than you and have recently done the very job the employer is trying to fill?

The definition of frustration is when you are treated like an ant at a picnic because you're not perceived as an A- or B-list candidate.

Unfortunately, your exclusion rate from interview offers may be high when the employer uses online recruiting tools.

An answer to your dilemma. Get personal.

✔ Develop your own job leads by doing substantial research, and then target your resume.

✔ Network your way to a referral chain, asking each of 20 or more people whom you call daily: "Who else should I be talking to?"

✔ Follow up on job ads, but diffuse the crushing competition by figuring out who the hiring manager is and contact that decision-maker directly. You can even write a resume letter (see Chapter 9) to that person, but do not mention the job ad. Your approach is that you've been researching companies where your excellent qualifications may be a good fit. Even if this "happy coincidence" causes the hiring manager to send your resume to the HR department, now it arrives from an important executive and is likely be examined.

✔ Remember that the vast majority of jobs are found in small businesses. Some aren't yet using modern job-search tools and will value your person-to-person approach.

You can protect your identity in its purest Web form by buying a domain for your name — YourName.com. You can also purchase a URL (Web address) for your resume — YourNameresume.com. See chapters 2 and 5 to see why owning your own name has gained red-alert status in a digital age. Claim your name!

Chapter 2

Finding Your Next Job in the Wide World of Social Media

In This Chapter

▶ Appreciating what social job search can do for you

▶ Tying into top-rated social networking sites

▶ Creating profiles and bios you're proud of

▶ Discovering a treasure trove of social networking tips

*T*he familiar adage claiming the secret to landing a good job "is not what you know, but who you know" is hereby officially stamped incomplete in this era of online social connectivity. Consider this revised version: The secret to landing a good job is what you know, who you know, who knows you, and who your friends know.

All this knowing is exploding on the Web on *social networking sites,* a big part of *social media.* The terms overlap in popular usage and definitions vary widely. Here's my take:

✔ **Social networking sites** are Web venues with huge online databases of information individuals have uploaded about themselves. They do it to mingle with other people in the site's database — to put themselves "out there." Their autobiographical information is public or semi-public and usually includes a description of who they are (a *profile*) and/or a short biography (a *bio*).

Many social networkers just want to hang around with each other. Others aim to grow their circle of acquaintances. Still others are interested in a specific subject (like dating or business). Social networking sites typically have a personal focus, but a growing number operate with a professional purpose.

✔ **Social media** — also known as *new media* — is a set of technologies and channels that enable a virtual community to interact in the same space. Social media includes a wide variety of forums, ranging from social sharing sites, such as YouTube and Flickr, to social networking sites, such as LinkedIn and Facebook.

There's little question that two-way communication on the interactive Web is dramatically changing the game for job seekers and recruiters alike. If you're scratching your head about how social networking actually works, and are unsure how to use it to find a job and promote your career, this is a chapter you won't want to miss.

The Sweeping Reach of Social Networking

Reflecting the shape of job search now and job search to come, social networking dominates Internet use. At a half-billion strong, Facebook alone claims 54 percent of the world's Internet population as visitors. Bigger than most countries, Facebook has more users than the United States has citizens.

What's more, the growth rate of social networking is startling: The number of people visiting social media sites keeps rising — the numbers increased by 24 percent between 2009 and 2010. Social networking doesn't appear to be a fad but an honest-to-goodness paradigm shift in the way people do business on the globe, including the business of finding employment.

Begin now to think about how to harness this new power that offers a double rainbow of job-search help — from direct access to hiring managers and quick identification of potential allies at prospective employers, to easy look-ups on company profiles and obtaining posted endorsements from your network. Just to keep it interesting, different services offer different features. (Similarly, some charge fees and others are free.)

But, at root, the many benefits of using social networking services for career management and job-hunting fall into two basic categories. In signing on with one or more social networking services, you are

- **Showing the world how hirable you are.** By filling out profiles and list-ing your credentials, you advertise your potential or immediate avail-ability on an "e-billboard" that helps recruiters and employers find you.

- **Gathering supporters to hold open doors.** When you collect, connect, and network with friendly contacts, you gain a potential source of refer-rals, get updates on their employers' hiring modes, receive insider fill-ins on company culture, and uncover other useful information.

Scout sites that may be useful for a job search in the social networking clouds by running a Web search for "List of social networking websites." You're rewarded with a hearty list of active (non-dating) sites.

Eyeing the Big Three of Social Networking Job Search

Of the countless social networking services available to you, three services top the charts in career management and job-search potential: LinkedIn, Facebook, and Twitter.

Because the music plays on but the lyrics keep changing in online networking tools, jump on the Web site of each social network to obtain the service's latest operating guides and opportunities. Here's a starting peek at each of the three industry leaders.

LinkedIn keeps focus on professionals

If you're a professional, managerial, or executive job searcher, LinkedIn (www.linkedin.com) is the big-league social site you want. Its 80 million worldwide members swing for the fences. Totally business focused? LinkedIn is your online chance to put a home run up on the board.

Unsurprisingly, case histories of LinkedIn members using the professional social network to find jobs keep rolling out. Here are the LI experiences of three people in the Pacific Northwest:

- ✔ A laid-off engineer landed a promising new post paying more money at a financial services Web site. This happened shortly after a headhunter found the engineer's job status on LI had been changed from "current" to "past."

- ✔ A radio station marketing manager lost his job and decided to post a forthright status note: "I'm up for grabs, who wants me?" Someone in his network saw it and referred him as a candidate for the position of programs and events manager at a city's chamber of commerce organization. The former radio man cinched the job offer a week later.

- ✔ A woman decided to dramatically refocus her employment pursuits on outer space. Lacking contacts with specialists in that part of the universe, her career coach suggested she use LinkedIn to find industry contacts. The wannabe E.T. expert used LinkedIn to land two relevant internships, plus a volunteer gig promoting a space frontier conference.

Sampling LinkedIn benefits buffet

LinkedIn keeps new service features coming at a brisk pace while extending its global reach around the world. Already LinkedIn overflows with free ways job seekers can work the job market scene. The following options are the tip of the iceberg:

✔ **Posting a profile.** An LI profile contains the same information as your generic resume. (See Chapter 6 to find out more about generic and customized resumes.) You include your work history, education, competencies, and skills. "Open to opportunities" means you're unemployed or about to be, trying to move from part-time to full-time work, or just seeking greener pastures.

✔ **Expanding your network.** By "working social," you can continue to add voices to your chorus of colleagues, creating a strong source of referrals and endorsements. You want to stand out, but you don't have to stand alone when you need professional helping hands.

✔ **Joining groups.** Much like participating in traditional professional associations and trade groups, LI affinity groups offer camaraderie according to particular occupation, career field, or industry. If no existing group zeroes in on your requirements, start your own.

Each group maintains a job-posting area where recruiting and hiring managers post their openings before word gets out; as a group member, you see all the posted job openings while they're fresh. Each LI member can join up to 50 groups.

✔ **Periscoping your future.** When you're puzzling over how next to position yourself to reach career goals, LinkedIn Career Explorer can help. Based on its database of real-life personal and company profiles, the LinkedIn service shows what happened to others in your shoes, names companies where you might work, forecasts how much money you can make, and identifies by name the kinds of people you might meet along the way.

✔ **Consuming news.** LinkedIn's Signal is an innovative service that saves you time and annoyance at TMI (too much information). By using a series of filters — such as network, industry, company, time published, school, and the most popular hashtags for Twitter — members cut through news feeds and Twitter tweets to get only what they select. Signal enables you to search for specific keywords or topics you'd like to keep up to steam on, such as colleagues or business rivals, or a company you'd like to work for.

✔ **Premium search tools.** If you want to rev up your free search, choose the enhanced version of LinkedIn by paying between $20 and $50 a month for one of three premium levels and get benefits like these:

- Top billing for your profile (comparable to a sponsored link on Google's first page)

- The ability to communicate with hiring managers, even those outside your network

- Access to full profiles of hiring decision makers

LinkedIn upshot

If you feel you can devote serious job search and career management time to only one social network, make it LinkedIn, the recruiters' favorite. According to a recent social recruiting survey, 86 percent of hiring companies in the United States use LinkedIn in their recruiting process. (The same survey reports 60 percent of recruiting responders use Facebook, and 50 percent use Twitter.)

The orientation time to sharpen your skills on LinkedIn may cost you a few nights out on the town, but after you get the hang of it, you'll be glad you're linked in with other people who are as willing to help you as you are to help them.

Facebook hands adults important search tools

The age curve of the world's half-billion Facebook users still breaks along generational lines — the vast bulk of Facebook membership remains on the sunny side of 40. But an older demographic is moving in like a carrier task force sensing professional networking and job-finding opportunities in uncharted waters.

Newbies and long-time Facebook users alike lose if they snooze past the frequent site remodels. In late 2010, for example, the site created a new tool called "Download Your Information." It enables you to download to your computer everything you've ever posted on Facebook, including your messages, wall posts, photos, status updates, and profile information.

Facebook is wonderful for chat, status updates, or wall posts to keep your friends and family wired into your life. The social site is also a convenient way to remind your contacts to keep you in mind if they get wind of a job that could blow in your direction, as indicated by the story of a young woman in the American capitol:

> I used Facebook to get my current job and I couldn't be happier. Last year I posted several status updates about my job. A friend of a friend saw the posts and e-mailed me about an opportunity at [the federal agency where she worked]. I went in for an interview and three days later (light speed in the federal government), I had a job offer.

Sampling Facebook benefits buffet

Facebook is a runaway success offering a heavy slice of opportunities to move forward with your plans for the future. Here are a handful of those opportunities:

✔ **Networking to useful faces.** Many of your colleagues and the professionals in your field are on Facebook — or likely soon will be. Remember to update your status with your current job situation and what you're looking for. When you're in full job-hunt mode, keep your network in the loop with regular progress reports — you don't want them to forget to help you.

The interactive Facebook crowd includes prospective employers (solo operators, recruiters, hiring managers, and human resource specialists). Because Facebook is not a professional network (like LinkedIn), contacting employers through FB can help you get noticed because there's less competition from other job seekers.

✔ **Looking at job listings.** Check out Facebook Marketplace for local job listings. Although Facebook's Marketplace isn't comprehensive, you likely face less competition for jobs posted there.

✔ **Milking groups.** Groups on Facebook are virtually the same as groups on LinkedIn — a place to share breaking news and developments of collective interest. Join up or start groups for a topic, industry, or interest. By hanging out with people who care about the same things you do, you'll be noticed and in a good spot to hear about unadvertised jobs in the hidden job market, as well as advertised jobs you might otherwise overlook.

✔ **Cruising relevant pages.** Stay abreast of what's up on Facebook's job site pages and company pages. When you spot a company you'd like to work for, click that you "like" its page and get company news that may aid your job search.

✔ **Personalizing your search.** Because Facebook has integrated with prominent job search engine SimplyHired, you can try to find jobs through your Facebook friends. After you hop on `www.simplyhired.com`, find jobs you want, click on the "Who Do I Know" button at the top of search results to see your Facebook friends at the company and send private "can you help me?" inquiries to them.

✔ **Creating a Web presence.** Even when you don't operate your own Web site (most people don't), you can be on digital deck with a profile on Facebook. Direct viewers to your profile with a vanity address that reflects your name, like this: `www.facebook.com/NathanJoseinsky`.

Facebook upshot

Facebook has won the hearts of a big slice of the younger population for finding friends, classmates, staying in touch, gossiping, and more. A number of late-to-the-party older (that is, above age 35) members find Facebook useful as a communications bonanza for job searching and promoting their personal brands.

Twitter opens quick, slick paths to employers

Free, personal, and highly mobile, Twitter is a Web-based message-distribution system for posting messages of up to a concise 140 characters. (If you guessed that the preceding sentence was, with spaces, exactly 140 characters, you're right. Like wit, brevity is the soul of Twitter talking.)

Twitter talk describes your activities for *followers* — people who want to keep track of what you're up to. You can include links to other content in your messages, including a resume you've stashed on the Web. A Twitter message is known as a *tweet;* the verb is *to tweet;* the forwarding of other people's tweets is *retweeting.*

Until recently, Twitter was commonly seen as the social site for trivial pursuits — specializing in the "I'm having a veggie sandwich for lunch" kind of thing. But current traffic counts changed that perception, giving Twitter new respect.

Statistics suggest that about 200 million visitors worldwide now use Twitter, generating about 70 million tweets a day. Americans who are familiar with Twitter surged to 87 percent in 2008, up from 5 percent two years earlier. A recent study for marketing and advertising firms reveals Twitter's power in spreading messages far and wide: "The majority of Twitter users never post anything . . . but they are definitely reading and clicking."

Twitter offers a stable of techniques to make a successful job search materialize for you, including bumping up your visibility and connecting with employment targets.

One of the techniques — inspiring a friend to tweet for you — is illustrated by the case of a young Chicago woman who told a pal she hoped to find an internship in public relations but was having zero luck. Her friend tweeted a marketing pitch: "Anyone hiring for a PR internship? I know a well-qualified candidate on the hunt." A follower of the tweeter immediately responded with an offer. An internship was born at a start-up PR firm in Chicago that, after graduation, morphed into a full-time job.

Direct pitching for yourself on Twitter is another way to go. When a woman was laid off from an Idaho-based computer company, she packed up her desk and on the way out tweeted: "Just been laid off from XYZ computer company." By the time the newly minted employment seeker left the parking lot, she had a job offer from a friend who ran a local Web development company.

Sampling Twitter benefits buffet

"Short is sweet" describes Twitter's ability to communicate big ideas in a few words, a feature increasingly appreciated by job searchers and those who advise them. Here's a taste of Twitter.

- **Speeding toward jobs.** In a job market where every opening attracts unbelievable numbers of resumes and often closes application within the first 24 to 48 hours, speed counts. Through Twitter, you can get new openings sent to you before most recruiters get them by following the right tweeters.

- **Getting tweets from job boards.** Monster reaches out to job seekers in its database to encourage them to apply on Monster for jobs matching their qualifications. Other job boards that tweet jobs announce the collaboration on their Web sites.

- **Following recruiters and hiring managers.** You can seek out and follow recruiters and get early dibs on breaking job opportunities.

- **Tweeting for help.** Here are examples of tweets you can send to kick-start a job search:

  - I'm looking for a sales job. Not retail. Here's resume link. Can anyone push it around?

  - I'm trying to get hired in accounting by XYZ corp. Know anyone inside who could walk my resume to HR or acct. mgr?

  - Will you set up meeting, or can I call using your recommendation?

  - Have you seen any great job postings for insurance claims adjusters? Pls advise.

  - Hey, 300 pals: Who'll rehearse me for big job interview?

  - Just interviewed for job you don't want? Maybe I do. Try me.

- **Researching with hashtags.** A *hashtag* is any word in Twitter immediately preceded by the pound symbol (#). Examples: #marketing, #healthcare, #engineering. Hashtags corral all tweets that contain the same hashtag, letting you easily track down a topic.

- **Teaming up with Twitter sidekicks.** Twitter Search (`www.twitter search.com`) is a Twitter-operated service that searches the service for jobs. Additionally, legions of third-party ancillary Web sites have appeared to cash in on the enormous volume of data Twitter generates. The third-party sites are free. Examples:

  - JobShouts.com (`www.jobshouts.com`) tweets job openings to Twitter-users.

  - Twitjobsearch.com (`www.twitjobsearch.com`) is a job search engine that scrapes Twitter for the jobs that match keywords you enter, and you can apply if the particulars are right for you.

- JobDeck (www.jobdeck.com) searches for jobs and connects you with your contacts on Twitter, Facebook, and LinkedIn.

- TweetMyJobs (www.tweetmyjobs.com) compiles open positions from thousands of companies worldwide.

- Listorious.com (www.listorious.com) lists people of interest in your target companies or profession.

Twitter upshot

Twitter is a great channel for quickly sharing news, asking questions, and connecting. At a basic level, it's simple to use. You can find helpful insider employment news by following the right people. Unlike LinkedIn and Facebook, you need not ask for anyone's acceptance — you just click "follow" on a Twitter user's name and you're in the game.

Making Sure Online Profiles Capture Your Best Side

Social networking is an A-team option in today's job market because job seekers want to be where recruiters and hiring managers can find them. But the truth is that online profiles on networking sites can help or harm your job search. I discuss the upside and downside to online profiles in this section, and suggest tips to gain the best of all possible outcomes.

Let's hear it for profiles!

In the social networking job world, visibility is the name of the game, and that's why online professional profiles have become favorite self-marketing instruments. Consider the profile's virtues:

- **Get discovered.** Job finding is a numbers game. The more prudent information you include in your public profile about your marketable qualifications — and the more social networking sites where you post it — the more employers who can find you and the more they learn about you to incite their interest. The more employers who become interested in what you have to offer, the higher the bidding is likely to be for your services.

- **Advance references.** A public profile equips your networking supporters to recommend you as a candidate when they come across a job you may want.

> ✔ **Broadcast your branding.** By creating a potent online presence that sells your competencies, skills, and talents, you boost your personal brand. Your brand is the buzz about you, what you are known for, your personal reputation — how you are distinguished by accomplishments and characteristics.

For more information about branding, read *Me 2.0: Build a Powerful Brand to Achieve Career Success* by Dan Schawbel (Kaplan) and *Find a Job Through Social Networking* by Diane Crompton and Ellen Sautter (JIST Publishing).

Not all profiles should be cheered

Wait. Not so fast. Even the best of online profiling moves aren't immune from built-in problems that can leave craters in your search. As you craft a carefully written profile, be aware of potential troublemakers.

A public profile on a social networking site is a kind of generic resume. Because an online profile is static in the presentation of a job seeker's qualifications, it isn't changed and customized to match a specific job. (I discuss the vast advantages of customizing resumes in Chapter 6.)

The all-purpose profile works fine when you anticipate staying in the same field or career cluster. A *career cluster* is a grouping of occupations and broad industries based on commonalities, such as medicine, criminal justice, or construction.

But a public online profile can cause you to be passed over by recruiters when you're trying to change careers — when you're an editor who wants to become a chef, for instance. And a static public online profile can leave you out of consideration for jobs that your abilities and background qualify you for.

Employers perennially rank good communication as a must-have skill in candidates. Nothing shrieks poor communication skills and sloppy work louder than poor grammar and faulty spelling in online profiles. The eyes of the world are upon you.

A further risk in posting a public online professional profile is being *pigeonholed* — perceived as being a good fit for only one kind of professional role. When you're pigeonholed, boundaries are put up around you, limiting the directions in which you're free to move.

Even after you initially gain an employer's attention, an interested employer is motivated to turn over many online stones to confirm his or her original judgment. An inappropriate focus or stray fact on a static profile can cause reconsideration of your value — your customized resume says you're a marketing specialist, but your profile emphasizes your hotel management experience. Whoops!

Great tips for great profiles

Ensure that your social networking profiles produce big rewards and don't spoil your chances of landing the new job you want by following these suggestions:

✔ **Focus on workplace relevance.** A social networking profile can be much longer than a resume, but a profile is neither a life history nor an employment application. The trick is the right selection of content. Chapter 8 tells you more about the subject matter employers expect to see when reviewing your qualifications for employment.

✔ **Consider photo ops.** The way you look can draw viewers to — or away from — you. Think young, trim, good-looking vs. old, fat, ugly; human nature isn't always politically correct — or fair. Moreover, if a potential employer looks at your photo and is reminded of a much unloved relative or competitor, you're toast.

When you're undecided about using a photo in your online profile, you can play it safe by substituting an avatar, which is a graphical character representing a person. If you do use a photo, make it a professional-looking headshot.

✔ **Stay current with profile pages.** Technology changes with the season, and the flow of new products never stops. You can stay current by periodically checking SocialMediaToday.com.

✔ **Display your profile widely.** After you've sweated through the crafting of your perfect profile, link it with LinkedIn, Facebook, Twitter, and other social networking sites.

✔ **Load up on keywords.** After completing your profile (never leave it unfinished or you look like a quitter), review it for a healthy helping of search-engine friendly keywords that describe your qualifications that will help hiring honchos find you, maybe even before they post a job ad.

✔ **Entice with endorsements.** Include recommendations from former managers, colleagues, customers, and vendors. Shy about asking? Start by offering to write recommendations for them — maybe they'll return the favor.

✔ **Strike a balance.** If you're vulnerable to the pigeonholing trap — you are changing careers or you qualify for multiple roles — watch what you say in your social networking documents. And take care not to look like a liar by allowing your profile to unmask a history that contradicts the one you present in a customized resume.

Your best strategy: Selectively show the breadth of your capabilities without coming across as a jack of all trades but master of none. Except for small companies, employers prefer to hire a specialist for many of the best jobs. Balancing the appeal of your profile can be tricky, which is why you may want to consult an experienced professional resume writer for help with it. Chapter 20 contains guidelines for choosing writers and career coaches.

E-mail no longer king?

As a new generation of social networking services compete for a leading place in the new world's sun — just as e-mail did in the 1990s — forecasters speculate that the social shift will profoundly rewrite the way we communicate — in ways we can only begin to imagine. The reign of e-mail as king of communications is over, say some pundits. What do you think?

Scope Out Top Profile Samples

Trying to write an online profile for your job search but can't seem to come up with anything you think is good enough to post? Debating whether your profile should be compact or comprehensive? Puzzling over differences between a social networking profile, a resume, and a bio for the same individual? Heavy duty help is here in the next seven pages of sample documents.

These samples illustrate how today's classiest online documents can look. Study the samples and be inspired to bring your own career management products up to first-class quality.

The professionally produced samples include four documents: two profiles, a resume, and a bio — all written by world-class writers Louise Kursmark and Wendy Enelow, directors of the Resume Writing Academy (www.resume writingacademy.com), a leading comprehensive training program for aspiring resume writers. Here's what the samples show:

✔ Figure 2-1 is a one-page online profile for fictional Pilar Morales. Notice the simple but eye-catching screened summary at the top.

✔ Figure 2-2 is a five-page online profile for fictional Sarah Tobin, tailored for LinkedIn. Online profiles can run four or five pages, substantially longer than most resumes. Unlike resumes, profile pages after page one need not be name-labeled or numbered.

✔ Figure 2-3 is a two-page resume for Sarah Tobin. Tobin's resume is a handsome plain-text document that includes white space and is enhanced with design elements created by keyboard.

✔ Figure 2-4 is Sarah's short one-page bio. As social networking sites flourish, it's a good idea to create a polished and informative bio that you can place on many sites, including ZoomInfo (www.zoominfo.com). Notice that Sarah includes plenty of branding and accomplishments in this short, info-packed document.

In reviewing the last three documents for Sarah Tobin, note how her online profile, resume, and bio differ in layout and amount of information but remain consistent to a theme — Sarah Tobin is a high-end candidate.

PILAR MORALES

PROFESSIONAL PROFILE

Pilar Morales is a top achiever in sales and marketing of new home communities.

With experience in direct sales, sales management and training, marketing, and design for recognized leaders in residential development, she has closed millions of dollars in sales and played an influential role in the success of new home communities, innovative marketing strategies, and top sales teams.

After an early career in retail sales and management in Miami, Pilar transitioned to the real estate industry in Arizona in [date]. She quickly rose to top seller ranks for Regal Homes and Desert Builders, then relocated to California to join Adams Communities in Los Angeles.

RECOGNITION • EDUCATION • INDUSTRY CERTIFICATION
- Sales Team of the Year
- Lifetime Million Dollar Circle
- Platinum Million Dollar Circle (Sales Management)
- Prism Sales Awards
- Prism Design Awards
- CSP (Certified Sales Professional)
- MIRM (Member, Institute of Residential Marketing)
- California Real Estate Broker License

In [date] Pilar joined West Coast Homes in San Diego. Advancing rapidly to VP of Sales, Marketing, and Design, she held full responsibility for the company's 3500-sq.-ft. design center and all marketing, advertising, and sales programs. Under her leadership, sales revenues jumped 60% in [date] and 175% in [date], and members of her sales team earned Rookie of the Year, Salesperson of the Year, and Sales Manager of the Year at the [date] Star Awards.

As marketing manager, Pilar led a comprehensive rebranding for West Coast Homes and established the brand across all of the company's communities. Her design efforts transformed the sales centers and earned two Star awards for model merchandising. She increased the efficiency and effectiveness of the design center, enhanced sales training, and improved communication with buyers during the construction process. Her focus on customer service and customer needs assessment consistently resulted in exceptional customer satisfaction.

Since the acquisition of West Coast by Magna Homes in [date], Pilar has been working independently and with an established developer in direct sales of new and resale condominiums in Southern California. She possesses the expertise, drive, creativity, customer focus, and interpersonal skills to continue her record as a top performer.

Sane Diego, CA 92115
555•555-2345

Louise Kursmark and Wendy Enelow

Figure 2-1: Social networking profile of Pilar Morales.

Sarah Tobin, CNPDP
Product Development Leader – Technology & Telecom / CPG / Business Services
Gaining competitive edge through innovation

San Francisco Bay Area • Information Technology and Services

Current	• **Director Next Generation Product Development at SolutionTech**
Past	• **Director Product Development at XYZ Retail Networks** • **Manager New Product Development – Advanced Broadband Services** at Verizon • **Product Manager – Verizon@Home** at Verizon • **Teleconferencing Manager at AP Media Services**
Education	**California State University** BS Finance [dates] **ScrumMaster Certification** [date] **Villanova University** Six Sigma Green Belt [date] **Product Development and Management Association (PDMA)** Certified New Product Development Professional [date]
Recommendations	**13** people have recommended Sarah
Connections	**349** connections
Websites	• Solutiontech.com • Product Development and Management Association (PDMA)
Twitter	• ProductDeveloper
Public Profile	http://www.linkedin.com/in/sarahtobin

Louise Kursmark and Wendy Enelow

Figure 2-2: Social networking profile of Sarah Tobin.

Summary

I am a Product Development leader with a passion for delivering "what's next" and improving "what's now" for companies that value innovation as a market advantage. In a fast-track career through product development roles in diverse industries, I have had a measurable impact on revenue, market penetration, and product innovation.

An overview of my career includes these highlights:

* SolutionTech: Built a world-class product development organization for this global business outsourcing provider with clients in 52 countries on 4 continents.

* XYZ Retail Networks: Headed product development teams in repeated launches of new media products for some the world's largest retailers (Wal-Mart, Target, Costo, Best Buy).

* Verizon Broadband Division: Led innovations including orchestrating the development, testing and market launch of the company's first residential broadband service.

Primarily focused on technology innovation, I excel at both the art and the science of product development. Specifically, my expertise includes research and development (R&D), pipeline development, market-validity testing, co-development partnerships, technology transfers, technology joint ventures, customer presentations, and key account relationship management (in partnership with sales, marketing, and business development teams).

I am highly experienced in managing product teams and driving adoption of product development best practices that have been recognized as not only the standard within the company, but as the industry standard and model.

I thrive on challenge and am known as an innovator, change driver, and product evangelist. My expertise helps companies deliver on the promise of their ideas, capture new customers, expand into new markets, and outpace/outperform the competition.

* Next-Generation Product Development
* Technology Commercialization
* Team Leadership
* Continuous Process Improvement
* Six Sigma
* ScrumMaster
* CNPDP – PDMA

Specialties
Performance Highlights

* Twice built agile product development organizations from the ground up, keeping companies on the cutting edge.

* Thwarted competitive threat at XYZ Retail Networks by launching rapid-development process that speeded time-to-market by 60%.

* Built Verizon's first residential broadband service from zero to $6M annual revenue in 18 months.

Experience
Director, Next-Generation Product Development at SolutionTech
Global business outsourcing provider of business-support solutions
[dates]

Brought on board to create a world-class product development organization. Hit the ground running in entirely new industry and quickly ramped up product innovation while establishing the structure, processes, and metrics essential for a top-quality product-development function.

Won Internet Telephony "Product of the Year" award.

4 recommendations for this position

Director, Product Development at XYZ Retail Networks
World's leading retail media company
[dates]

Strengthened product-development capability, melding creativity with process/structure to harness innovation and ensure sustainable success. Recruited to company that was on the leading edge of a new advertising space (captive retail networks) but needed discipline, structure, and repeatability in its product development department. Provided expert leadership to build the idea pipeline, justify development, and quickly bring ideas from concept to customer.

Delivered multiple new products ahead of schedule and under budget and instilled innovation and process excellence as a way of life. Earned XYZ's "Outstanding Achievement Award."

5 recommendations for this position

Manager, New Product Development, Advanced Broadband Services at Verizon
Leading American broadband and telecommunications company
[dates]

Designed and executed strategic roadmap for next-generation products. Improved and accelerated product-development process; boosted productivity 30%; initiated and managed relationships with co-development partners. Developed product strategy and business plans for entry into digital music, online gaming, and e-health.

2 recommendations for this position

Product Manager, Verizon@Home at Verizon
[dates]

Launched the company's first broadband residential service, Verizon@Home, and grew to 150,000 subscribers and $6M annual revenue in 1 year. Spearheaded aggressive development, introducing 25 new product features in 18 months. Cut $5M from development costs by rationalizing features to meet customer expectations. Achieved 90+% customer satisfaction rating for 7 consecutive quarters.

No recommendations for this position

Teleconferencing Manager at AP Media Services
[dates]

Managed high-volume, high-profile calls involving some of the world's leading business, financial, and political leaders. Became recognized for innovative problem-solving skills and was subsequently recruited by a key client (Verizon) to lead a groundbreaking product initiative.

No recommendations for this position

Additional Information

Interests   Bike touring, traveling, California history and geography

Groups and   Product Development and Management Association
Associations

Honors and Awards "Product of the Year" – Internet Telephony, [date]
                                "Outstanding Achievement Award" – XYZ Retail Networks, [date]

Personal Information

Phone   415-555-1234

Contact Settings

I love to share product development ideas, success stories, and best practices. Always happy to advise if I can be of help.

Interested In
- career opportunities
- new ventures
- expertise requests
- reference requests
- consulting offers
- job inquiries
- business deals
- getting back in touch

SARAH TOBIN

415-555-1234 San Francisco, CA 94133 s.tobin@mac.com

PRODUCT DEVELOPMENT LEADER

Technology & Telecommunications / Consumer Goods / Business Services

Delivering "what's next" and improving "what's now"
for companies that value innovation as a market advantage.

Expert at driving all phases of the product development lifecycle in diverse industries. Combine vision, strategy, process expertise, and business/financial acumen with a passion for innovation and the drive and discipline to bring the most viable products to market at the lowest development cost.

Highly effective at building strong teams and generating support for new ideas across large, dispersed organizations. Creative in involving partners, vendors, and internal champions and challengers. Energized by tough challenges.

Performance Highlights
- Twice built cutting-edge product development organizations from the ground up.
- Thwarted competitive threat at XYZ by speeding product time-to-market by 60%.
- Introduced Verizon's first residential broadband service and built to $6M annual revenue in 1 year.

EXPERIENCE AND ACCOMPLISHMENTS

SolutionTech, San Jose, CA [dates]
Global business outsourcing provider of pioneering solutions for critical business support processes.

DIRECTOR, Next-Generation Product Development

Brought on board to create a world-class product development organization. Hit the ground running in entirely new industry and quickly ramped up product innovation while establishing the structure, processes, and metrics essential for a top-quality product-development function.

- Midstream, took control of pilot project and led to Internet Telephony "Product of the Year" award.
- Created concept for new product line, the next generation of staffing outsourcing. Developed to pre-production in 8 months and under $275K budget.
- Commercialized/productized customer analytics technology, creating $2M annual revenue source for SolutionTech and delivering new source for voice-of-the-customer metrics to our clients.
- Built firm foundation for innovation and execution within the product development organization:
  - Defined and implemented time-to-market process including Stage-Gate steps.
  - Built internal team of both "product champions" and "product challengers."
  - Established and evangelized methodology to stimulate pipeline concepts from all areas of the company; 2 ideas introduced by sales successfully transformed into products.

Louise Kursmark and Wendy Enelow

Figure 2-3: Resume of Sarah Tobin.

415-555-1234   **Sarah Tobin**   s.tobin@mac.com

XYZ Retail Networks   San Francisco, CA, [dates]
World's leading retail media company; clients include Wal-Mart, Target, Sears, Costco, Best Buy.

DIRECTOR, Product Development

Strengthened product-development capability, melding creativity with process/structure to harness innovation and ensure sustainable success. Recruited to company that was on the leading edge of a new advertising space (captive retail networks) but needed discipline, structure, and repeatability in its product development department. Provided expert leadership to build the idea pipeline, justify development, and quickly bring ideas from concept to customer.

- Retained company's #1 line of business (+50% of revenue) by designing, developing, and installing next-generation retail broadcast systems ahead of inflexible deadline and under $29M budget.
- Managed simultaneous release of multiple new products—consistently on schedule, on budget, exceeding performance targets, and delivering measurable benefits to clients.
- Drove continuous improvement and innovation in the product-development process and instilled both process and innovation as a way of life. Key elements and results:
  - Innovation instigation. Modified process to drive creativity and build R&D pipeline.
  - Rapid development. Grew number of projects 40% while reducing time-to-market by 60%.
  - Product-line rationalization. Improved existing products and boosted revenue metric by 19%.
  - Quality audit process. Reduced installation errors by 27% in first 6 months.
- Earned XYZ'S "Outstanding Achievement Award" within 6 months of hire.

Verizon, New York, NY   [dates]
A leading American broadband and telecommunications company

MANAGER, New Product Development, Advanced Broadband Services   [dates]

Designed and executed strategic roadmap for next-generation products. Improved and accelerated product-development process; boosted productivity 30%; initiated and managed relationships with codevelopment partners. Rolled out successful 300-customer trial ahead of schedule and under budget.

- Increased sales opportunity 25% for Broadcast Interactive TV.
- Cut development costs in half by designing a prototype "fast-track" product development process.

PRODUCT MANAGER, Verizon@Home   [dates]

Launched the company's first broadband residential service, Verizon@Home, and grew to 150,000 subscribers and $6M annual revenue in 1 year. Achieved 90+% customer satisfaction rating.

EDUCATION AND PROFESSIONAL CERTIFICATION

BS Finance [date], **California State University**
ScrumMaster Certification [date] • **Six Sigma Green Belt** [date], **Villanova University**
Certified New Product Development Professional [date], **PDMA**

SARAH TOBIN

415-555-1234 San Francisco, CA 94133 s.tobin@mac.com

Sarah Tobin is a Product Development leader with a passion for delivering "what's next" and improving "what's now" for companies that value innovation as a market advantage. She has had a measurable impact on revenue, market penetration, and account retention in product-development leadership roles for companies in diverse industries, from telecom to media, consumer goods, and business services.

Primarily focused on technology innovation, Sarah is a master of both the art and the science of product development. With a deep understanding of technology capabilities and the R&D function, she knows how to stimulate idea generation, drive pipeline development, and execute co-development partnerships with vendors to build better products at lower cost. Yet she also understands market realities and has repeatedly put in place the disciplined processes, metrics, and validity testing essential for new ideas to thrive in a competitive marketplace. She is highly experienced at managing product teams and driving adoption of product development best practices.

Currently Sarah is Director of Next-Generation Product Development for a global business outsourcing provider. She has generated millions in revenue, introduced a technology "product of the year," and established robust methodologies for idea generation and concept development.

Previously, as Director of Product Development at XYZ Retail Networks, Sarah created a disciplined, structured, repeatable product-development process that was used to launch products for some of the world's largest retailers.

Sarah began her career in Product Development with Verizon, where she launched the company's first broadband residential service (Verizon@Home) and created the strategic roadmap for next-generation products. She is a Certified New Product Development Professional, a ScrumMaster, and a Six Sigma Green Belt with a Finance degree from California State University.

Sarah thrives on challenge and is an innovator and change driver. Her expertise helps companies deliver on the promise of their ideas.

Louise Kursmark and Wendy Enelow

Figure 2-4: Bio of Sarah Tobin.

URL shorteners can time out

A URL is the address of a Web page on the World Wide Web. URL shorteners are handy helpers for connecting recruiters and other important viewers to your Web-hosted resume or profile.

URLs as long as a city block are hard to pass along. Long-winded links not only take up too much space in text resumes, they can break in e-mail, and they are hard to handle in general. Enter more than two dozen free shortening services, such as Bit.ly (`www.bit.ly`), TinyURL (`www.tinyurl`), and Goo.gl (`www.goo.gl`). Just visit one of the sites, and a shortening service replaces your excruciatingly long link with its short little Web address, making everyone happier.

One watch-out: Shortened links can expire. When you're in full job-search mode, you certainly don't want links to your resumes or profiles to be no-shows. Like a pilot inspects an aircraft before taking off, check your important URL shorteners weekly.

Put Your Best Face Forward

A problem with some social networking online profiles is the tendency to share insider stuff that seems okay when you're speaking to friends but may not be perceived favorably by potential employers. One job seeker wrote that she rides a motorcycle with her husband, which can raise questions about risk taking and health insurance costs. Her revelation would have been positive had she been applying for a job marketing Hogs or as a stunt double, but, alas, she wants to be a court reporter.

Another job seeker led off his profile with the good news that he is a cancer survivor. Health insurance costs? Reliable attendance? Longevity on the job?

The litmus test for revealing personal data in a professional online profile is the same as that for a resume: Does including this information enhance my perceived qualifications for the type of job I seek?

Chapter 3

Going Mobile: Resumes on Smartphones and Tablets

In This Chapter

▶ Job searching anytime, anywhere, any way

▶ Saving time with tips for mobile job search

▶ Avoiding common mobile job-search mistakes

*T*he world is mobilizing (pun intended). Nearly five billion mobile phones are in use across the globe, and nine of ten people in America are mobile phone subscribers. That's a bunch. While total figures aren't yet in for tablet computers, their numbers are going through the roof: Nearly five million have been sold during their first eight months on the market. In a nutshell, numbers of mobile devices and their users are heading in one direction — straight up!

This moment of historical mobile impact is obvious in everyday life: When the majority of mobilized people now leave their houses, they pack along these three things: keys, wallet or purse, and a mobile phone or tablet. How different is that from ten years ago?

A sizable and growing proportion of people — including resume-writing job seekers — get their daily information fix via their mobile devices. Many are members of Generation Y, a force of as many as 70 million. Generation Y-ers were early adopters of mobile technology. Most are still in their 20s and are just warming up to the best ways of conducting their adult job chases. But not all mobile-device-using job seekers are under 30; older job seekers are going mobile as they look for every advantage when surfing difficult employer-driven job markets.

Earning New Rewards with Mobile Search

Looking for a few reasons to add mobile to your job search mix — or not? This section shares the potential benefits for taking your job search with you wherever you roam:

- ✔ You're not tied down waiting to send or receive a resume or job message. You can job search while you're on the bus, waiting for a friend in a restaurant, or sitting in a dentist's or doctor's office.

- ✔ If you set up job alerts, you can respond quickly to opportunities even when you're out and about. Response time is a big factor in crowded job markets because there are so many people looking for jobs that the recruiter has plenty of candidates to consider within a day or two.

- ✔ You can seize unexpected opportunities to market yourself. Suppose you're on a commuter train or a plane, chatting with a seatmate who shows a legitimate interest in your resume. You can instantly display your resume on your mobile device, as well as immediately send it to your seatmate's e-mail address.

- ✔ You can invest more effort into your search because you don't have to wait until you're home to use your desktop computer. Mobile search bridges the gap between online and offline.

- ✔ Mobile devices are helpful for short-notice interview invitations. Suppose your resume was strong enough to attract a recruiter's interest, and the recruiter phones to ask if you can meet the same day. You say yes, but realize you're short on information about the employer. Pull out your smartphone or tablet to research quickly.

Perish the thought of going on a mobile job search using a work phone provided by your employer. Your employer owns what's on it and can check the content at any time. For your personal phone, make sure all security patches are installed to keep your business *your* business. Be sure you have all the new bells and whistles that enhance your mobility.

Knowing When to Stick to Home Computer Searches

For a growing segment of the population that is nearly always connected with smartphones and other digital devices, mobile job searching around the clock is a natural expectation. But not every job situation is ideal for mobile search. For example, the level of responsibility for the job you seek is one cause for pause.

Glossary for mobile devices

Mobile Web means Web access from a mobile device, such as a smartphone, tablet, or laptop. It enables the use of Internet-connected applications or browser-based access to the Internet. Here are other simple definitions of mobile terms to demystify any geek speak you encounter when becoming a confident job searcher on the go.

✔ *Apps* are convenient programs that make your life easier when you're on the go. Apps turn your smartphone into a little computer in your hand. The word *app* is short for *application,* a software program that runs inside another service. Digital devices — such as smartphones, tablets, and e-readers — expand their functions by allowing apps to be downloaded. Apps are available for a wide variety of purposes, including scouting for jobs.

Job search apps offer job postings, job hunt advice, and related content. Many job search apps are free or modestly priced.

✔ *Smartphones* make and receive phone calls, text, take and send photos, are Web-enabled, can send and receive e-mail, edit MS Office documents and Google Docs.

The five main types of smartphones generally are considered to be BlackBerry, iPhone, Android, Palm, and Windows Mobile.

✔ Apple's iPad is the best known among a growing group of competitive *tablets* (also called tablet PCs or tablet computers). These sleek, light devices are the bigger brothers and sisters to the smartest of the smartphones. They can handle many tasks once performed only by personal computers: check e-mail, surf the Web, edit photos, compose documents, and more. Tablets can connect with computers to transfer files, and new ones will have ports connecting with printers or USB (flash) drives.

✔ *E-readers* are devices used solely for reading, such as the Amazon Kindle and Barnes & Noble Nook. They are portable, have excellent readability in bright sunlight, and long battery life. Some people think the reading experience is better on e-readers than on tablet screens.

✔ Mobile devices transfer information over a distance without being fettered by cable or wire. *Wi-Fi* is short for Wireless Fidelity, referring to the standard way computers connect to wireless networks. This is the technology that most mobile devices use now. What's next? Super WiFi, or WiFi on steroids, is coming on fast. If WiFi were a city street, Super WiFi would be an expressway.

Executive and managerial job seekers are more likely to gain interviews through traditional channels because the cost of a poor management hire to a company's bottom line can be extreme. Companies take their time on these decisions and often engage outside recruiters to scour the range of potential talent. By contrast, mobile search works very well for high-turnover industries, which usually have available positions and welcome walk-in candidates, such as retail outlets, restaurants, theaters, hotels, and hair salons.

Another reason to think through your approach before relying on mobile job search to connect you with interviews is when you're a professional (pharmacy supervisor or electrical engineer, for example) shooting for a job that probably requires robust pre-employment testing. Technical incompatibility between devices is a barrier.

When you're using a smartphone to scare up job leads but remain uncertain about applying for those jobs mobile-style — or perhaps you just want time to think over your response — choose the half-and-half solution: E-mail the job link to yourself and use your desktop or laptop computer to apply when you get home. Proceed as you would if you had found the job on your computer instead of on your smartphone.

Powering a Mobile Search

Embarking on any endeavor in which you are a novice carries a certain amount of uncertainty and frustration. To increase your productivity and save you time from chasing dead ends, consider the following basic advice.

Choose job-search apps wisely

Cheerleaders for employment-related apps explain that they are super-convenient, offer intuitive and user-friendly interfaces, and are plentiful. That's true, but your best bet is researching the apps for your own preferences. Here's a mere snippet of what's available in the apposphere:

- Many popular job-search Web services have created apps that search their own sites, such as Monster.com, CareerBuilder.com, Indeed.com, SimplyHired.com, and Beyond.com.
- Staffing companies are fielding such creations as Adecco Jobs, produced by employment service Adecco USA.
- Not to be left behind, employers are joining the app crowd, as illustrated by Hyatt Job Search for Hyatt Hotels.

Most job apps enable you to apply for a job on the spot, but some ask you to e-mail the job's link to yourself. (Faithfully check your options on how to respond.)

Beyond personal experimentation, seek referrals from fellow job seekers and media experts. Analysts for *PC Magazine* and Web site Mashable.com regularly comment on the quality of specific apps, as well as report what's coming up next in the app business.

Watch type size and font

Readability is the password to your resume. In typefaces, serifs are the small elements at the end of strokes. Typefaces come with or without serifs. What I say in Chapter 11 about typefaces and fonts relates to print. But my guidelines for mobile resumes and Web pages are different.

For print, I favor Times New Roman, and other serif typefaces for body text. But for online body text, and especially for mobile resumes, I prefer sans serif typefaces, such as Verdana, Helvetica, and Arial.

Font sizes smaller than 12- or 14-point are often hard to read on mobile devices and Web pages.

Empower RSS to send job news

Before you launch a mobile search, download a free Really Simple Syndication (RSS) reader — which I describe in Chapter 4 — to your smartphone or tablet. Subscribing to a reader means you get immediate notice of new jobs in your industry or career field.

The free Google suite for mobile phones works on all the top smartphones and gives you an RSS reader, Gmail access, Google Docs, and more. For additional information, use your mobile phone or tablet to visit `www.m.google.com/search`.

Do sign up for free job alerts offered by job boards and job search engines (using RSS or e-mail), but less may be more. Unless you are selective in choosing to hear about jobs that meet your criteria, you may suffer from too much information. If you find yourself oversubscribed, cancel some of them. Choose the best and lose the rest.

Stay in the running with a rehearsed salary strategy

Using the correct salary strategy is critical when filling out online applications. Being overpriced or underpriced screens you out of consideration for a job that's already been priced in a company's budget — computer software will see to it. When you're on the fly, possibly distracted, and a hot job pops up on your mobile device, automatically fill in the blanks about salary requirements with an effective salary response strategy you've memorized.

Here's solid counsel to help you work out your best strategy from the best salary coach I know, Jack Chapman. Chapman is the author of the classic guide, *Negotiating Your Salary: How to Make $1000 a Minute.* Here's what the salary coach tells me.

As a job hunter, your priority No. 1 is to first get an interview, and then maintain your integrity — no lying. Among your choices, pick one you like:

- In the unlikely event the online application box accepts text, write "competitive." That's the raw truth: You want a competitive wage. This answer should not screen you out.

- Usually only numbers are allowed. Research a competitive salary using Salary.com, Payscale.com, Indeed.com, or GlassDoor.com, and see whether you can enter a numerical range in the application box. A range has better results than a single number. A range says "competitive wage."

- When the application box won't accept a range, but requires a single number, state a number that is in the 50th percentile of the range — even if you want more. Salary research sites list salary ranges by percentiles. (Example: For a range of $30,000 to $50,000, the 50th percentile is halfway between, or $40,000.) This isn't the time to negotiate; it's a time to say, "Let me interview! All I need is a competitive salary." Remember your priority No. 1: Get into an interview. Negotiate when the time is right.

- If you think the company is gathering ammunition to lowball you, apply twice if the system will allow it. (Use a different phone number.) Write a number in the 25th percentile in your second application. (Example: The 25th percentile of a $30,000 to $50,000 range is $35,000.) Again, focus on your priority No. 1: Getting into an interview. Negotiate the pay upwards when the time comes.

Pick your work site with GPS

When you live in the north end of a city and have zero interest in commuting to work in the south end — or when you want to work in a specific geographically desirable area — use a location-finding app equipped with GPS (global positioning system) technology, such as CareerBuilder's free Jobs. This tool tracks down jobs in your target area by keywords. Location-finding apps are increasingly available for mobile job search apps.

Score with proven keywords

You can use your mobile device to send an employer a *resume note* — a synopsis or summary of your resume — with a link to your full-design resume that resides on a Web-hosting site. (Check out Chapter 7.) Your note won't have the space to say much, so what it does say had better be choice, or your note will be deleted as text spam.

When you know the specific keywords that target a job you want, use them. If not, game the process by using universally effective keywords that identify the professional attributes employers most value. Chapter 5 gives you a list of the most commonly requested professional attributes.

Avoiding Mobile Job-Search Mistakes

Experience is the name everyone gives to their mistakes but here are three you can easily sidestep in your quest to make mobile search provide paychecks for you. (I'm all ears if you discover other "experiences" you'd like to share; you can reach me at jlk@sunfeatures.com.) As you fire up your mobile job search, avoid this trio of errors.

Thinking technology overcomes poor resume quality

No matter how impressive the technology that puts it into a hiring manager's hands, your resume speaks loudly about who you are and what you offer. Expecting anything other than that document to do your talking is a mistake. This caveat applies to all age groups, but has special relevance for the Boomers-and-beyond crowd.

Older workers know they can illustrate they work on today-time, not yesterday-time, by job hunting with the latest technology and techniques. But eye-popping technology won't cover over weak resumes that fail to address a job's requirements, lack accomplishments, and are missing other persuasive qualities revealed in these pages.

Fail to create a first-rate, customized resume before you master technology, and you'll have wasted your time figuring out how to make mobile job search work for you.

Going on too long when going mobile

Because the screens of smartphones are in the three-inch neighborhood, consider sending in plain text a *resume note* (synopsis or summary with fewer than 500 characters) that links to your full-design resume stored on a Web hosting site.

The screens of tablets and readers can handle total resumes, but hold the size to one or two pages. Consider using a 12- or 14-point font and sending the document as a PDF. Size counts. If the resume reader doesn't have 20-year-old eyes and literally can't read your resume, you're out of luck. Chapter 7 gives you the complete scoop on how to send your resume in which situations.

If you're errand-hopping and standing in the store's long returns line getting set to send an e-mail with your resume attached when suddenly you arrive at the front of the line and the helpful store clerk is giving you the stink eye for not moving forward, don't panic and fire off your resume without a message. Odds are blank-screen messages will be forgotten or ignored. Wait until you have the time to include a well-crafted cover note. (See my book, *Cover Letters For Dummies,* 3rd Edition [Wiley].)

Looking naïve in following up

Because the process of sending resumes through mobile platforms is still in its early years, when you don't hear a peep back after sending yours, you may wonder whether your resume was lost in the weeds of the mobile Web. Should you call the recipient company to ask? Not immediately. Most resume-intake specialists view such calls as flat-out nuisances.

There's a better way to deal with the question of whether your mobile resume arrived at its destination: When you don't receive even a computer-generated acknowledgment within a few days, resend your resume on a desktop or laptop computer to the employer's e-mail address.

Still no response? Okay, call. But make yourself appear more knowledgeable by asking: "Has my resume arrived and has it been routed? To whom? Is there any other information you'd like me to provide?" (For more tips on resumes gone missing, see Chapter 7.)

Search management saves sanity

Other than road warriors, job seekers using mobile search moves often combine them with home-based search, bringing opportunity to achieve chaos. Imagine frantically hunting for a critical but missing little slip of paper last remembered as being in your pocket, or trying to make sense of a bunch of online tidbits that now appear to be orphans. (Disclosure: I speak from experience: Some days my office is a candidate for the cover of *Home and Landfill*.)

Ward off the headache of disorder by managing your job search with JibberJobber.com, a free service that enables you to track where you've sent resumes and the jobs you've applied for, as well as to record your progress as you pass through the hiring process. Additionally, you can keep a nose count of your networking contacts and comment on how they have provided assistance.

JibberJobber.com remains available online for desktop Internet job search, but use your smartphone to check out its mobile address at www.m.JibberJobber.com.

Money talk: CEO Jason Alba confirms the free service at entry level is "forever," but moderately priced upgrades are available if you choose.

Mobile: From Novelty to Necessity

How encouraging are future prospects for mobile job search? Fantastic! In late 2010, the U.S. Federal Communications Commission announced the opening up of unused airwaves for wireless broadband networks that will be more powerful and can reach much farther than today's WiFi hotspots. Think Super WiFi — ultrafast, longer range, and more reliable connections. Pundits say the FCC decision frees up the most unlicensed spectrum in 25 years. Because mobile search runs on wireless technology, the FCC decision speeds the use of mobile job search enabled by smartphones and tablets.

How fast will mobile communications grab big chunks of the world's attention? About five years passed for the Internet to come of age as a leading player in the job market. Mobile job search is claiming star status even faster because more of today's working adults grew up with the Internet and simply expect technological change. Additionally, the recruiting media industry is working around the clock to create products to fill all the new wireless broadband space the FCC has handed it on a platter. The signals are green for mobile job search.

So don't be afraid to try something new just because you don't know as much about mobile search today as — with practice — you will a year from now. And, as an unknown someone has said, don't refuse to go on an occasional wild goose chase — that's what wild geese are for.

Chapter 4

Familiar Search Tools That Haven't Gone Away

*W*hile not all Web technology tools have held up under the rigors of time and progress, some are still favored job finders in the 21st century. Job boards and company Web sites, for instance, retain star status in determining where to send your resumes. The handsome full-design resume is another tool that remains on job seekers' hit parade. (Chapter 11 gives you the scoop on resume design.)

The opposite of full design, the plain-text resume — once headed for oblivion because it's a drab pain to read — is coming back largely because many job boards accept only plain text. Why? Because plain text (unlike a word-processed document) can't harbor a harmful virus, as well as other technical reasons related to time and cost.

Other tools from the 1990s — such as scannable resumes — are showing their age. And instant messaging has virtually given way to Twitter and texting.

In this chapter, I describe a carousel of familiar job-search tools with a broad brush because technology changes rapidly. Some observers estimate the average lifespan for much current technology is about 24 months. Whatever the time frame of change, its warp speed renders many details quickly obsolete in a book. Not only does technology move forward, but companies marketing and using it come and go.

Plain-Text Resumes Stay on the Scene

The *plain-text resume* (also known as an ASCII resume) is an online document constructed without formatting in plain-text file format. The main characteristic about this resume is its looks (or lack of same). Figure 4-1 shows a plain-text resume. The creature's so ugly only a computer could love it. But for the foreseeable future, the job market is stuck with plain-text resumes. As Jim Lemke, a human resources executive and this book's technical reviewer, says:

> *"A plain-text resume is still good to have to use when you need it. Some lower-end applicant tracking systems require that you paste a resume in a text window. A pasted formatted text resume will come out much better than a pasted MS Word resume. A formatted text resume also comes in handy to send to handheld devices. Although the scannable resume is almost extinct, the plain-text resume will be around for a long time."*

Companies sometimes require that you submit a plain-text resume. Create your resume in your favorite word-processing program, save it, and then convert it to plain text (ASCII) by following these steps:

1. **Click Edit → Select All.**

2. **Click Edit → Copy.**

3. **Open Notepad.**

   To get there click Start → Programs → Accessories → Notepad.

4. **Click Edit → Paste.**

5. **Turn on the word-wrap feature in the Format drop-down menu.**

6. **Save the resume as "yourname.txt" (for example, "CarolynChase.txt").**

Not all versions of Notepad have a spell-check feature, so be sure to spell check *before* you save your resume as an ASCII file.

Because your resume now has ASCII for brains, it won't recognize the formatting commands that your word-processing program uses. Don't use any characters that aren't on your keyboard, such as smart quotes (those tasteful, curly quotation marks that you see in this book) or mathematical symbols. They don't convert correctly, and your resume will need fumigating to rid itself of squiggles and capital *U*'s.

```
Plain Text Resume

        Della Hutchings
        890 Spruce Ave.
        Las Vegas, NV 22222
        945-804-9999
            E-mail: dellah@aol.com
        Admin Assist, 4 yrs exp, 6 software pgms, time mgt skills

        SUMMARY
        ================================================================
        Word. WordPerfect. Lotus. Excel. PageMaker. QuickBooks
        Bilingual: Spanish. Time management. Budgeting. Organizational
        skills.

        EMPLOYMENT
        ================================================================
        University of Upper Carolina                           [dates]
        Church Knoll, NC


        ASSISTANT TO DIRECTOR OF ACADEMIC TECHNOLOGY
        Use and support a wide variety of computer applications
        Work with both Macs and Dell computers
        Communicate with clients in South America
        Apply troubleshooting and problem solving skills
        Maintain complex scheduling for employer, staff, self
        Responsible for dept. budget administration; 100% balanced

        Mothers for Wildlife Inc.                              [dates]
        ADMINISTRATIVE ASSISTANT

        Edited/wrote newsletter
        Organized rallies and letter-writing campaigns
        Maintained mailing lists
        Saved organization $5,000 changing equipment

        EDUCATION
        ================================================================
        University of Upper Carolina at Chapel Hill, NC        [dates]
        BA with honors in International Studies

        Won Gil award for best honors thesis on Latin America
        GPA in Major: 3.8/4.0

        AFFILIATIONS
        ================================================================
        Carolina Hispanic Students Association
        Amnesty International
        Concept of Colors (Multicultural modeling group)

        HOBBIES
        ================================================================
        Like details: Writing and Web design

        AWARDS
        ================================================================
        On present job: Administrative Assistant of month four times  [dates]
        Recognized for productivity, organization, attention to detail
        and interpersonal skills
```

Figure 4-1: This sample resume for Della Hutching is included solely to illustrate the appearance of a plain-text resume. It is not intended to convey strong content.

Ed's attachment etiquette

Ed Struzik knows what recruiters want. Struzik, president of BEKS Data Services, Inc. (www.beksdata.com), speaks from the vantage point of years' experience in providing outsourced resume-processing services and consulting to many major companies. Here are a few pitfalls Struzik says to avoid when e-mailing attachments:

✔ ***Do not*** **attach EXE files.** An Executable file can contain a virus, and no one will chance having the hard drive or network infected.

✔ ***Do not*** **attach ZIP files.** Who's to say the ZIP file doesn't contain an infected Executable. And besides, can your resume be so large that you have to ZIP it?

✔ ***Do not*** **attach password-protected documents.** How would you expect someone or something to open it without the password?

You know that you're off in the wrong direction if you have to change the preferences setting in your word processor or otherwise go to a lot of trouble to get a certain character to print. Remember that you can use dashes and asterisks (they're on the keyboard), but you can't use bullets (they're *not* on the keyboard).

Although you can't use bullets, bold, or underlined text in a plain-text document, you can use plus signs (+) at the beginning of lines to draw attention to part of your document. You can also use a series of dashes to separate sections and capital letters to substitute for boldface. When you don't know what else to use to sharpen your ASCII effort, you can always turn to Old Reliable — white space.

Be on guard against other common ASCII landmines:

✔ **Typeface/fonts:** You can't control the typeface or font size in your ASCII resume. The text appears in the typeface and size that the recipient's computer is set for. This means that boldface, italics, or different font sizes don't appear in the online plain text version. Use all caps for words that need special emphasis.

✔ **Word wrap:** Don't use the word-wrap feature when writing your resume because it will look weird. Odd-looking word wrapping is one of the cardinal sins of online resumes. Set your margins at 0 and 65, or set the right margin at 6.5 inches. Then end each line after 65 characters with hard returns (press the Enter key) to insert line breaks.

The subject line online

When you're sending an online resume in any form, the subject line of your e-mail can bring you front and center to a recruiter's attention:

- In responding to an advertised job, use the job title. If none is listed, use the reference number.

- When you send an unsolicited resume, write a short "sales" headline. For example: Bilingual teacher, soc studies/6 yrs' exp. Or, Programmer, experienced, top skills: Java, C++.

Never just say *Bilingual teacher* or *Programmer*. Sell yourself! Keep rewriting until you've crammed as many sales points as possible into your "marquee."

Should you show a "cc" for "copy sent" on your resume? If you're e-mailing a hiring manager (such as the accounting manager), copy the human resources department manager; that saves the hiring manager from having to forward your resume to human resources and is more likely to result in your landing in the company's resume database to be considered for any number of jobs.

- **Proportional typefaces:** Don't use proportional typefaces that have different widths for different characters (such as Times Roman). Instead, use a fixed-width typeface (such as Courier) so that you have a true 65-character line. For example, if you compose and send your resume in Courier 12 and it's received in the Arial typeface, it should still work well with most e-mail programs, surviving transport with a close resemblance to the original line length.

- **Tabs:** Don't use tabs; they get wiped out in the conversion to ASCII. Use your spacebar instead.

- **Alignment:** Your ASCII resume is automatically left-justified. If you need to indent a line or center a heading, use the spacebar.

- **Page numbers:** Omit page numbers. You can't be certain where the page breaks will fall, and your name and page number can end up halfway south on a page.

When you send your ASCII resume, paste it with a cover note (a very brief cover letter) into the body of your e-mail.

E-Forms: Fill in the Blankety-Blanks

The e-form is just a shorter version of the plain-text resume, and you usually find it on company Web sites if the company doesn't accept full-design resumes. The company encourages you to apply by setting your plain text into designated fields of the forms on the site.

Stop and ask directions

You can never be 100 percent sure what technology is being used where you want to send your resume. The solution is to ask — by telephone or by e-mail — the company human resource department or the company receptionist the following question:

I want to be sure I'm using your preferred technology to submit my resume. Can I

send it as an attachment, say in MS Word or Adobe PDF?

Alternatively, if you don't have a clue, you can send your resume within the body of your e-mail as plain text and also attach it as a word-processed document.

The e-form is almost like an application form, except that it lacks the legal document status an application form acquires when you sign it, certifying that all facts are true.

Follow the on-screen instructions given by each employer to cut and paste the requested information into the site's template. You're basically just filling in the blanks with your contact information that's supplemented by data lifted from your plain-text resume.

Remember that e-forms can't spell check, so cutting and pasting your resume into the e-form body, instead of typing it in manually, is your best bet. Because you spell checked your resume before converting it to ASCII (of course, you did!), at least you know that everything is likely to be spelled correctly.

E-forms work well for job seekers in high-demand occupations, such as nursing, but they don't work so well for job seekers who need to document motivation, good attitude, and other personal characteristics and accomplishments that computers don't search for. When you rely on an e-form to get an employer's attention, you're playing 100 percent on the employer's turf.

Scannable Resumes Get Used in a Pinch

A *scannable resume* is a resume that a recipient, usually a clerk in an employment office, scans into a computer as an image. Because you don't know what technology the employer is using and computers read resumes differently than people do, you still should stick to the inconvenient rules that follow.

A scannable resume may start life as a paper resume that you can postal mail, hand deliver, or fax; the employer uses a scanning machine to enter your hard-copy resume into a candidate database. Next, computer software extracts from it a summary of basic information, pulling out factors like your name, contact information, skills, work history, years of experience, and education.

Scanned resumes and their extracted summaries sleep peacefully until a human resource specialist or recruiter searches the summaries by keywords to retrieve candidates who match the requirements of a job opening. The technology ranks candidates, from the most qualified to the least qualified. The most relevant resumes get a wake-up call and pop to the recruiting screen, where human eyes take over the recruiting tasks.

Scannable resumes are on their way out, joining the MS-DOS operating software in computer museums. Recruiters prefer newer intake systems that enable resumes to travel smoothly online and move straight into a resume-management database.

Even so, don't trash your scannable resume know-how just yet. If an employer asks that you send a resume by postal mail or fax, assume that it will be scanned. Take the following steps to prevent scanning errors from putting you on the sidelines:

- ✔ **Use type that's clear and readable.** Don't use a condensed typeface. White space separates letters; no space smushes them together. Letters must be distinctively clear with crisp, unbroken edges. Avoid arty, decorative typefaces.

- ✔ **Avoid these bad-scan elements:**
  - Italics or script
  - Underlining
  - Reverse printing (white letters on a black field)
  - Shadows or shading
  - Hollow bullets (they read like the letter *o*)
  - Number signs (#) for bullets (the computer may read what follows as a phone number)
  - Boxes (computers try to read them like letters)
  - Two-column formats or designs that look like newspapers
  - Symbols, such as a logo
  - Vertical lines (computers read them like the letter *l*)
  - Vertical dates (use horizontal dates: 2006–2011)

✓ **Feel free to use larger fonts for section headings and your name.** A font size of 14 to 16 points is good. Larger headings look better on the electronic image of your resume when humans read it (which doesn't always happen). I recommend you format the body of your resume in a 12-point font size, the section headings in 14-point, and your name in 16-point.

✓ **Do keep your scannable resume simple in design and straightforward.** Recruiters call this approach "plain vanilla," and they like it because it doesn't confuse computers.

✓ **Do send your paper resume without staples.** Paper clips are okay. Follow this tip for all resumes that you mail or hand deliver because staples are a pain to pull out before feeding into a scanner one page at a time.

Online Screening Guards the Employment Door

Your OnTarget resume may never be read if an employer's online screening program decides in advance that you aren't qualified for the position's stated — or unstated — requirements. In essence, screening software has the first word about who is admitted for a closer look and who isn't.

Online screening is an automated process of creating a blueprint of known requirements for a given job and then collecting information from each applicant in a standardized manner to see whether the applicant matches the blueprint. The outcomes are sent to recruiters and hiring managers.

Online screening is known by various terms — *prescreening* and *pre-employment screening,* to mention two. By any name, the purpose of online screening is to verify that you are, in fact, a good candidate for the position and that you haven't lied about your background. Employers use online screening tools (tests, assessment instruments, questionnaires, and so on) to reduce and sort applicants against criteria and competencies that are important to their organizations.

If you apply online through major job sites or many company Web site career portals, you may be asked to respond *yes* or *no* to job-related questions, such as:

✓ Do you have the required college degree?

✓ Do you have experience with (specific job requirement)?

✓ Are you willing to relocate?

> ✔ Do you have two or more years' experience managing a corporate communications department?
>
> ✔ Is your salary requirement between $55,000–$60,000/year?

Answering "no" to any of these kinds of questions disqualifies you for the listed position, an automated decision that helps the recruiters thin the herd of resumes more quickly but that may be a distinct disadvantage to you, the job searcher. (Without human interaction, you may not show enough of the stated qualifications, but you may have compensatory qualifications that a machine won't allow you to communicate.)

On the other hand, professionals in high demand categories benefit by a quick response, such as nursing. Example: *Are you an RN?* If the answer is "yes," the immediate response, according to a recruiter's joke, is "When can you start?"

Sample components of online screening

The following examples of online screening aren't exhaustive, but they are illustrations of the most commonly encountered upfront filtering techniques.

- ✔ **Basic evaluation:** The system automatically evaluates the match between a resume's content (job seeker's qualifications) and a job's requirement and ranks the most qualified resumes at the top.

- ✔ **Skills and knowledge testing:** The system uses tests that require applicants to prove their knowledge and skills in a specific area of expertise. Online skills and knowledge testing is especially prevalent in information technology jobs where dealing with given computer programs is basic to job performance. Like the old-time typing tests in an HR office, there's nothing subjective about this type of quiz: You know the answers, or you don't.

- ✔ **Personality assessment:** Attempts to measure work-related personality traits to predict job success are one of the more controversial types of online testing. Dr. Wendell Williams, a leading testing expert based in the Atlanta area, says that personality tests expressly designed for hiring are in a totally different league than tests designed to measure things like communication style or personality type.

  "Job-related personality testing is highly job specific and tends to change with both task and job," he says. "If you are taking a generic personality test, a good rule is to either pick answers that fall in the middle of the scale or ones you think best fit the job description. This is not deception. Employers rarely conduct studies of personality test scores versus job performance and so it really does not make much difference."

✔ **Behavioral assessment:** The system asks questions aimed at uncovering your past experience applying core competencies the organization requires (such as fostering teamwork, managing change) and position-specific competencies (such as persuasion for sales, attention to detail for accountants). I further describe competencies in Chapter 8.

✔ **Managerial assessments:** The system presents applicants with typical managerial scenarios and asks them to react. Proponents say that managerial assessments are effective for predicting performance on competencies, such as interpersonal skills, business acumen, and decision making. Dr. Williams identifies the many forms these assessments can take:

- **In-basket exercises** where the applicant is given an in-basket full of problems and told to solve them.

- **Analysis case studies** where the applicant is asked to read a problem and recommend a solution.

- **Planning case studies** where the applicant is asked to read about a problem and recommend a step-by-step solution.

- **Interaction simulations** where the applicant is asked to work out a problem with a skilled role player.

- **Presentation exercises** where the applicant is asked to prepare, deliver, and defend a presentation.

- **Integrity tests** measure your honesty with a series of questions. You can probably spot the best answers without too much trouble.

Pros and cons of online screening

Here's a snapshot of the advantages and disadvantages of online screening, from the job seeker's perspective:

✔ **Advantages:** In theory, a perfect online screening is totally job based and fair to all people with equal skills. Your resume would survive the first cut based only on your ability to do well in the job. You are screened out of consideration for any job you may not be able to do, saving yourself stress and keeping your track record free of false starts.

✔ **Disadvantages:** The creation of an online process is vulnerable to human misjudgment; I'm still looking for an example of the perfect online screening system. Moreover, you have no chance to make up for missing competencies or skills. (An analogy: You can read music, but you don't know how to play a specific song. You can learn it quickly, but there's no space to write "quick learner.")

Can your resume be turned away?

What if you get low grades on answering the screening questions — can the employer's system tell you to take your resume and get lost? No, not legally. Anyone can leave a resume, but if they don't pass the screening, the resume is ranked at the bottom of the list in the database.

The bottom line is that if you don't score well in screening questions, your resume is exiled to a no-hire zone even if it isn't physically turned away.

Blogs Give a Global Brand

Career experts recommend blogging as an extraordinary opportunity to become better known in a profession or career field — a branding tool. You can headline your own blog or write entries for someone else's blog. Millions of blogs operate around the globe, with new ones launching every day.

A *blog* is a Web site, or part of a Web site, that features regular updates of commentary on anything from politics to celebrity gossip to whatever the blogger ate that day. The term itself is a blend of the words *Web* and *log*. Keeping a blog running requires a fair amount of work. Because most blogs are maintained by an unpaid individual with regular entries of commentary, one-person blogs come and go. Sometimes the bloggers become guest commentators on blogs maintained by others.

Blogs are the ultimate Web insider's clubhouse. They attract loyal readers who hold an avid interest in a blog's topic. Recruiters understand that to hire the right people, you should go where the right people hang out. That's why recruiters cruise career-field-related blogs, looking for top talent in a specific occupation — or for experts who can steer them to top talent.

Finding blogs for role models takes a bit of shopping around. Try these suggestions to kick off your hunt:

1. **Browse for a topic and add "blogs" to the search term.**

   For example, "employment blogs" brings up a zillion possibilities, such as George's Employment Blawg (`www.employmentblawg.com`).

   You can also turn to a blog search engine, such as Search4Blogs (`www.search4blogs.com`).

2. **When you find a blog you like, check out the site's *blogroll* (links of blogs on similar topics).**

   George's Employment Blawg, for example, lists several pages of other employment and recruiting blogs.

To establish your own blog, find a host site that offers free service for beginning bloggers — such as Typepad (`www.typepad.com`) — and start writing.

Keep up with blog-based job ads by visiting Blogs with Jobs (`www.blogs withjobs.com`).

RSS Delivers Job Alerts on Your Time

The evolution of *really simple syndication* (RSS), the technology designed to give you a heads-up when a job you want becomes available, reminds me of the difference between periodic television network news programming and all-news cable television. Instead of having to watch the news at 6 p.m. or 11 p.m., you can watch late-breaking news on your timetable 24/7.

Familiar free online job search agents at major job boards periodically send you e-mail alerts about jobs that meet your specific search criteria. But the modern and also free RSS technology whisks *live feeds* to your computer or mobile devices around the clock with the latest jobs from thousands of employers and job sites.

RSS is a rapidly growing service for the immediate distribution of online content — in this case, job postings.

How does RSS beat the older e-mail job agents? Three ways: efficiency, relevance, and timeliness. Sending RSS job feeds to your RSS reader prevents e-mail job alerts from clogging your in-box.

Moreover, RSS feeds more closely match your stated requirements. Like an advanced search, you get a closer match to what you want. For example, if you're an accountant and you want a job in Milwaukee, an e-mail search agent might return everything with the term "accountant" or its variations, such as accounting for lost automobiles in Milwaukee. RSS job feeds are programmed to mirror your specific wishes.

RSS job feeds are a wonderful way to get the first word when a new job is posted. And you can program the feeds to include breaking news in industry concerns, information that can put you at the head of the line in job interviews. Jobs are filled quickly these days and you know the old saying about early birds.

You can receive RSS feeds in a few different ways. You can download a free RSS reader, or use the RSS reader built into Web sites you want to follow. For example, the job search engines I describe in Chapter 7 give simple instructions on how to add their live job feeds to your computer or mobile devices.

Resume Blasting: A Really Bad Idea

Resume blasting services (also jokingly known as resume spamming services) advertise their willingness to save you time and trouble by "blasting" your resume to thousands of recruiters and hiring managers all over the Internet — for a fee, of course. The pitches are tempting, but should you avail yourself of this miraculous service? Just say no!

Resume blasting can bring you big trouble, from making identity theft easier for crooks, to irritating your boss, to making you an untouchable for recruiters. Moreover, as I explain in Chapter 6, customized resumes are a short cut to job interviews.

Privacy and identity theft problems

Concerning identity theft issues, privacy expert Pam Dixon advises being cautious with your resume's information. Read about it on her nonprofit World Privacy Forum (www.worldprivacyforum.org), where Dixon continually updates a must-read report titled "Job Seeker's Guide to Resumes: Twelve Resume Posting Truths."

Admittedly, merely being careful about releasing your resume information online won't keep you safe from Identity theft in these days when the guardrails on privacy are coming down in so many ways in so many places. But do be stingy with your private information — in particular, omit your home address.

Identity theft may be the worst-case scenario, but it isn't the only life-altering problem that can arise when you put your business on the Web. Use a resume-blasting service while you're employed, and you may lose your current job. Experts say that employers do search for their employees' resumes in job site resume databases.

"When employees' resumes are found grazing in someone else's pasture before noon," says CareerXroads' Mark Mehler, who consults with countless company managers, "they may be on the street by the end of that same day."

Get your resume past spam gatekeepers

You may not know whether your resume becomes cyber-litter because a spam or virus filter deletes it unread. Susan Joyce, who operates Job-Hunt.org (`www.job-hunt.org`), offers good tips for getting your resume where you want it to go.

✔ **Do** send e-mail to only one employer at a time. Do not send e-mail to more than five people at that employer's address at the same time. (It's okay to send to a single person, with copies to others at the same employer, but don't send the same message to a large group of people at the same employer.) The employer's spam filter may see all the messages from one source and conclude that you are sending spam.

✔ **Do** send your resume to yourself and a few friends using different Internet service providers, like AOL, Gmail, Verizon, and Yahoo, to see whether your message arrives with your resume still usable.

✔ **Don't** use junk-mail type subject lines. Examples: exclamation points, all capitals, or spam buzzwords, such as *free, trial, cash,* or *great offer.* Even appropriate phrases like "increased sales $10,000 a month," can trigger spam filters, thanks to junk pitches such as "Make $10,000 a month from home working part time." When you're in doubt, try spelling out dollar amounts.

✔ **Don't** use too many numbers in your e-mail address, such as jobseeker12635@yahoo. com. Filter software may think the numbers are a spammer's tracking code.

Overexposure to recruiters

One more reason not to spread your resume all over the map: When you're targeting the fast track to the best jobs, nothing beats being brought to an employer's notice by an important third person — and an independent recruiter qualifies as an important third person.

Employers are becoming resistant to paying independent recruiters big fees to search the Web when they theoretically can save money by hiring in-house corporate recruiters to do it. That's why recruiting agencies need fresh inventory that employers can't find elsewhere. If you want a third-party recruiter to represent you, think carefully before pinning cyber-wings on your resume.

In addition to losing control of your resume, its wide availability can cause squabbles among contingency recruiters over who should be paid for finding you. An employer caught in the conflict of receiving a resume from multiple sources, including internal resume databases, will often pass over a potential employee rather than become involved in deciding which source, if any, should be paid.

Job Search Technology Is Here to Stay

Whether you're a job seeker with a streak of ambition a mile wide or a person who just wants to go with the flow but keep an escape hatch handy if your job starts to sink, now's the time to bone up on the rudiments of how technology can serve you in the job market. It's not going away.

Chapter 5

Do Due Diligence, Ditch Digital Dirt

In This Chapter

▶ Waking up: More employers trolling for online dirt

▶ Going all out when your reputation screams for repair

▶ Sidestepping future digital damage to your good name

▶ Proactively building a good name for yourself

· ·

A 40-something job seeker in the Northeast felt as though life was kicking him to the curb after four weary months of chasing job after job and never being called to interview. Eventually he discovered he was being mistaken for another man with the same name who had serious digital dirt: His namesake was involved in a Supreme Court obscenity case.

A 30-something single mother in the Midwest was fired from her job at a nonprofit organization — for something she did on her own time — the day after her boss Googled employees and discovered the mom was writing a sex blog.

A 20-something banking employee in the South was disappointed to learn that his good friend, who was interviewing for a job in the bank, lost out to another applicant because the interviewer checked the friend's Facebook page and was turned off by photos of the candidate drinking and cavorting with buddies.

These three incidents reflect a new reality in today's world: Your online image has become as important to your career as your customized resumes and your carefully managed references.

This chapter examines in understandable, low-tech terms, how your digital footprint can make you or break you.

Online Life Is an Open Book

The digital boom has given social media recruiting a prominent seat at the meet-up table where employers and job seekers connect. Recruiters who chase data on social networks now have the tools to add their own insight to the formality of information fed to them by candidates. As they click through the pages of Facebook, Twitter, LinkedIn and other sites, hiring authorities discover hidden areas of people's lives, and the outcome of social search isn't always to a job seeker's advantage.

The numbers of employers using social search keep heading higher. At least half of employers questioned in recent surveys now use online information to screen job candidates.

A look at the dark side

In a recent CareerBuilder survey, 35 percent of employers said they decided not to offer a job to a candidate based on the content uncovered on a social networking site.

From most to least common, the following are reasons employers cited for not hiring a candidate:

- ✔ Posting provocative or inappropriate photographs or information
- ✔ Posting content about drinking or using drugs
- ✔ Bad-mouthing previous employer, coworkers, or clients
- ✔ Showing poor communications skills
- ✔ Making discriminatory comments
- ✔ Lying about qualifications
- ✔ Sharing confidential information from previous employer

Some research shows that even higher percentages of hiring authorities search for online information about job candidates. A recent Microsoft study found that 79 percent check out potential hires online, and of those, 70 percent said they have rejected candidates based on what they found.

As a job seeker, you have a real chance of being prejudged or eliminated if digital dirt stains your reputation. Why take that chance?

A look at the bright side

In the same CareerBuilder survey, 18 percent of responding employers reported they found content on social networking sites that caused them to hire a candidate. From most to least common, those reasons include

- A profile that provided a good feel for the candidate's personality and fit
- A profile that supported the candidate's professional qualifications
- Creativity
- Solid communication skills
- Being well-rounded
- Good references
- Having received awards and accolades

Why Clean Up Your Act

Perhaps you've heard the joke about young people having to change their names on reaching adulthood to disown youthful hijinks stored on their friends' social media sites. It's a gag, but an important gag because we live in an age where your posted past can haunt your real-life future.

I asked Susan Estrada, a preeminent Internet pioneer and authority, this question: "What happens to all the data that floats in cyberspace? Is it possible to totally erase information that you or others have posted about you on the Web?"

Estrada's candid answer: "Nope. So much of the stuff, once in the cloud, is out of control. You should figure it will live forever. I have stuff out there from the '80s and '90s that I can't touch."

Google CEO Eric Schmidt agrees; he once told pundit Stephen Colbert: " . . . just remember that when you post something (online), the computers remember it forever."

Moreover, here's a wild card: What eventually happens to your posted information on a social site remains legally unclear when, by its rules, the site claims ownership of your personal data and everything you share on its space. Reading a site's privacy rules is a good idea.

Moving to other places on the Web and starting all over again as a virgin may be difficult, but do the best you can to shape up your hirable image before you head out to search for a job.

Restore Your Online Reputation

A recent Pew Research Center Internet report cements the general belief that search engines and social media sites now play a central role in building a person's identity online. The majority, 57 percent, of adult Internet users say they have used a search engine to look up their name and see what information is available about them online.

Many users in the Pew study refine their online reputation as they go by changing privacy settings on profiles, customizing who can see certain updates, and deleting unwanted information about them that appears online.

What's the Internet buzz about you? If you discover your reputation is crippling your job search efforts, I offer suggestions to help kick those skeletons out of your online closet.

Your first move requires research to uncover exactly what, if any, reputation problems are holding you back. Google your name and see what turns up. (In the vernacular of discussion threads, this is called "doing a self-Google.") Check Bing and Yahoo, too. And don't forget Pipl (www.pipl.com), a people-search engine where you may discover forgotten clues to your behavior on sites you no longer use.

When the news is bad, first try simple remedies. When you find something you don't like, e-mail the person responsible and ask that it be taken down.

Sometimes asking nicely is all you need to make negative news about you disappear. If not, here are additional steps to consider whether your online distress is self-inflicted or someone else is out to get you.

1. **Vacuum any crime scene.**

    Remove photos, content, and links you control that can torpedo you in an employer's eyes. If you don't control the posting site, ask the individual who does control it to ditch it. When in doubt, take it out.

2. **Overwhelm the bad stuff.**

    Smother indiscretions you've committed with a lot of new and favorable photos, content, and links — and endorsements from upstanding people (teachers, clergypersons, employers, coworkers, for example.) Google searchers normally read only the first few pages of results, not page 38. When you can't convince a site owner to make harmful content go away, your best bet is to entomb the hurtful data six feet under on page 38, 39, 40 — or deeper.

Check for your attacker, or else!

As good-name hits keep rolling off the line online, a new industry has emerged: reputation management services. At least a dozen firms have sprouted in the past several years to defend clients against bad-mouthing on the Web. Businesses hire them to avoid lost business, and individuals hire them to keep the bad-reputation monkey off their busy backs.

Most rep management firms offer both repair and maintenance services. How do they work? I discuss the essence of their efforts in this chapter: They strive to maximize positive content and bury

offending content deep in search results. There's even a trade association for the fast-emerging field: The Online Reputation Management Association (www.ormassociation.org).

Search engine optimization (SEO) is the practice of manipulating aspects of a Web site to improve or change its ranking in search engines. SEO techniques are used widely in professional-level reputation management to bury digital dirt. Find out how SEO works in *Search Engine Optimization For Dummies,* 3rd Edition (Wiley) by Peter Kent.

3. Call in a SWAT team.

Some people become the victims of malicious smears and psycho-talk that can wreak all kinds of damage even if it is patently false. In an age when the Internet does not forget, active self-defense is the only way to protect your online reputation.

In worse case situations, you may have to turn to professionals, such as Defend My Name (www.defendmyname.com) or ReputationDefender (www.reputationdefender.com). If the substantial cost is too much for your budget, study advanced techniques to clean up your own act. Start with a reputation management book written by experts.

The best book I've seen about surviving a rough-and-tumble Internet is *Wild West 2.0: How to Protect and Restore Your Online Reputation on the Untamed Social Frontier* (AMACOM) by Michael Fertik and David Thompson.

Fertik is chief executive officer, and Thompson is chief privacy officer, of ReputationDefender, a comprehensive online reputation management and privacy company. They've had a lot of experience helping people for whom the Internet has become an indelible scarlet letter.

Keep Watch on Your Online Reputation

Your digital good name comes from everything you do online that can be viewed by others. Anything and everything! This includes social media like Twitter, LinkedIn, and Facebook. It includes blogs, forums, and Web sites where you leave comments. It even includes the kinds of products and services that interest you.

Don't fool yourself with wishful thinking — "Oh well, my online reputation isn't the real me." Real or not, it *is* you, and your digital presence indicates how employers are likely to perceive you. Perception rules. As inconvenient as it is, in the online world, perception is reality.

Staying out of trouble online

Think down the road, and think twice before engaging in a flame war or lighting one up with firecrackers that carry your name tag. How do employers and recruiters ferret out your faults? They search for your name on various Web sites and search engines. The following recommendations help you put your best digital footprints forward.

Set up a free Google Alert on your name

The alerts you receive offer early warnings about identity mix-ups — those evil twins who have your same name and are out there online ruining it. Go to Google.com/alerts and type your name (surrounded by quotation marks) into the "Search terms" box. Select "Everything" as the "Type."

To be double-sure you're free, clear, and clean, perform a daily search for your name on Google or a search engine of your choice. Even if an employer doesn't check social networks or blogs, you can bet a basic Google search is part of how you're researched. Pages from social media and blogs may appear at the top of such a search.

Beware the overshare

Don't post trash you don't want everyone to know — no one cares how drunk, stoned, or loose you were last night. Don't post anything about your dating life. Don't post your birthdate. Don't post anything that may embarrass you five years down the road. Unless you're posing with the president of a nation or the Dalai Lama, don't post your name on party photos. Don't mix business and personal details online.

Most of all, if you're employed, don't post news of your job search in tweets or status updates, which is as dangerous as the boss finding your resume in the office copy machine.

Select Facebook friends with caution

To friend or not to friend bosses and coworkers? The jury's still out on that question but remember this: No matter whom you allow past the velvet rope and into your Facebook life, lock down privacy filters to create different levels of friends, such as professional and personal, and to select how much information each group can see.

All the security settings under the sun won't protect you if one friend decides to share your content with the rest of the world. Ignoring friend requests isn't rude, and gathering friends competitively opens you up to privacy problems. But it is a myth that you can see who has viewed your profile — that's technically impossible.

Keep an eye on MySpace comments

Remember that you're not the only writer on your account. Any of your friends can comment on your profile, which other friends can read. Daggers have been known to slip in among the diamonds.

Network building is a worthy pursuit, but a huge number of pseudo friends doesn't count for much in your career world and creates needless risk. Moreover, becoming online pals with celebrities and politicians isn't always a hot idea: It may cause employers to wonder whether you're too full of yourself and will be overly demanding.

Don't go naked on Twitter

Letting it all hang out on the tweet line invites everyone to follow and see what you're up to. That's not only unsafe, it's uncool. Instead, open multiple free accounts (no limit) and make sure the one with your real name on it is pure as a falling snowflake. If you feel you must pass on frisky questionable links, use an alias account.

List respected groups on LinkedIn

Give thought to which interest groups and associations claim you as a member, and give deeper thought as to whether all of them do you proud on your professional profile.

In the United States, civic groups such as Kiwanis and Rotary contribute to your good name, but Vampire Cretins of America cause pause because . . . well, it may lead some people to perceive you as a weirdo. (Chapter 8 tells you more about the kinds of organizations that look good on your profile.) Unlike data that search engines dig up about you, information in your profile is under your control.

Bird-dog your blog tracks

If you're blogging on your own creation and other blogs, be mindful of what you're saying (and have said) as it relates to your job life. Maybe you ranted something you regret, like a previous depression or law case, and would like a rematch. If you haven't already done it, use Google Blog Search (www.blogsearch.google.com) to see what's up and what you'd like to take down. If the search engines aren't indexing your personal blog, look into registering it with the likes of Google, Yahoo, and Bing.

Keep mum on grievances

Bellyache elsewhere when you please, but not in the land of cyber-please. Stay positive. And don't overlook specific accomplishments that boost your brand. (See Chapter 2 for more about branding.)

Remember that turnabout is fair play

Don't sabotage others by indiscreetly spilling unsavory beans, or playing jokes that can provoke injury to a friend. For example, don't comment online to someone starting a new job, "Congrats! Hope you break your record and last three months!" Blabbing "state secrets" invites reciprocal action.

Join the right armies

Participate on forums, discussion threads, groups, and so on that create positive content and jibe with your career plans. Comment on Web sites and blog postings with high traffic.

For example, adding your profile to LinkedIn, which has a high rank with search engines, pushes your profile higher in Google search results. You can also publish your profile on Plaxo (www.plaxo.com) and VisualCV. com (www.visualcv.com) and connect them to each other. Check possible cross-reference links on each Web site where you post a profile.

Not only does being seen in the right places give you online credibility, these mentions help crowd out dirt and relocate it to the back of the line.

Looking like a champ online

If the Internet is one giant resume, as comedian Stephen Colbert says it is, use online reputation management to boost your appeal as an ideal job candidate. The rise of social media and advances in technology can make favorable words about you sound like confidence, not bragging. The following tips deal with your routine behavior when you open doors to the way you think and what others think about you.

Make cheerful comments

Even when you're down and out and suffering a bad case of the blues, don't make those feelings part of your online persona. Employers aren't looking to hang crepe. They try not to hire Gloomy Gus or his sister, Dora Dour. Instead, employers look for new hires who radiate a positive attitude. To paraphrase your mother's admonition: "If you can't say something nice, say nothing at all on the Internet." (Or use a screen name.)

Mention popular traits

Although they may be clichés, certain keywords for personal attributes and abilities have not outlived their usefulness. Major job search engine Indeed. com analyzed millions of job ads on its site over a six-month period in 2010. The object of the analysis was to find out which popular traits employers ask for again and again.

In descending order, expressed in keywords, the top 15 professional attributes or abilities employers want in the people they hire are

- ✔ Leadership
- ✔ Interpersonal skills
- ✔ Problem-solving
- ✔ Motivation
- ✔ Efficiency
- ✔ Attention to detail
- ✔ Ability to prioritize
- ✔ Teamwork
- ✔ Reliability
- ✔ Ability to multitask
- ✔ Time management
- ✔ Passion
- ✔ Listening skills
- ✔ Outgoingness
- ✔ Honesty

Look for ways to incorporate these wanted traits into your comments. You may say, for example, "My boss was highly complimentary about my last report, saying it showed leadership and solved key problems in holding the line on material cost."

Post kudos on social media

Have you won an award? Has someone praised you? Don't hold back. Just post the facts on your page — "I was excited to get these good words from Carl Case, the head official of the Little League where I coach: "We're proud of Jake's great 9–1 win record this year. The kids think he's Superman."

Announce your promotions

Let friends know when you move up a notch. Don't forget to add how much you appreciate working for such a fine employer. You look successful and loyal.

Social media absenteeism also risky

"There was a time when you went full bore on a job search where you mainly concentrated on proofing your resume and cover letter for typos, checking out your interviewing wardrobe and performance, and giving your references a heads-up," says Scott Swimley, sales vice president for Alumwire, a San Francisco-based company that provides a social media platform created for interaction by individuals, schools, and corporations.

"Change happens," Swimley adds. "Not only can Internet information about you hurt your reputation, employers may not hire you — especially if you're a young adult working in marketing or communications — if you entirely lack a social networking presence."

Relate growth experiences

Relate on your page or blog the life or professional experiences that are helping you to mature into a better person or more competent worker. Education is an obvious topic. But think about other positive shaping experiences as well. Perhaps you worked in a soup kitchen or helped build housing for the poor. Maybe you read a book on time-management skills or a guide to managing the friction between generations in the workplace. You are painting a picture of who you are and what you can do.

Look Who's Talking . . . About You

It seems that the younger you are, the quicker you're getting the memo about the career-risky behavior of living out loud and having bad news about you infest the Web. People 18 to 29 are more apt to vigorously scrub unwanted posts and limit information about themselves than are older adults, according to surveys. Why is that? My guess is older adults come later to social media, have already established their careers, and spend little time thinking about digital dirt.

That characterization certainly described me until the day a friend called my attention to a Web site that reviews products and services. Checking out the site, I was shocked to see an anonymous blistering attack on the superb veterinarian who has long done a great job of caring for my pets. Furious at the unknown critic's fact-free character assassination, I quickly went tit for tat with a glowing evaluation of my pets' vet.

That was the day I moved from passively understanding there's a very real threat of accidental damage and malicious attacks on the Internet to actively advocating the care and feeding of online reputation management.

Part II

Customizing Resumes: Your Many Faces in Many Places

The 5th Wave   By Rich Tennant

"Do you think I'm padding my resume by including work experience revealed in my Past Life Regression Therapy?"

In this part . . .

Forget the one-size-fits-all resume. That thing is kaput. Today's hiring managers rely on sorting tools that show no mercy about your qualifications, which means that you absolutely, positively must show each employer exactly how well your skills align with their needs. This part of the book fills you in on ways to tailor-fit your value to the job you want.

Chapter 6

Target! The Generic Resume Has Nearly Dropped Dead

In This Chapter

▶ Selling yourself as custom match for each job

▶ Moving instantly with Plug-and-Play resumes

▶ Tailoring your resume from A to Z

*Y*our old one-size-fits-all resume is dated, obsolescent, moth-eaten, passé, antediluvian, and otherwise dumpster-ready.

Blame it on technology. Today's employers are drowning in digital resumes because job seekers find them so easily clicked and sent — and send them they do! By the hundreds, by the thousands, by the millions! What's a resume-soaked employer to do?

The 21st Century Resume Rush has caused most companies to use an automated applicant tracking system (ATS) to make the first cut of people applying for a job opening. After the software separates the possible from the worthless, human eyes take over. Recruiters surf the surviving database of possible hires to identify the best matches of candidate and job. After additional cuts, only the last candidates standing get the recruiter's interviewing nod.

This chapter explains why your resumes go missing and reveals new time-saving techniques to increase your odds of making it over early hurdles.

Targeted Resumes Conquer Generics

When you're on the outside looking in at recruiting gates and going nowhere, suspect that your standard-issue generic resume is stopping you cold. Once a staple of job search, today's generic resume model has become merely a shot in the dark, ricocheting about a murky marketplace of endless competition — a shot far more likely to miss than hit your target. This is especially true if you're on the high end of the age scale, or have been unemployed for a long while.

When you're tired of being kicked around in the job market, reflect on the differing initial impressions a generic resume and a targeted resume make:

✔ **A generic resume is candidate-centered.**

   Translation: Here's my resume, Mr. or Ms. Employer. Hope you can find something you like about me. I'm too busy and I lack motivation to show you exactly why you want to hire me. You're on your own. Good luck. Signed: *No one you ever heard of.*

✔ **A targeted resume is employer-centered.**

   Translation: Glad to see you, Mr. or Ms. Employer. I'm so right for your job I've gone the extra mile to make it easy for you to spot the fabulous match between my qualifications and your job's requirements. I promise it will be well worth your time to look me over more closely. Signed: *Someone you want to meet.*

With the exception of a handful of situations (see the sidebar in this chapter, "Special cases when going generic is okay"), the all-purpose resume is in a hearse headed for a final resting place behind history's hill. Rather than join the funeral procession, discover the rewards of creating a customized, targeted resume for each job you seek.

This chapter emphasizes how to do just that with the least fuss and muss. It reveals two Custom Lite approaches that deal in quick fixes. In contrast, the Full Custom approach requires a more comprehensive makeover.

By boosting the odds, you won't be screened out before you get a chance to interview; both the Custom Lite and Full Custom approaches can put new fire in the belly of your job search.

Welcoming a Custom Lite Approach

In case you're wondering how the generic resume became the norm, national career expert Peter Weddle explains that way back when the typewriter was king, customizing resumes was a time wipeout — like re-chiseling a statue.

Even though the computer age is upon us, fully customizing a resume remains a time-sucker in busy lives — like preparing a five-course meal from the beginning. That's why you want to check out two quick-fix Custom Lite treatments to tailor your resume for each specific employment opportunity:

✔ The first technique is based on *design;* the recruiter gets a glimpse of your matching value at first glance.

✔ The second technique is based on *words;* the recruiter grasps your matching value at first read.

Design-based approach: Two columns

The *two-column resume* — also called a *T-resume* or *ledger resume* — is a custom quick fix that immediately tells recruiting eyes: "I have exactly what you're looking for." The two-column layout is appropriate for most resumes, other than top executive resumes and academic CVs.

A popular treatment of the two-column resume opens with a summary featuring bullets:

✔ The left column of a ledger design is typically titled something along the lines of "You Ask For" or "Company Requires." It identifies the position's requirements — the qualities and capabilities a given employer seeks to hire.

✔ The related right column of a ledger design typically has a title like "I Offer," or "I Deliver." It confirms the job seeker provides the specific requested qualifications.

The remainder of a two-column profile design is identical to the remainder of a generic resume.

You can extend the two-column format beyond the summary to a larger portion of the resume — or even throughout the entire resume. For convenience, I show the two-column design only as a first-page summary presentation.

I illustrate the two-column look with a pair of first pages of resumes for mythical lawyer Mark Thomas. Mark's *generic* resume (Figure 6-1) reflects a lawyer with general qualifications who writes to benefit himself. Contrast this document with Mark's *targeted* resume (Figure 6-2), which reflects a lawyer who writes to benefit the employer.

Mark Thomas
San Diego, California
(555) 555-5555
mthomas@gmail.com

Professional Summary

Well-qualified attorney seasoned in civil litigation and trial practice. Extensive experience in business litigation, construction defects, homeowner association law, employment law, and personal injury. Solid record in all aspects of litigation—from client interaction and court appearances to written discovery, depositions, alternative dispute resolution, and appeals. Strong research and legal writing skills; taught legal writing at respected law school for six years.

- Solid 9-year record of litigating cases. Licensed to practice in State and Federal Courts
- Taken, defended more than 100 depositions of parties, witnesses, experts
- Proven ability to draft winning arguments, prevail in oral law and motion practice
- Handled mediations, settlement conferences, and arbitration hearings on matters ranging from small business partnership disputes to complex litigation involving more than 100 plaintiffs and 75 defendants
- Actively seek out advice and critical suggestions from supervisors. Managed extensive case loads on diverse issues in multiple jurisdictions
- Created systems to regularly and timely inform clients, attorneys, paralegals, and support staff of deadlines, procedures, and other significant developments

Legal Experience

Dewey Cheatem & Howe [Dates]

Associate Attorney

Drafted successful motion for determination of good faith settlement, leading to compromise of $1.8 million damage claim for $200,000. Defended client general …

Figure 6-1: The first page of Mark Thomas' generic resume fails to show potential employers what they'd gain from hiring him for a specific employment opportunity.

Mark Thomas

San Diego, California
(585) 555-5555 ❖ mthomas223@gmail.com

Tenacious │ Intrepid │ Conscientious │ Cool -headed

Well-qualified attorney seasoned in civil litigation and trial practice. Extensive experience in business litigation, construction defects, homeowner association law, employment law, and personal injury. Solid record in all aspects of litigation— from client interaction and court appearances to written discovery, depositions, alternative dispute resolution, and appeals. Strong research and legal writing skills; taught legal writing at respected law school for six years.

You Ask For	*I Deliver*
☐ Minimum 7 years' experience in State and Federal Court.	☑ Solid 9-year record litigating cases. Licensed to practice in State and Federal Courts.
☐ Ability to take and defend depositions.	☑ Taken and defended more than 100 depositions of parties, witnesses, experts.
☐ Ability to draft pleadings and motions, make court appearances.	☑ Proven ability to draft winning arguments and prevail in oral law and motion practice.
☐ Ability to handle mediations, settlement conferences, and arbitration hearings.	☑ Handled 85 mediations, settlement conferences, arbitration hearings from small business partnership disputes, to complex litigation with 100 plaintiffs, 75 defendants.
☐ Ability to take direction and work independently on cases and projects assigned.	☑ Actively seek advice, critical suggestions from supervisors. Managed extensive case loads on diverse issues.
☐ Good communication skills and heavy client contact.	☑ Created more than 25 systems to timely inform clients, attorneys, paralegals, support staff of deadlines, procedures, developments.

Legal Experience

Dewey Cheatem & Howe   [Dates]

Associate Attorney
Drafted successful motion for determination of good faith settlement, leading to compromise of $1.8 million damage claim for $200,000. Defended client ....

Figure 6-2: The first page of Mark Thomas' targeted two-column resume makes clear the benefits he offers for a specific employment opportunity.

Word watchers: Know your synonyms

Generic resumes are also known as:	*Targeted resumes are also known as:*
one-size-fits-all	customized
all-purpose	tailored
universal	personalized
all-in-one	job-specific

If you submit a two-column resume to a company Web site or to a job board, remember to attach it as a PDF (Portable Document Format by Adobe). Otherwise, the formatting will go berserk. Chapter 7 gives you further guidelines for determining which format is best for which kind of electronic recipient.

Words-based approach: Plug and Play

If the future of snagging job interviews is in personalizing the approach, the question is, why don't more people create targeted resumes? Probably because crafting a Full Custom resume for every job you go after is as tiring as tap dancing your way across a continent very slowly.

The answer lies in a groundbreaking approach that relies on shortcuts. The big idea is to create a *starter* (basic) resume of one to three pages that you change as needed to fit each job goal.

Although a number of people have noodled around with quick fixes for 21st century targeted resumes, top career strategist Kathryn Troutman has nailed the technique, creating the Troutman Plug and Play Resume Method. She is president of the Resume Place (www.resume-place.com), a large Baltimore-based writing and publishing firm.

The Troutman Plug and Play Resume Method is a systematic process in which you mix and match prepared modules of personal information as a jiffy shortcut to customizing each resume. You store, sort, and speedily retrieve information as needed. And because you cut and paste, you do it fast!

Although Troutman's Plug and Play (PnP) approach fits into the Custom Lite category, her method packs a powerful punch in targeting job searches.

The PnP technique enables you to almost instantly send out a targeted online resume for any opportunity *for which you qualify*. The PnP approach won't work if you're an artist applying for a finished carpentry job. It could work like a charm if you're an artist applying for a position as a museum exhibit designer.

When you're unsure whether your qualifications for a specific job are adequate, review the relevant occupational brief in the Occupational Outlook Handbook (www.bls.gov.oco), a free federal government publication revised every two years.

After you make practice runs with the Troutman Plug and Play Resume Method, you can create a first-rate tailored resume in under an hour; I've seen Troutman whisk out an impressive PnP resume in 20 minutes flat.

Plug and Play Resumes in Five Easy Steps

When your time management budget won't stretch to include crafting a Full Custom resume hearty enough to survive software and human recruiter screening, don't give up — call PnP to the rescue with these steps.

Step 1: Create a core resume

Compile every career-related factor in your background. Include data ranging from experience and education, to competencies and skills. Everything! (For content suggestions, see Chapter 8.)

Don't forget to include accomplishments you can back up with true brief stories in an interview.

Think of your core resume as a comprehensive career inventory — a trip down memory lane. The finished product may spread over a dozen pages; no matter — only you lay eyes on this valuable resource document that saves you exasperation and time in the long run.

Step 2: Create information modules

Stockpile data on your computer in the form of personal information modules — paragraphs of autobiographical facts you copy and paste into many targeted resumes. Begin this step by drawing content from your core resume (Step 1). Add more data as needed.

Create one or more modules in each of the following categories:

- ✔ **Keywords:** Gather industry and typical position requirements for the kind of job you're targeting: job titles, job duties, and industry jargon. Web browse for online lists of additional keywords in the same job families; try searching for "keyword generators" and "keyword lists."

- ✔ **Accomplishments:** Choose accomplishments related to the jobs you're targeting; this selectivity is especially important if you're changing career fields. (Never say your greatest accomplishment is in a field from which you're trying to escape.) You can create various types of accomplishment categories, such as accomplishments saving or making money for an employer.

- ✔ **Work experience:** Construct a module of your previous job titles, employers, and years worked. Focus on paid work but include unpaid work as well, especially if you're short on the former. Internships are valuable. (Work is work, paid or unpaid.)

- ✔ **Skills:** Put together paragraphs naming your skills aimed at specific functions — a good start is management skills, administrative skills, budgeting skills, *hard skills* (the ones that help you do tasks specific to a particular job), and *soft skills* (the ones that help you work with people).

- ✔ **Competencies:** If skills are the activities people can see you do as you work at a given job, competencies are the knowledge and experience you use to do the skills well. Compile paragraphs describing your competencies and how you use them. You can separate competencies by specific categories — work-based competencies, and behavior-based competencies, for example. (See Chapter 8.)

- ✔ **Education and professional development:** Assemble a module detailing a reverse chronological history of your education, including continuing education, seminars, and distance learning.

  Limit your list of professional development courses to the past five years. Your chances of remembering anything from a training course you attended five years ago are slim. Additionally, the world has changed enough to make training older than five years somewhat outdated.

- ✔ **Credentials:** Make a module identifying relevant licenses and current professional certifications. Omit any credentials from a field you hope to see only in your rear-view mirror.

- ✔ **Awards, honors, memberships:** Record your professional kudos and memberships. For these paragraphs, select only those with relevance for your target.

When the name of the award doesn't show its impact, tell what it was for as opposed to what it was called. Thanks to career expert Don Orlando for the following examples that illustrate this tip.

The "President's Award" in one company may be for exceeding sales goals by 10 percent, while an award with the very same name in another company may be given for just meeting the goal. Avoid confusion by

- Showing the competitiveness of the award — relate how many people competed for it.

- Adding any unusual context — were you the only person to win the award back-to-back in the 50-year history of this honor? Say so to get full credit for what you've done.

✔ **Organizations:** A module mentioning both professional and civic membership groups to which you belong deserves careful thought, for both relevance and impact. Mention the fact if you were an officer.

✔ **Profiles:** Build modules of your favorite summary profile for each kind of job you're targeting.

✔ **Endorsements:** Keep a module on standby of two- or three-line testimonials (like very short book blurbs) from anyone who has seen you solve problems. Likely sources include bosses, coworkers, customers, and vendors. Endorsements from well-known individuals in a community are helpful, too. Specific comments are more powerful than generalities.

For more suggestions on the content of your modules, skip ahead and read content categories in Chapter 8, and read about keywords in Chapter 10.

Step 3: Create a starter resume

Select information from your core resume in Step 1 to produce a starter (basic) resume of one to three pages. (Yes, you may be able to use, with modification, your old generic resume.) Save your starter resume on your computer — it's the foundation for all your targeted spinoffs.

Step 4: Research target job positions

When you respond to an advertised job, analyze the specific job description for employment you hope to snare. Zero in on keywords.

Alternatively, when you park your targeted resume in a job board database, or shop it around your network, study a dozen job ads to find the most common requirements for the work you want. Again, remember to use plenty of keywords.

Although job duties also reflect keywords you can use in your response, don't confuse job duties with job requirements. A requirement may be a college degree; a job duty may be managing workers. In lining up keywords, choose requirements first because they are primary indicators you are qualified for the position.

Step 5: Create a targeted resume

Lead with strength in your PnP resume even if you have to bend some conventional rules and reshuffle your personal chronology.

For example, graduates generally start listing work experience before education on their resumes after one year of full-time work, or after their first full-time job. But in PnP resumes, a decade-old education may appear before work history in situations where a job seeker is starting over in a different career, or needs to be appreciated as a proven learner.

Consider the following points to keep your PnP resume from premature crashing-and-burning by immediately showing how your qualifications jibe with a job's requirements:

- ✔ In most situations, change the summary bullets (relevant skills) at the top of your resume's first page to make them instantly perceived as relevant to the targeted job.

- ✔ Sometimes — to establish immediate relevancy — you alter the chronological order of your work experience and education.

  You may, for example, lead your work history with a job you held five years ago when the older job is a better match than a more recent job. But don't lead with a job you held 20 years ago even when it's a close match. Remember that recency is next to relevancy in PnP resumes.

- ✔ When you can't decide whether to (a) present a strongly preferred traditional reverse chronological history with no gaps, or (b) to showcase certain relevant items by moving them forward out of traditional order, ask yourself whether altering how you present your work history or education will improve your chances of surviving the screening process.

  If your answer is "yes," go for it! If your answer is "no," stick to the traditional, no-gap lineup.

When you're ready to cut and paste your way to a targeted resume, don't forget to change the job objective at the top of your starter resume. A surprising number of job seekers overlook this essential step.

Plug and Play Resume Sketches

Look over the following backstory for Allen C. Trenton, followed by his three-page starter resume and its five spinoff *resume sketches (*one page each*)*.

Resume sketches are not resumes. Instead, they are brief educational illustrations of how the PnP concept works. I have purposely omitted much detail in these sketches to make the PnP process easier to observe.

Allen's starter resume and his five resume sketches were created by Resume-Place.com president Kathryn Troutman. (Although based on a real person, names and other identifying data have been changed for privacy reasons.)

Allen's backstory

Thirty-three-year-old Allen lives in Baltimore, Maryland. Voluntary relocation would be a last resort. Now unemployed except for temporary work, Allen is in the career-change mode, hoping to get a job he wants with the skills and experience he already has.

While a college student, Allen began his studies and work experience at a recording studio, hoping to become a recording and sound engineer. Later he switched to selling high-end sound equipment for a prominent retail chain and continued there after graduating with a bachelor's degree in psychology.

When, in a down economy, the retail chain shuttered a few years later, Allen discovered comparable employment wasn't available locally. Now married, Allen decided to make a course correction and began to teach substitute classes for the Baltimore public schools. The substitute teaching assignments patched holes in his family budget, as Allen and his wife struggled to pay their bills.

To clone or not to clone: Mirroring ad language

Must you use the exact words you find in a job ad or position description? In a word, yes. Although sophisticated software may give you points for synonyms, the human recruiters that rule the second round of screening may not. Junior recruiters can't be counted on to recognize subtle differences in terminology. And high-volume recruiters racing through enough resumes to wear out a dozen pairs of eyes in eight hours may not take the time to carefully consider slight changes of expression. So, for now, you should stick with the ditto school of content and keywords, advises Jim Lemke, this book's technical editor.

In addition to his ease in communications pursuits, Allen's managerial skills include computer systems operation, planning projects, and coordinating events.

He is scouting professional positions in a number of career fields for which he likely qualifies — positions that are interesting to him and offer employee benefits.

As soon as his employment is stable, Allen will evaluate distance learning options to earn a master's degree in education, as well as prepare for secondary teaching certification.

Described by friends as "a walker and a talker," Allen much prefers interacting with people to toiling alone at a desk. Allen, who can sell Christmas trees in February, is looking with creative eyes at employment opportunities in both the private and the federal sectors.

Allen's starter resume

Allen's starter document is the basis for each resume sketch, as described in Step 3 in the above section "Plug and Play Resumes in Five Easy Steps." His starter resume (Figure 6-3) is the framework Allen uses to spin off customized resumes.

ALLEN C. TRENTON
Baltimore, MD

Cell: 443-333-3333   Email: actrent@yahoo.com

TITLE OF TARGET JOB

RELEVANT SKILLS

- Skill
- Skill
- Skill
- Skill
- Skill

WORK EXPERIENCE

Substitute Secondary Education Teacher, Baltimore County Public School System, Baltimore, MD   [Date to Present]

- Teach courses in multiple disciplines and at all grade levels. Apply established educational evaluations, models, rules, and guidelines to establish individual student goals. Establish safe, stable learning environment. Exhibit positive behavioral models.

- Develop and follow curricula for history, social studies, geography classes. Engage students with text and class exercises. Conduct research. Lead discussions about historical events.

- Communicate effectively orally and in writing with parents, guardians, school administrators. Monitor progress. Help students overcome obstacles and achieve personal goals.

- Successfully inspire diverse student audiences; including emotionally disturbed students, ADD, ADHD, various other psychological disorders. Also work with low-income, minority, and recent immigrant students with poor prior academic achievement. Prepare students for required benchmark examinations; provide testing accommodations for special needs students.

Key Accomplishments

Successfully taught challenging 5th grade class of 8 special needs minority students for 5 months.

Ensured all students matriculated to 6th grade. Improved behavior and academic achievement. Commended by teachers and administrators as the only Sub to succeed with this class in two school years.

Figure 6-3: Allen's starter resume is a framework document used for instant customization.

Allen C. Trenton, Page 2   443-333-3333
_____

Worked late and stayed after normal school hours to make every group feel welcome.

Took time to really understand learning requirements of 5th grade, minority, and special needs students. Teacher with 20 years' experience said: "Allen's the best substitute we've had in two years!"

All my students successfully moved on to the next grade—the only teacher among the 12 educators employed by this school to deliver results like these.

Marketing Specialist, The A-Place, Inc., Catonsville, MD   [Date to Present]

- Work 10 hours a week.
- Design and assist with marketing efforts and plans. The A-Place, Inc. is a contractor, publisher, and provider of federal services for private industry and federal jobseekers.
- Book fulfillment services: Assist with book purchases by government agencies, military customers, Amazon.com, book distribution groups and wholesalers seeking popular federal publications.

Key Accomplishment

Complimented by company general manager for reliability and careful work; awarded highest performance rating for effective inventory management; no stock losses.

Census Enumerator, US Census Bureau, Baltimore, MD   [Dates]

- Worked 20 hours a week.
- Managed a tight schedule to interview hundreds of people.
- Collected and developed high quality reports from a variety of sources.
- Used my uncommon problem-solving skills to conduct one of the largest surveys done in America in the last ten years.

Key Accomplishments

Completed interviews within deadlines with a safe track record.

Found just the right balance between interpreting rules and regulations and resourceful interviewing needed to get reliable results from complete strangers. Supervisor with ten years' experience in census operations complemented me for the top-notch interviewing skills.

Allen C. Trenton, Page 3   443-333-3333

Sales Manager/Sales Associate, Tilling Audio-TV, Owings Mills, MD   [Dates]

- Expert in meeting and greeting visitors. Built rapport with strangers; managed rush of customers with unique needs. Seven years' experience in retail sales and business development. Skilled in interpreting complex technology environment. Genuinely listened to clients and responded with relevant and engaging information.

- Coached, trained, motivated sales team of 11 professionals. Covered product interpretations, demonstrations, customer service, conflict resolution and negotiation.

- Project manager for commercial and residential installation contracts. Researched, negotiated, evaluated, managed, scheduled, and served as point of contact for 5 professional installers.

- Oversaw and monitored contractor performance. Maintained procurement records. Developed vendor contacts. Collected funds, Prepared invoices. handled retail sales and reports.

Key Accomplishment

Led sales team to consistently achieve personal and company benchmarks. Inducted into the Winners' Circle for five consecutive years — a rare accomplishment as the Circle is limited to our top five producers.

EDUCATION AND RECENT PROFESSIONAL DEVELOPMENT

Pursuing M.Ed., University of Maryland, Baltimore, MD [Expected Date]
Used my strong problem-solving skills to complete Praxis 1 and 2 Social Studies, placing in the top 10%

University of Maryland, Baltimore, MD   [Date]
BS, Psychology,
GPA 3.25. Dean's List. Worked 20 hours a week carrying full academic load

Omega Recording and Engineering School, Rockville, MD   [Date]
Certificate, Recording and Sound Engineering

Spinoff 1: Permanent substitute teacher

Permanent substitute teachers earn higher pay in this school district than temporary substitute teachers. So although Allen already works as a temporary substitute, understandably he would like to transition to permanent status. Figure 6-4 shows his targeted resume sketch.

In addition to aiming his bullets of relevant skills directly at his teaching expertise, Allen's education module appears before his work experience to highlight his intent to invest in graduate study and to acquire the required credentialing for permanent status. He displays his major, psychology, in boldface type because educators view knowledge of the science of human behavior as a plus in education. His statement that he worked while earning high grades is also viewed as a plus (think dedicated workhorse). His next module, work experience, shows valuable work experience in teaching; note key accomplishments in teaching and in interacting with a wide variety of people.

Spinoff 2: Training coordinator

Allen looks for connections between teaching children and training adults. In retargeting the relevant skills bullets, he mentions his skill with office and training software. (See Figure 6-5.) Allen leads with his education paragraph and follows with his work experience in teaching for the same reasons he did in Figure 6-4. Allen includes key accomplishments proclaiming not only does he work well with almost everyone, but he's a standout professional who succeeded where others failed.

Spinoff 3: Background investigator

Background investigators do the kinds of things Allen identifies in Figure 6-6, which shows his resume sketch's bullets of relevant skills for this federal job. (This is not a job for Sam Spade chasing murder suspects but a government national security function.) Although the Census Bureau job was temporary, Allen presents it first to communicate his ability to productively interact with large numbers of strangers in any setting. He follows with the substitute-teaching job because it shows that he's currently employed. (Employers typically prefer to hire employed candidates.)

Spinoff 4: Contract specialist

The relevant skills bullets in this version of Allen's Plug and Play resume sketch (Figure 6-7) use a lot of keywords to indicate he knows his way around negotiation and contract management. His referral to statistical analysis software (SPSS and PASW) adds to the presumption of professional competence. Allen leads with his work experience module, starting with his substitute teaching job to show he is employed. Allen immediately follows with his retail experience in the Tilling Audio-TV store, which is his strongest qualification for work as a contract specialist.

Spinoff 5: Park guide

Walker-and-talker Allen lays out his relevant skills, using many of the keywords he found in the job announcement. (See Figure 6-8.) Allen immediately follows his skills bullets with his work experience module to communicate his ease with crowds of strangers. Allen's education module comes next to indicate his interest in dealing with information as well as with people.

Special cases when going generic is okay

Although targeted resumes outperform generic resumes by a three-planet radius, a one-size-fits-all document can be effective in some circumstances.

✔ **Job fairs:** Customized resumes are impractical for wide distribution at dozens of employer booths. That's why I suggest you write the best all-purpose resume you can; when you get a nibble from a company you'd like to work for, quickly get back to the company recruiter with a targeted resume. Your willingness to go the extra mile makes you stand out from the competition.

✔ **Similar career pursuits:** When you have a single job goal — such as working only in the biotech industry developing new wonder drugs — you can work with one really good resume. But when posting your resume in online databases, you need a resume customized for each additional career field or job function you pursue.

✔ **Networking contacts:** If you hand out generic resumes to your inner circle of friends to help them help you in your search, mark them, "For Your Eyes Only." Ask them to contact you when they hear of job leads so you can respond with a targeted resume.

✔ **Reference refresher:** Send a generic resume or a bio to people who have agreed to serve as a reference in your job search.

✔ **Social media:** Profiles and bios are also in the one-size-fits-all family of information about you. When posted online, both bios and profiles defy customization. (Read about pigeonholing in Chapter 2.)

ALLEN C. TRENTON

Baltimore, MD

Cell: 443-333-3333   Email: actrent@yahoo.com

Permanent Substitute Teacher

RELEVANT SKILLS

- Gift for clarity: speak, explain, instruct; inspire, motivate students
- Proven success interacting with individuals in diverse settings
- Strong problem-solving skills. Excellent in social skills and conflict resolution
- Earned Bachelor's degree. Solid GPA

EDUCATION

Pursuing M.Ed, University of Maryland, Baltimore, MD   [Expected Date]

BS, **Psychology,** University of Maryland, Baltimore, MD   [Date]
GPA 3.25 Dean's List. Worked 20 hours a week
while carrying a full academic load

WORK EXPERIENCE

Substitute Secondary Education Teacher   [Date to Present]
Baltimore County Public School System, Baltimore, MD

Train and motivate students—including special needs students—for required benchmark examinations

Communicate and instruct clearly so students get seamless learning and motivation

Communicate in writing to get support of parents and administrators

Key Accomplishments

All my students successfully moved to the next grade—the only teacher to deliver these results.

Balanced pressing coordination, multi-tasking, and class scheduling needs with teaching special needs students. Teachers and administrators said: "Allen's the best we've had in two years!"

Census Enumerator, U.S. Census Bureau, Baltimore, MD   [Dates]

Managed tight schedule. Used uncommon problem-solving skills to conduct hundreds of interviews.

Key Accomplishment

Interpreted rules to interact resourcefully with interviewees.

Figure 6-4: In this resume sketch, Allen's starter resume is turned into a marketing document for a permanent substitute teaching job.

ALLEN C. TRENTON
Baltimore, MD

Cell: 443-333-3333   Email: actrent@yahoo.com

Training Coordinator

RELEVANT SKILLS

- Communicate and instruct clearly
- Track record of motivating people
- Effective coordination, multi-tasking, class scheduling
- Keyboard skills: 60 wpm; fluent MS Office, plus current training software
- Bachelor's degree with strong GPA

EDUCATION

Pursuing M.Ed, University of Maryland, Baltimore, MD   [Expected Date]

BS, **Psychology,** University of Maryland, Baltimore, MD   [Date]
GPA 3.25. Dean's List. Worked 20 hours a week while
carrying full academic load.

WORK EXPERIENCE:

**Substitute Secondary Education Teacher, Baltimore County Public
School System, Baltimore, MD**   [Date to Present]

- Train, inspire, and motivate audiences.
- Communicate and instruct clearly so students get seamless learning and motivation.
- Communicate in writing powerfully enough to enlist and maintain the support of parents, guardians, and administrators.

Key Accomplishment

Balanced pressing coordination, multi-tasking, and class scheduling needs
with the requirements of teaching special needs students. Teachers and
administrators with 20 years' experienced said: "Allen's the best substitute
we've had in two years!"

Census Enumerator, U.S. Census Bureau, Baltimore, MD   [Dates]

Managed tight schedule to interview hundreds of people. Collected
and developed high quality reports from a variety of sources.

Key Accomplishment

Found the right balance between interpreting rules and regulations and resourceful
interviewing needed to get reliable results from strangers. Supervisor with 10
years' experience in census operations complemented me for my top-notch
interviewing skills.

Figure 6-5: In this resume sketch, Allen's starter resume becomes a sales tool for a training position.

ALLEN C. TRENTON

Baltimore, MD

Cell: 443-333-3333   Email: actrent@yahoo.com

Background Investigator

RELEVANT SKILLS

- Top-notch interviewing skills; resourceful, good judgment
- Proven ability to collect and develop information from variety of sources
- Reliably prepare investigation reports with document quality controls
- Strong time-management skills to plan, conduct surveys
- Uncommon problem-solving skills
- Attentive to Interpreting rules and regulations
- Bachelor's degree – solid GPA

WORK EXPERIENCE

Census Enumerator, 20 hrs/wk   [Dates]

**US Census Bureau
Baltimore, MD**

Managed tight schedule to interview hundreds of people. Collected, developed high quality reports from variety of sources.

Key Accomplishments

Safely met deadlines. Gained confidence of public. Supervisor with 10 years' experience in census operations complimented me for my top-notch interviewing skills.

Substitute Secondary Education Teacher   [Date to Present]

**Baltimore County Public School System
Baltimore, MD**

- Communicate effectively orally, in writing with students, parents, school.

- Successfully interview, teach, inspire diverse student audiences. Prepare students for required benchmark examinations; provide training and testing for special needs students.

Key Accomplishment

Commended by teachers and administrators for only Sub to succeed with special needs class for two years.

Figure: 6-6: Allen's starter resume is tailored for the job of a federal background investigator in this resume sketch.

ALLEN C. TRENTON
Baltimore, MD

Cell: 443-333-3333   Email: actrent@yahoo.com

Contract Specialist

RELEVANT SKILLS

- Experienced contract negotiator, marketer, business development specialist
- Effective developing, tracking, managing contracts
- Cheerfully support senior management, providing careful contract oversight
- Strong multi-tasking skills coordinating large-scale projects
- Reliable knowledge of Microsoft Office Suite, SPSS, and PASW
- Bachelor's degree, solid GPA

WORK EXPERIENCE

Substitute Secondary Education Teacher   [Date to Present]

Baltimore County Public School System
Baltimore, MD

Teach courses in multiple disciplines, all grade levels. Evaluate students' progress with federal, state, and local academic goals. Apply educational assessments, curriculum-based measurements. Check every detail for timelines, accuracy, conformance.

Sales Manager/Mentor   [Dates]

Tilling Audio-TV
Owings Mills, MD

Negotiated pre- and post-award contract functions, procurement. Monitored delivery of goods and services with multiple installers. Oversaw and validated contractor performance. Collected funds, prepared invoices, handled retail sales and reports. Researched, evaluated, managed, scheduled, and served as point of contact for up to 5 professional installers.

EDUCATION

University of Maryland,
Baltimore County, Baltimore, MD

Bachelor's Degree - Psychology – [Date]
GPA 3.25, Dean's List. Worked 20 hours a week with a full academic load

Figure 6-7: Allen's starter resume is reframed for a contract specialist position in this resume sketch.

ALLEN C. TRENTON
Baltimore, MD

Cell: 443-333-3333   Email: actrent@yahoo.com

Park Guide

RELEVANT SKILLS

- Proven ability to meet strangers and make them feel welcome
- Skill to help visitors learn useful things during their time with us
- Dedication to keep information up to date
- Capability to schedule events that attract visitors and keep them coming back
- Computer skills — MS Word, Excel, online searching — make me efficient

WORK EXPERIENCE

Substitute Secondary Education Teacher,   [Date to Present]
Baltimore County Public School System, Baltimore, MD

- As substitute teacher, consistently respond to needs of strangers.

- Help students learn useful things during their limited time with me.

- Schedule classes, events, and homework dedicated to keeping information up to date.

- Attract parental support and keep them involved.

- Use computer skills daily — MS Word, Excel, online searching.

Key Accomplishments

- Worked late and stayed after normal school hours to make every group feel welcome.

- Took time to really understand learning requirements of 5th grade, minority and special needs students. Teacher with 20 years' experience said: "Allen's the best substitute we've had in two years!"

EDUCATION

University of Maryland, Baltimore, MD
Pursuing Master's Degree in Education   Expect graduation [Date]

University of Maryland, Baltimore, MD
Bachelors Degree - Psychology, [Date]
GPA 3.25 Dean's List. Worked 20 hours a week with full academic load

Figure 6-8: In this resume sketch, Allen's starter resume is personalized to apply for a park guide job.

Two-page resume tip

When you frequently construct a two-page resume, customize the first page and save time, whenever possible, by keeping the second page the same each time. Freezing the second page isn't always possible, but the concept is a good starting point.

When Only Full Custom Resumes Will Work

At some points in a hunt for ideal employment, everyone needs market-driven, full-blown, totally customized job search communications.

When you come across an opportunity that can literally change your life — and you want it more than you've ever wanted another job — pull out all the stops and start from scratch. Put your watch in a drawer and don't count the hours needed to do a first-class Full Custom resume in which you tell the employer such critical facts as these:

- ✔ How you plan to make the company more money than it costs to recruit and employ you
- ✔ Why you are an excellent match for the job
- ✔ The power of your network as it relates to the industry the company serves
- ✔ What competencies and skills you bring to the organization
- ✔ Your good reputation and its ability to attract and keep good customers and team members
- ✔ Your capacity for doing the work better than other candidates
- ✔ Your ability to solve company or industry problems
- ✔ Why the employer should believe you

To prepare an OnTarget custom resume, follow these three clear steps.

Step 1: Prepare your core resume

Probe your memory to jot down every factor in your background you can use to customize a resume, from experience and competencies to skills and education. You don't submit this inventory document to an employer but you use it as a rich personal resource. Use as many pages as you need. (For pointers on content, check out Chapter 8.)

Step 2: Research requirements of the job

If you're responding to a specific advertised job, jot down the requirements listed in the job ad. If you really want an edge, call the company's human resources department and ask for the position description. That's the document the company uses to evaluate your qualifications for the opening, and to evaluate you should you win the job. If you sense any reluctance by HR to provide you with the position description, ask for a copy with any proprietary information (including salary range) blacked out. Promise you'll treat what they send you as completely confidential. Address all job requirements in your Full Custom rewrite.

Step 3: Customize your resume

After drafting the must-haves in your Full Custom resume, review your core resume to see whether you can add secondary items mentioned in the ad or position description to further improve your chances.

Is Targeting Your Resume Really Necessary?

Sprinting ahead in today's candidate-cluttered job market gobbles up more research effort than the last time you baited your resume hooks. When there were plenty of jobs to go around, you may have needed to apply for, say, ten openings in a job search before meeting success. Now, to land a job you want, don't be shocked to find that you have to step up your game to go after ten times that number.

What's more, when a job opening draws your attention, respond at first light. In these tight times, employers have plenty of talent from which to choose, a development that causes the application window to snap shut in as few as 48 hours.

So, yes: Customizing your resume really is necessary. Full Custom is the ideal approach, but Custom Lite is a powerful close second, and its racing speed probably meshes better with your way-too-busy lifestyle.

If you're inclined to pooh-pooh the research required to effectively customize your resume, consider this sage insight from Winnie-the-Pooh's creator, A.A. Milne: Organizing is what you do before you do something, so that when you do it, it is not all mixed up.

Chapter 7

Chart a Cool Course
to the Right Jobs

. . . .

In This Chapter

▶ Presenting resumes on the new digital docks (platforms)

▶ Scouting what's happening on the best job boards

▶ Zeroing in on company Web sites

▶ Speeding up your hunt with job search engines

. . . .

Although the Internet makes uncovering a gold mine of job possibilities easier than ever, your mission is to separate the gold from the sand in finding the right opportunities for you.

This chapter aims to help you get your resume to the right eyes for the right jobs without fumbling around and wasting time. You discover new advice about effective ways to send your resumes to market, as well as updated information about the digital tools you already may be using.

From the gobs of new Web products and services that keep popping up, only some survive and thrive, while others drop out quickly. In an effort to avoid describing developments whose shelf dates expire too soon, I cover this chapter's list of resources as a digest with relatively few illustrations.

Different Docs for Digital Docks: Sending Your Resume in the Right Tech Form

The job search process is becoming ever more digitized, producing a variety of devices and Web sites where your online resume can be marketed. Early adopters collectively call these places *digital docks* or *platforms*. Beyond the terminology of digital docks or platforms, confusion reigns.

This section shows you how to navigate the evolving and confusing technical landscape to successfully transmit your resume to the people who can give it a thumbs-up welcome.

Resume question of the decade

The big question savvy job seekers are asking right now is which exact form they should use to send resumes to a specific digital dock. Read the instructions on each digital dock, of course, but you have the following three basic options:

- The **full-design resume,** when used as an online document, conveys a visual message as well as information expressed only in typographic text. Graphical design elements vary — the most popular are lines, white space, bullets, columns, graphs, symbols, and colors. The advantage: Human eyes find full-design resumes far more inviting to read than plain-text resumes.

- The **plain-text resume** is an online document constructed without formatting in plain-text file format. You can use any character that's on your keyboard, including dashes, asterisks and plus signs, capital letters, and white space. But you can't use bullets, boldface, or underlined text. The plain-text advantage: Citing technical reasons, digital docks — especially online resume databases — that rely primarily on computer software accept only documents submitted in plain text.

- The **hyperlinked** (or *linked*) resume is an online document that anyone can access easily by moving from one Web site to another. When used for resume transmission, you store a full-design resume on a Web site, and then, within a plain-text resume, embed a link that connects to it.

A full-design resume has loads more pizzazz for human eyes than a plain-text resume, which has all the visual appeal of a pimple on a wart on a fruit fly. But remember that not only do some digital docks accept only plain text; the screens of some mobile devices are too small to effectively display a full-design resume. The linked resume is a workaround when you want to put your best self forward with a full-design resume, but — as a practical technical matter — can't.

Essential new chart answers question of the decade

Comments of growing confusion about the technical aspects of conveying resumes have been showing up in my mailbox for months, but the point was hammered home as I worked on this book.

Tim, a neighbor and job-searching information technology specialist, proudly showed me his terrific full-design resume. Button-popping with pride, the IT specialist felt sure his effort would blow recruiters away. But the next day, Tim was considerably subdued: A major resume database had declined his full-design resume with the explanation that only plain-text resumes need apply. At that moment, I realized that if an IT guy doesn't know how to handle the technical digital-dock challenge, a lot of other people don't either. Solution: A handy chart to solve digital missteps.

When you want to toot your resume horn, but find yourself in a fog about what a digital dock will accept or reject, stay on course with *The Lemke Guide,* the helpful chart in Figure 7-1.

James M. Lemke, this book's perceptive technical reviewer, created the world's first guide to making resumes rock on digital docks. Jim was ably assisted by recruiting aces Mark Sugalski, general manager–sourcing, SunGard Higher Education in Malvern, Pennsylvania; and Scott Swimley, vice president–sales, Alumwire, San Francisco, California.

Web hosting sites

Before launching your job search, find an online home to park your full-design resume — either your personal Web site, or a free or fee Web hosting site. Plenty of Web sites enable you to post a full-design resume.

Some sites operate as paid hosting services and charge a low monthly rate (under $10 a month) for small personal Web sites you can use to host the link to your full-design resume and your professional portfolio, if you wish.

Others are free, but read the fine print.

Still other sites are free and mean it, but understandably encourage you to eventually upgrade to a modestly priced paid membership — such as Yola.com — a service that gets rave reviews from pundits and users alike.

When you need a hosting site for a multimedia resume, remember to choose one — such as VisualCV.com — that can accommodate images, charts, references, awards, and more.

To view a list of more than 200 free Web hosting services, go to `www.free-webhosts.com/free-web-hosts.php`.

Digital Dock	Full Design	Text Only	Link	Comments
Job Board	✓	✓	✓	If the job board has an Import Resume or Browse button, you can upload your full-design resume and include a hyperlink to your personal resume site. If not, use your text resume.
Job Search Engine				These search tools aggregate (collect) job listings from the Web, directing job seekers to respond through the original source.
Company Web Site	✓	✓	✓	Check the Web site to see whether it accepts full-design resumes in MS Word doc or PDF form. If not, send text only. When you have a personal Web site, embed the URL in your resume text as a hyperlink.
Recruiting Firm (Third Party)	✓			Third-party firms prefer a good-looking resume not limited to text. Always verify the format with the recruiting agent. If you work with placement agency firms (which get paid by the employer after you are hired through their efforts), do not include a URL to your Web resume. Some employers may claim that your information is public domain and try to avoid paying the placement agency, so if an agency recruiter sees that you have a Web resume URL, the recruiter may not want to work with you.
Web Hosting Site	✓			Post your full-design resume on a free Web hosting site.
Personal Web Site	✓			Post your full-design resume on your own Web site.
Smartphone	✓	✓		Some of the new smartphones can save and forward documents in formats such as MS Word and PDF. If your smartphone cannot accept these formats, use a plain-text resume synopsis. Consider also the technology of the recipient. When in doubt, go with plain text.
Tablet	✓	✓	✓	The iPad and competitive tablets can save and send a resume in most commonly used styles.
Platform Destination	**Full Design**	**Text Only**	**Link**	
LinkedIn	✓	✓	✓	LinkedIn requires you to use its resume-building tool; however, you can create a link to a personal Web page where you keep your full-design resume, or you can use the free SlideShare application and upload your full-design resume in MS Word, PDF, or PowerPoint.
Facebook		✓	✓	Facebook requires you to enter specific information in a structured way. Facebook includes a link option, so if you have your resume posted somewhere on the Web, you can direct people to it.
Twitter		✓	✓	Twitter enables you to post a very basic profile; however you can provide links to LinkedIn or to your personal Web site.
Google Profile		✓	✓	You can add a link connecting to your full-design resume on your personal site or on a Web-hosting site.

Figure 7-1: The Lemke Guide removes the guesswork from how effectively your resume will hook up with different types of digital docks.

Job Boards Are Alive and Changing

How many job boards are there in the world? The count is elastic from year to year, but estimates place the number operating globally as high as 50,000. Job boards have become the dominant information source for identifiable open jobs. Even newspapers, in addition to printed pages, now post their help-wanted ads online in job-board style.

This portion of the chapter suggests efficient ways to steer through an ocean of job boards. Despite the rise of social media (Chapter 2) as a job-search tool, abandoning job boards (and their relatives, job search engines) would be a mistake. Here's the deal on what is taking place in the job-board industry, and my take on what's likely to happen to it next.

Basic job board categories

The industry can be divided into two basic groups:

✔ **General job boards** include all kinds of jobs and are usually big and well-known national enterprises that offer a long list of features attractive to job seekers. Examples include Monster, CareerBuilder, and Job Central.

✔ **Niche job boards** focus on a specific group of jobs, separated by such affinity factors as career field, function, industry, location, diversity, or other job seeker criteria. Examples:

  • Temporary/part time: SnagAJob.com, Net-Temps.com

  • College: CollegeRecruiter.com, CollegeGrad.com

  • Executive: TheLadders.com, Jobs.WSJ.com

  • Occupations: JobsOnTheMenu.com, MarketingJobs.com

  • Diversity: LatPro.com, DiversityJobs.com

  • International (English): Naukri.com, JobsDB.com

Weddle's names best job sites

Weddle's, a top consulting firm in the recruiting industry, annually conducts the Oscars of online employment boards. CEO Peter Weddle says they do it, not in a backroom somewhere, but by maintaining a year-long ballot for recruiters and job seekers to identify which sites they like best. Each year 30 employment sites cop top honors and are listed on both Weddles.com (`www.weddles.com`), and the International Association of Employment Web Sites (`www.employmentwebsites.org`).

Mobile's wave of the future

Steven Rothberg is an acknowledged leader in the integration of mobile technology into job board offerings. Rothberg, president of CollegeRecruiter.com, explains how it works in his service: "Job seekers can sign up to receive their job match alerts sent by text so they find out about new jobs immediately."

Rothberg forecasts a paradigm shift in resume viewing practices coming soon. He projects the shift will be away from laptops and desktop computers, and toward mobile devices such as smartphones and tablets.

But what if you want to sit at your desk and type all day? "No problem," says Rothberg. "Merely connect your mobile to your flat-panel monitor and full-sized keyboard, much like we've done for 15 years with docking stations on laptops. But a big difference is your mobile will connect wirelessly. Mobile is the wave of the future."

A snapshot of job-boards evolution

For the past two decades, a typical job board has been a free Web site for job hunters to apply online for advertised jobs and stash resumes in the board's database. Additionally, job seekers can choose to receive free collateral services, such as job match alerts, salary surveys, and privacy options. Employers pick up the tab, paying fees to advertise jobs and search the board's resume database.

Job boards are evolving with innovations unheard of five years ago, notably the following:

- Digital tie-ins embracing Twitter, LinkedIn, Facebook, and other social media.
- Resume displays on mobile docks — smartphones and tablets.
- An emerging closed apps (applications) environment. The apps are available by subscription on mobile devices, replacing the previously open environment on the Internet.

Forecasting job boards' future

Debate on the future of job boards is loud and noisy. Three main viewpoints hold center stage:

- **Jobs boards are doomed.** Job boards are deadheading to oblivion because, critics say, employers are finding it cheaper to recruit by using social media. Google counts nearly 280,000 references in my recent search for "job boards dead or dying."

> ✔ **Job boards are forever.** "Not so fast!" fire back defenders of the job-board faith — employers will continue to support boards because they have the proven ability to deliver candidates.
>
> ✔ **Job boards are adapting.** Job boards are morphing with the times — not only are they integrating mobile and social capabilities, but some are cutting rates to compete on price with start-up competitors, and even considering rebranding themselves away from the term "job board."

So who's right? I agree with the recruiting media industry consensus, which embraces the third viewpoint, arguing that job boards aren't going to depart this planet anytime soon — but they will continue to evolve.

Hunting on Company Web Sites

Legendary bank robber Willie Sutton said he targeted banks because "that's where the money is," suggesting that his listeners "go there often." Similar advice can be given about company Web sites because "that's where the jobs are — go there often."

Thousands of companies big and small have career sections on their Web sites. They don't necessarily advertise all of their openings on pay-to-post job boards, meaning you may discover hidden jobs by trolling company sites.

As you scan a company site, back up to its home page and click to press releases, annual report, about us, and relevant general areas for any edge you can use to enhance your application when you move to the careers area.

Meet CareerCast.com: 1,001 job boards

When you're trying to decide which jobs mesh with your talents, interests, and qualifications, here's a tip: Check out the annual free *Jobs Rated Report*. The report appears on CareerCast.com, a job portal containing 1,001 job boards that are powered by Adicio in the United States and Canada.

CareerCast.com publisher Tony Lee explains how the report works: "The *Jobs Rated Report* offers in-depth reviews of 200 jobs based on a range of criteria, including work environment, income, outlook, stress, and physical demands. Additionally, CareerCast.com provides links from each position to actual jobs available in its huge North American database of job boards."

Frequent winners: actuary, software engineer, computer systems analyst, biologist, and historian. Bringing up the rear: roustabout, lumberjack, ironworker, dairy farmer, and welder.

Susan P. Joyce, the talent behind Job-Hunt.org, reminds you: "In addition to visiting the employer's Web site to see what the company does, check it out on Yahoo Finance, BusinessWire.com, Hoovers.com, and similar digital compilers of information to discover the latest news about the employer and the employer's industry." Joyce also recommends that you set up Google Alerts on target employer names and products or services so that you're continually updated about your target company's operations. Follow these steps to do so:

1. **Go to www.google.com/alerts.**

2. **Type company name, in quotation marks, into the "Search terms" box.**

3. **Select "Everything" as the Type; Select "Once a day" as "How often."**

When you reach the careers area and begin submitting your resume in earnest, remember to pay close attention to each requirement of the position and customize your resume to show your qualifications are a bull's-eye for those requirements. (Review Chapter 6.)

Pay attention to specific instructions on each company's site. And don't be surprised if you're asked to take online pre-employment tests or respond to screening questions.

Some job seekers use anonymous resumes to maintain their privacy and stay out of trouble with their current employer. An anonymous resume is stripped of the subject's name and contact information, and generic descriptions are substituted for company names in the experience section. Anonymous resumes are distributed by job sites or third-party employment services, but employers often consider them to be a waste of time and won't accept them.

Fast-Forwarding: Job Search Engines

A job search engine (JSE) races across the Internet scooping up job listings from job boards, company sites, newspapers, and associations. The big idea is free one-stop shopping for job seekers.

These collector sites allow you to view in one place virtually all the jobs posted on the Internet that fit your personal criteria. Job search engines let you slice and dice results, based on what you seek, such as career field or occupation, full- or part-time work, large company or small, geographic location, and so forth. And they reveal when each job was posted. (The newer the posting, the more likely the employer is still accepting applications.)

Job search engines rarely engage in job transactions themselves; instead, they pass users along to the source of the information.

Five clues to identifying the best job search engines include these features:

✔ A search-and-match technology that works correctly

✔ Wide coverage of available jobs with dates of postings

✔ Easy-to-use delivery options: e-mail, mobile, RSS feeds

✔ Tools to save and manage searches

✔ Integration of social media resources

Using job search engines

While each job search engine includes specific instructions on the best way to use it, you can expect certain basic information to apply across the board. Here are the general steps you're likely to follow when using a job search engine:

1. **Create a personal account.**

   Register with one or more job search engines. Many job listings appear on all the engines because, with exceptions, they pull their inventories from the same places.

2. **Decide how to receive the jobs.**

   You may prefer daily or semi-weekly job alerts. Or you may choose an RSS feed (see Chapter 4) to have job ads sent as they are posted directly to your computer, smart phone, tablet, or other digital dock.

3. **Set preferences.**

   Use the preferences setting to select the jobs you want to show on your results page. You may, for example, choose to show results based only on location or pay levels.

4. **Become familiar with related options on the site.**

   Options vary but may include such extras as a map of the job's location, salary market information, company research, or potential contacts inside the target company.

5. **Narrow your search.**

   Drill down through the job listings to be as specific as possible to get to the jobs you want. Quality — not quantity — counts most. Look for freshness of the listing and those jobs relevant to your preferences. Search on skills, industry, and location.

6. **Track and save your searches.**

   Each job search engine allows you to save your searches on its site. Doing so enables you to manage the most current and desirable listings.

7. **Upgrade to advanced search, if you need it.**

   If you're running into dead ends, try using the site's advanced search feature. You can prowl by such criteria as keywords, job title, company, type of job, and location.

8. **Review potential for social media and mobile integration.**

   Calculate the advantages of combining social media (for example, LinkedIn, Facebook, or Twitter), and apps (applications) with job search engines; typically social media provide a source for finding jobs at friends' workplaces.

Alison Doyle's informative book, *Internet Your Way to a New Job — How to Really Find a Job Online,* 3rd Edition (HappyAbout.com) provides additional information on using job search engines to scout job leads. Doyle is a pioneering and widely lauded leader in digital job search; find her at Jobsearch.About.com (www.jobsearch.about.com).

Meeting job search engines

Similar to the classification of job boards, job search engines can be split into two broad groups: general job search engines, and niche job search engines. Both are small categories. Here's a thumbnail of the best-known job search engines.

General job search engines

When you want to go to a kind of "job mall," rather than to individual job-board stores, head for general job search engines. The following roundup of marquee names in job search engines will put you on the pathway to jobs galore.

- **Indeed.com:** "One search. All jobs." Indeed.com's signature catchphrase pretty well sums up its mission. It's the world's most popular job search engine, and it's free to job seekers. Indeed.com relentlessly gathers listings from job boards, company Web sites, newspapers, associations, and any other sources that cross its bounty-hunting 'bots (software that crawls the Internet). It's full-featured, including social networking integration galore.

- **SimplyHired.com:** Another popular and free JSE, SimplyHired.com, also gets my thumbs up. Heavily endowed with social networking and other most-wanted features, SimplyHired.com lets you track down jobs by occupation, job title, or location, and filter by job type, work experience, company revenue, and size. Disclosure: I'm a dog lover, so I flipped over the feature naming dog-friendly companies that allow employees to bring Fido to work.

- **LinkUp.com:** In a class by itself, LinkUp.com lists only jobs taken directly from more than 22,000 company Web sites. Companies range from large to small across the United States. Listings disappear as soon as they're filled. Job seeker tools include hook-ups with social media, mobile services for smartphones and tablets, bookmarking of favorite listings and searches, and job alerts with RSS feeds. You apply directly to listed company sites for any job that catches your eye.

✔ **TwitJobSearch.com:** This job search engine sweeps the Web for job postings on Twitter's tweets. You can "follow" people of your choice (somewhat like signing up for job alerts on other sites), as well as retweet (passing on jobs to your Twitter network). Competition to TwitJobSearch.com is growing, leaving the impression that many entrepreneurs are hoping to harvest Twitter's job potential. Browse for "job search engines Twitter."

If you're uncertain what tweets have to do with charting a cool course to the right job, read *The Twitter Job Search Guide* by Susan Britton Whitcomb, Chandlee Bryan, and Deb Dib (JIST Publishing). It clearly explains what you need to know. Visit the book's Web site at www.twitterjobsearchguide.com.

Niche job search engines

Niche job search engines are new kids on the block and the ultimate time savers for job hunters searching in the categories they serve. Don't confuse them with niche job boards. The boards maintain resume databases and charge employers to view them; the engines do not maintain resume databases and instead refer job seekers back to the original job posting. The following two niche job search engines illustrate the growing category:

✔ **GreenJobSpider.com** collects openings from more than 50 green job boards, company Web sites, and Twitter.

✔ **SEOJobsFinder.com** corrals jobs requiring Search Engine Optimization, social media, Web, and copywriting skills.

Preventing Resume Black Holes

Even when you consciously make sure your resume is in the correct form for digital docks, you may still be frustrated by silence from employers. No calls. No e-mails. No carrier pigeons. Nada. What could be wrong?

When your efforts are hitting resume black holes — those cyberspace caverns where unclaimed resumes go to die — the following tips can help route your resume to the right jobs.

Forget chasing every job

Are you part of the resume mob, applying for anything and everything that doesn't crawl? Two words: Stop it! From this moment on, let loose your online resume only when you have serious qualifications (like you have four of the four "must have" qualifications in the job posting). What's in a selective distribution policy for you? Plenty:

✔ You don't waste your time, leaving more of it to thoughtfully respond to job postings for which your prospects are realistically bright.

✔ Your hopes aren't dashed for something that's not going to happen, causing you to suffer the black-hole blues.

✔ You don't blemish your image with recruiters, one of whom may someday shepherd you to a terrific job. Recruiters, whose income depends upon finding "perfect" candidates for specific positions, are likely to be annoyed if you send them generic resumes over and over.

As a swamped recruiter said: "When I'm looking for a chief financial officer and an industrial engineer applies, why should I spend time I don't have to personally respond?" He has a point.

Hit bull's-eye with your resume

Most generic resumes are now goners (as I discuss in Chapter 6). Make it easy for employers to consider you for a specific job by matching your resume to the job description for each job you target.

If you submit your resume without knowing the particulars of an open job, you probably won't organize your information to exactly match. Use the exact words the job description calls for. If the job says you must have "more than three years of experience," say precisely that; don't assume the applicant tracking system (ATS) software will figure it out from the dates. Never try to impress by overstating what you offer — if the job posting calls for five years' experience, for example, say you have five years' experience; don't say you have 22 years' experience.

In customizing your online resume, pay special attention to the requirements section (qualifications required) of the posting. Tailor and submit a different resume for each position you qualify for within the same company (see Chapter 6).

Give your database-dwelling resume new life every three days. Refreshing your resume is especially important on general job boards. Recruiters scour them all day long and rarely look back more than two days. Make a minor revision, such as deleting an insignificant word, typing it back in, and saving the change. This simple action lifts your resume to the top of the pile again.

Move fast, follow guidelines

When you're hotly pursuing a job opening, timing is destiny. Jobs are flying off the shelves in today's economy. Back in the day, you may have been smart to wait a couple of weeks to make your move after the first wave of candidates had passed through the resume pile. Not anymore. Those who apply first have an advantage: As soon as a recruiter finds several promising people, interviewing begins.

Pay attention to the date a position is posted because listings more than a few days old may already be filled. You can still apply, of course, but don't be surprised if you don't hear back because the job is no longer available.

Follow directions given in the job posting, even the tiresome tasks of cutting and pasting job applications and answering questionnaires.

You may be able to save time filling out online job applications with an automatic form filler, such as FillPerfect.com, which was designed for the job hunt. (Unless you're technically inclined, the learning curve may be bumpy.) Most auto form fillers are either free or offer free trials.

Neutralize chilling information

Use your e-mail to skirt two knock-out punches that can cause a screener to fly over your resume:

- ✔ **Location:** Employers resist the expense of relocation unless your talent is unavailable in their locale. Tell a true version of a story like this: Suppose you're in Montana and the job is in Atlanta. Say in your e-mail that you went to school in the South (or vacationed there), love it, and, at your own expense, hope to return to Dixie as soon as possible.

- ✔ **Money:** A job posting asks for your salary history or salary requirements; you fear you're a little rich for the company's budget but that as soon as they appreciate the value you bring, it won't be a problem. Say in your e-mail that you look forward to disclosing the personal information at a job interview and ask whether you should bring copies of your W-2 forms.

Enhance the power of keywords

When your resume contains too few of the employer's preferred mix of job-specific keywords, it may remain twisting in the windy void of the resume black hole. Forever.

Keywords tend to be hard skills, and industry- and job-specific terms employers look for in a job candidate (Chapter 10). Categories to mine for keywords include these examples:

- University or college names
- Degrees and certifications
- Job titles and company names
- Product names
- Technical terms and industry jargon
- Software and hardware
- Industry and job skills
- Years of experience
- Professional associations

To feed ATS software a nourishing keyword diet, repeat the same keywords and phrases you find in the job description. Include slight variations, such as accounting, accountant, and accountancy.

Keywords are usually nouns. When you use Web resources to research keywords, do not confuse nouns with action verbs. Action verbs animate your resume; keywords communicate your qualifications.

Using enough of the right keywords on your resume gooses an ATS to rank you as a higher and better match for a specific job, putting you in the running for the interview list.

Go directly to the decider

When your resume is stuck in a black hole, send another copy to the hiring manager — the decider. But how do you find the name? A quick-and-simple search is adequate for most jobs. At small companies, the decision-maker may be the head of your function; at larger companies, the decider may be a few notches down from the vice president of your function. Other easy-button tips:

- Call the company and ask.
- Research the company's Web site, which usually displays leadership bios and main phone numbers; decode the formula for the decider's e-mail address by looking at the company's press releases.

✔ Try a Web search for the company name plus the decider's function or likely title.

✔ Check out people-finding sites, such as ZoomInfo (www.zoominfo.com) and Spokeo (www.spokeo.com).

✔ Reach out to your networks on social media, such as Twitter, Facebook, and LinkedIn. Send word to all your connections that you're interested in the job and ask whether they can name that name.

✔ Consider using fee services to reach hiring managers. LinkedIn, with 80 million members worldwide, offers both free accounts and fee accounts. Among the paid variety are the Job Seeker premium accounts, which enable you to send messages straight to hiring managers who aren't in your network.

✔ If you're a college student or graduate, your alumni office or career center may provide alumni contacts at companies you're targeting.

Find an inside advocate

Assuming your uncle doesn't own the company where you want to work, your No.1 best way to get hired is to find a valued company employee who is willing to act as a conduit to the hiring manager.

Harried and hurried hiring managers may decide the best way to hire good people is to consider those recommended by satisfactory employees on the theory that birds of a feather flock together.

Your next best move: Find an inside advocate who will deliver your resume to the company's HR recruiters and say a few encouraging words about you.

For a decade or so, CareerXRoads recruiting consultants Mark Mehler and Gerry Crispin have annually surveyed large, highly competitive, high-profile corporations on their sources of hire. Excluding inside promotions and transfers, the sourcing study always reveals that referrals win out, numbering more than a quarter of all external hires.

When you're on the outside looking in and don't have a clue about who you can deputize as an inside advocate, turn to social media and professional organizations, asking (or tweeting) "Who do you know who works at — ?"

Keep on keepin' on

When you don't hear a word back, it may not have been your fault but the employer's fault that your resume got lost in a black hole. Here are a few things that could have ruined your day:

- ✔ The job was cancelled or frozen, denied budget approval, or never existed outside the hiring manager's wish list.

- ✔ A job listing may have been contracted for 30 days but the job was filled on day five and the recruiter simply forgot to take down the listing.

- ✔ The job was a high-turnover gig and posted even when there was no immediate opening because managers like to have replacements standing by.

- ✔ An employee in the job was on the firing line but received a last-minute reprieve. Unfortunately, no one told you.

- ✔ Worst of all, a job may have been locked up for a friend or internal candidate but posted to prove the employer abides by fair hiring practices.

Seeking and Finding Is Easier Than Ever

While eye-popping technical wizardry on the Web is indisputably the engine driving big changes in the job market, the Internet is not the end-all and be-all in finding career gold.

Southern California career coach Mark James (www.hireconsultant.com) puts its value in perspective for most people:

> *A recipe for unemployment: Click and send, cross your fingers, and hope your smartphone rings. A recipe for employment: Press a full-bore campaign that includes human networking and researching job leads from all media.*

Chapter 8

Content Makes the OnTarget Difference

· ·

In This Chapter

▶ Understanding the parts of your resume

▶ Dumping content that doesn't open interview doors

▶ Deciding whether to use an objective or summary

▶ Using good judgment on salary requests

▶ Shaping your content in application forms

· ·

A prospective employer makes a leap of faith investing money in you as a new and untried employee. Are you really a good match for the position and the company? A resume's content is the first step toward answering that question.

How important is content? In comparing a position's requirements to your qualifications (see Chapter 6), what your resume says is mission-critical.

The Parts of Your Resume

To make your contents easy to access, organize the facts into various categories. Here are the essential parts that make up a resume:

✔ Contact information

✔ Objective or summary statement

✔ Education and training

✔ Experience

✔ Skills

✔ Competencies

✔ Activities

> ✔ Organizations
>
> ✔ Honors and awards

You may also include:

> ✔ Certifications
>
> ✔ Licenses
>
> ✔ Work samples
>
> ✔ Endorsements

To increase the likelihood that your resume positions you for an interview, take the time to understand the purpose of the different resume parts, which I explain in the following sections.

No more than you want to carry around 30 pounds of extra weight do you want fat in your resume — family, early education, favorite things, and so forth. Trim it! The rule for including data on a resume is simple: If the data doesn't support your objective to be invited for an interview, leave it out.

Leading with Contact Information

No matter which format (Chapter 9) you choose, place your name first on your resume. If your name isn't first, a computer may mistake Excellent Sales Representative for your name and file you away as Ms. Representative.

Use boldface to display your name in a size range of 14- to 20-point typeface, depending upon your preference. The rest of your contact information can appear in 10- to 12-point typeface. Keep adjusting type sizes until you get the effect you prefer.

Here's a shocker: Except for specific and overriding reasons, limit contact information to your

> ✔ **E-mail address.** This is your single most important contact data point because that's how the majority of employers will initially contact you.
>
> Additionally, if you have them, you can add a space and then your Web or blog site, Web portfolio, and social media pages. (Caveat: Don't go overboard with social media extras or readers may wonder whether you're too busy being social to work hard.)
>
> ✔ **Mobile phone number.** Some employers prefer to pick up the phone and give you a call.

✔ **City and state of residence.** This information shows you have roots. Employers understandably resist springing for relocation costs unless the talent they seek isn't available locally.

Why has there been a reduction in the recommended amount of contact information? Long answer short: technology and crime. The need for a home street address has passed into history because employers are now far more likely to communicate by Internet than by postal mail. What's more, rising concerns about identity theft and privacy loss argue against listing a home street address unless there is an overriding reason to do so.

The first page of your resume is valuable real estate: Ditching unnecessary text like your street address is akin to clearing weeds out of your lawn. Why not leave blank any unused white space to make your resume more open and readable, or use it for information that markets you?

Hooking the Reader with Summary or Objective

Your OnTarget resume needs a hook to grab attention. The hook immediately follows your name and contact information and is expressed as an objective or as a summary.

A summary is known by many names. Among the most popular are skills summary, highlights summary, asset statement, power summary, career highlights, career summary, career profile, career focus, summary of qualifications, and accomplishments profile.

The two types of hooks — objective and summary — differ in emphasis:

✔ The **objective** is self-centered, stating *what you want.* For example, your resume might include an objective line like this one:

Objective: Assistant to Executive.

✔ The **summary** is work-centered, stating *what you offer.* Here's how a summary line might look on your resume:

Summary: Over 10 years of progressively responsible office support experience, including superior computer skills, with an earned reputation for priority-setting and teamwork.

Sometimes you combine the job objective and summary. Here's how an unlabeled combined objective and summary might look:

Assistant to Executive, to keep operations under firmer control, using computer skills, contemporary office procedures, and pleasant manner with people.

However you fashion it, the hook tells the recruiter what you want to do and/or what you're qualified to do.

Debate rages among career pros over the topic of objective versus summary:

- ✔ Objective backers say that readers don't want to slog through a document, trying to guess the type of position you want and how you'd fit into the organization.

- ✔ Summary advocates argue that a thumbnail sketch of your skills and other competencies allows your qualifications to be evaluated for jobs you may not know about specifically, or offers an easy way to itemize your matching qualifications for a specific job's requirements. This factor is a serious consideration in resume database searches.

Focus speeds your resume to the eyes of people who can hire you, whether you style it as a job objective or as a summary — or as an unlabeled combination of both.

Choosing an objective

Your objective states what you want to do and the direction in which you're heading. It gives immediate focus to your resume and is the hub around which all the other information in your document relates.

When to use an objective

The time is right to use an objective when you

- ✔ Know the position being offered; make that job title your job objective.

- ✔ Have a greatly diversified background that may perplex some employers.

- ✔ Are a new graduate, a career changer, a service member exiting the military, a member of the clergy switching to the secular job market, an educator seeking another career field, or a homemaker reentering the paid workforce. A job objective says what you're looking for.

Advantages of an objective

Most studies show that employers prefer objectives for quick identification purposes. They like to see the name of their job openings at the top of a resume. Because you cite those qualifying accomplishments that support your objective and forget random experiences, the finished product shows that you and the desired job appear to be a well-matched pair.

Being objective about objectives

The debate over job objective or a variant of a skills summary continues unabated. I overheard these snatches of recruiters' opinions at a recruiting forum.

- ✔ "By including their desired job title in the online objective statement, job seekers increase the chances that their resume will match an employer's search."

- ✔ "I prefer to see 'Career Summary' in place of 'Objective.' If the objective doesn't match an employer's idea of the job, the resume will probably be discarded. By putting a one-paragraph 'commercial' as the very first thing the employer sees, you know that an overview of your qualifications is read."

- ✔ "As an in-house [corporate] recruiter, any resume I receive without an objective tells me the applicant is either a desperate jack-of-all trades who will take any job offered, or has not thought about his career enough to know what he wants. Both are huge red flags. I think an objective is essential."

- ✔ "We advise candidates to leave off the objective or we may remove it before sending to a client. Use the objective space to include more information on accomplishments and experience."

If you're responding to an advertised job, remember to match the basic qualifications it requires in the body of your resume even if the job seeks a "window pane technician" and your objective says "window pane technician." An objective that echoes the job title in the job ad is merely a first step toward showing that you're a great match.

Disadvantages of an objective

Ideally, you write a customized resume for each position (or career field) for which you apply. You should even write a different customized resume for each position for which you apply at the *same* company. The downside to a narrow job objective is that you may not be considered by the same employer for other open positions that you didn't know about. But if the objective is too broadly focused, your objective statement becomes meaningless.

Opting for a summary

If you choose to begin your resume with a summary, you can still target it to specific positions with the mix of strengths, skills, accomplishments, and other background elements that you include.

When to use a summary

The time is right to use a summary under these conditions:

- ✔ You have widely applicable skills (an administrative assistant, for example). Recruiters especially like a skills summary atop a reverse chronological resume because it lets them creatively consider you for jobs you may not know exist.

- ✔ You're in a career field with pathways to multiple occupations or industries (an electrical engineer, for example).

- ✔ You know that your resume is headed to a database. Because you want to be considered for multiple related positions you may not know exist — which may have the same or similar requirements — you try to design your summary broadly enough to accomplish this goal without sounding as though you're a jack-of-all-trades.

Soar with a summary

Accomplishments are the patron saints of OnTarget resumes. Part IV contains sample resumes that illustrate a variety of effective *summaries*. But here's a quick peek at a top-rated summary by Jan Melnik in *Executive's Pocket Guide to ROI Resumes and Job Search,* a book by Louise Kursmark and Jan Melnik (JIST Publishing).

Senior Marketing Executive

Providing Consistent Market Leadership to Leverage Exceptional Marketing & Sales Results

Outstanding record of highly focused, strategic marketing and sales leadership. Exceptional executive-leadership skills with talent for establishing and communicating vision, developing strategy, executing tactical plans, and motivating and empowering teams and individuals to achieve remarkable, sustainable results.

- Achieved rapid speed-to-market in successful product launches through hands-on leadership of brand and product development, strategic planning, packaging, marketing, and innovative distribution channels.
- Reputation for consistently creating value and delivering strong sales results.
- Precision focus on identifying and capitalizing on new business opportunities to generate profitable and sustainable growth.

Demonstrated Strengths...

• Profit & Performance Improvement	• Team Leadership/Motivation	• Strategic Planning
• Sales & Marketing Strategy/Execution	• Collaboration/Teamwork	• Results Orientation
• New Business Development	• Customer/Channel Expertise	• Brand Repositioning

A summary typically contains the three to five skills and competencies — sometimes more — that best support your job aspiration. The data in your statement need not be proven with examples in this brief section; for now it stands alone as assertions. In effect, you're saying, "Here's who I am. Here's what I can do for you." The summary is a tease, encouraging the reader to hang in there for proof of what the opening claims.

An exciting summary can revive a fading job accomplishment. Suppose you have an accomplishment that took place four or five years ago and is now needed to qualify you for a job. In a focused summary, the golden oldie achievement still sells for you as though it happened yesterday.

Advantages of a summary

Recruiters believe that what you're prepared to do next should be pretty evident from what you've already done. Another argument is premised on psychology: Employers aren't known for being overly concerned with what you want *from* them until they're sure of what you can do *for* them.

Summaries offer an easy way to identify the qualifications you have that match a particular job's requirements. Or identify qualifications that position you for related positions unknown to you in a given career field.

Disadvantages of a summary

A summary doesn't explicitly say what you want and why the employer would want you. The summary resume can backfire if it claims everything from soup to nuts yet misses the targets identified by employers for specific positions.

Making Education, Experience, Skills, and Competencies Work for You

When you begin drafting your core resume (see Chapter 6), carefully consider the following four categories of essential information. You include many other pieces of information for a core resume, but these four categories do the heavy lifting.

What's first — education or experience?

The general rule in resume-writing is to lead with your most qualifying factor.

With certain exceptions (such as law, where your choice of alma mater can dog you throughout life), lead off with experience when you've been in the workforce for at least one year. When you're loaded with experience but low on credentials, list your school days at the end — and perhaps even omit them entirely if you didn't graduate.

Education

List your highest degree first — type of degree, major, college name, and date awarded. Here are further tips for effectively highlighting your education:

- New graduates give far more detail on course work than do graduates who've held at least one post-graduation job for one year or more.

- Omit high school or prep school if you have a college degree.

- If you have a vocational-technical school certificate or diploma that required less than a year to obtain, list your high school as well.

- Note continuing education, including seminars related to your work.

- If you fall short of the mark on the job's educational requirements, try to compensate by expanding the continuing education section. Give the list a name, such as *Professional Development Highlights,* and list every impressive course, seminar, workshop, and conference that you've attended.

Experience

Describe — with *quantified* accomplishments — your present and previous positions in reverse chronological order. (See Chapter 18.) Include specific job titles, company names and locations, and dates of employment. Show progression and promotions within an organization, especially if you've been with one employer since the world was young.

Consider using more than one *Experience* heading on the same resume. Try headings such as *Accounting and Finance-Related Experience, General Business Experience,* and *Healthcare and Administration Experience.* Doing so is yet another way of reinforcing your qualifications for the job you seek.

Skills

Skills today are the heart and soul of job finding and, as such, encompass a variety of experiences. These are skills:

> Collaborating, editing, fundraising, interviewing, managing, blogging (Internet), researching, systematizing, teaching

And these are skills:

> Administering social programs, analyzing insurance facts, advising home-less people, allocating forestry resources, desktop publishing, coordinat-ing association events, designing home furnishing ads, marine expedition problem-solving, writing police reports, updating Web sites

And these are also skills:

> Dependable, sense of humor, commitment, leadership, persistence, crisis-resilient, adaptable, quick, results-driven

Skills are also keywords (Chapter 10). A *skill,* in job-search terms, is any iden-tifiable ability or fact that employers value and will pay for. That means that "five years" is a skill, just as "social media marketing" is a skill; employers pay for experienced provable skills.

Where do skills belong on your resume? Everywhere. Season every statement with skills. Skills are indispensable. You must name your skills or be left behind.

The Internet is awash in lists of skills. Web search terms such as *lists of skills, transferable skills checklist,* and *uncovering your skills.*

Top accomplishments

The accomplishments that lure most employers include:

- Increased revenues
- Saved money
- Increased efficiency
- Cut overhead
- Increased sales

- Improved workplace safety
- Purchasing accomplishments
- New products/new lines
- Improved record-keeping process
- Increased productivity
- Successful advertising campaign
- Effective budgeting

Competencies

Competencies include a combination of knowledge, skills, abilities, and personal attributes. These elements collectively translate into behavior, contributing to superior employee performance.

Put another way, business results are the *what* of employee performance, whereas competencies are the *how*. Because competencies are observable, they are measurable.

Compentencies are divided into two groups: *core competencies* for an entire function or company, and *role competencies* for a target position. Competency evaluation in hiring is used more often in large companies than in smaller firms.

If you're aiming for a job with a large employer, bone up on competency policy at each company. You can call the company's human resource department and ask, "Do you use a competencies model in recruiting?" If so, ask whether you can obtain a lexicon of the company's core competencies and the role competencies for the target position. Sometimes, the HR specialist will reveal the competencies and sometimes not. But ask.

A few examples of core competencies

Competencies do not come in a handy-dandy, one-size-fits-all package. They vary from industry to industry, and from company to company. The following very simple illustration of four competencies illustrates those a company might use for a technical sales representative.

Product knowledge	**Planning & organization**
Displays knowledge of products	Prioritizes and plans work activities
Explains product features and benefits	Uses time efficiently
Understands financial terminology	Plans for additional resources
Researches competitors' products	Integrates changes smoothly
	Sets goals and objectives
	Works in an organized manner
Technology usage	**Sales skills**
Demonstrates required skills	Achieves sales goals
Adapts to new technologies	Overcomes objections
Troubleshoots technological problems	Initiates new contacts
Uses technology to increase productivity	Maintains customer satisfaction
Keeps technical skills up to date	Maintains and promptly submits records

Including competencies in your resumes

Most good resumes focus on knowledge, skills, and accomplishments. They only hint at competencies required to do the work. To capture behavioral competencies on a resume, you must show how your accomplishments confirm your competencies. Or to turn it around, you must show how your competencies enabled you to rack up home runs.

To connect your behaviors with your accomplishments, you might say:

> **Product development:** *Created new midmarket segment supporting an annual growth rate of 20% in a flat industry, demonstrating high energy and business acumen.*

In the above example, the verb *demonstrating* connects the accomplishment (Created new mid-market segment supporting an annual growth rate of 20% in a flat industry) with competencies (high energy and business acumen). Other verbs you can use to bridge the two types of information include:

- ✔ Confirming
- ✔ Displaying

✔ Exhibiting

✔ Illustrating

✔ Manifesting

✔ Proving

✔ Revealing

✔ Verifying

Gaining Extra Points

You covered the meat and potatoes of your resume content. What can you add that will strengthen your image? You could, for instance, draw from your activities to show that you've got the right stuff. John Gill of Carlsbad, California, paid his own expenses to spend his college spring break building houses for the poor in Mexico. That act of sacrifice shows Gill's character; he goes out of his way to do important things for others. That's good resume content.

What's in your diary that may strengthen your image? Here are a few thoughts on buffing your image.

Activities

Activities can be anything from hobbies and sports to campus extracurricular participation. The trick is to analyze how each activity is relevant to the target job; discuss skills, knowledge, or other competencies developed; and list all accomplishments. Make sure that this section doesn't become meaningless filler.

In addition, avoid potentially controversial activities: Stating that you're a moose hunter won't endear you to animal-loving recruiters. If you've been able to research the reader and have found that you two have a common interest, list it on your resume so that it can become an icebreaker topic during an interview.

Organizations

Give yourself even more credentials with professional and civic affiliations. Mention all important offices held. Relate these affiliations to your reader in terms of marketable skills, knowledge, and accomplishments. A high profile in the community is particularly important for sales jobs.

Just as you should be careful about which activities you identify, so too should you be sensitive to booby traps in organization memberships:

✔ Listing too many organizations may make the reader wonder when you'd have time to do the job.

✔ Noting that you belong to one minority group organization may work in your favor, but reporting your membership in five minority group organizations may raise red flags. The recruiter may worry that you're a trouble-making activist.

✔ And, of course, you know better than to list your membership in religious or political organizations (unless you're applying for a job that requires such members hip). These affiliations don't apply to your ability to do the job, and some readers may use them to keep you out of the running.

Honors and awards

List most of the accomplishments for which you have been recognized. If the achievement had zero to do with work or doesn't show you in a professional light, don't take up white space with it; for example, you probably wouldn't list a Chili Cook-Off award unless you're applying for a job as a chef.

Certifications

A certificate verifies the qualification of a person. List on your resume the relevant certifications you hold in your field; they add luster to your qualifications and help you stand out from the competition. The heading can be a simple "Certifications" or "Professional Certifications."

Certification as a job-search tool is gaining renewed respect because of the following points:

✔ Certification is useful for resume triage by HR screeners who may not know the particulars of a given certification but nevertheless count it as a marker of extra knowledge and place resumes of cert holders in the coveted "interview" pile.

✔ Certification is valued by outsourcing firms because the credentials add credibility to project proposals. Employees with certs in outsourced departments are thought to be (but not proven to be) more likely to keep their jobs than those without the credentials.

✔ Certification is viewed as continuing education that indicates a job seeker has stayed up-to-date in a fast-moving field such as information technology.

✓ Certification for new college graduates shows they offer more than school-taught skills and are willing to make an extra effort to excel.

Licenses

If you're in a field or function that requires a license to do your work — such as legal, certified accounting, engineering, teaching, real estate, or medicine — show your license prominently on your resume. You can use a heading of "Professional Licensing" (if only one license) or "Professional Licenses" (for more than one license).

Endorsements

After citing an accomplishment, add immediately beneath it a short, flattering quote from your boss or a client. (Alternative placement: Present an endorsement in an italic typeface in a left- or right-hand column, or at the bottom of your resume.) Here are a few examples of endorsements:

✓ **For an information systems technician:** Bob Craigman (my boss) told the entire office: *I am basking in reflected glory that Charlie Pitman cut Internet access and telephone costs by 80%.*

✓ **For a sales rep at a toner and cartridge shop:** *Jennifer Robertson's resourcefulness in getting inside the SoapSuds account and expanding it by 15% after others had tried for months is truly impressive.* — Kevin Jones, General Manager

✓ **For an administrative support person:** *Tom is the first to greet me every morning and always projects a positive attitude.* — Kathryn Smith, Business Owner

Endorsements work, or advertisers wouldn't spend billions of dollars to use them. Be sure to check with your source before adding a quote to your resume.

Shaping Your Content on Application Forms

Application forms that you must sign aren't resumes. Once signed, an application form becomes a legal document. Lies can come back to bite and smite you. Stick to the facts by following these basic rules:

✔ Verify all dates of employment and salaries.

✔ Enter the full name and last known address of former employers. If former employers are no longer available, write "N.A." (Don't substitute names of coworkers.)

✔ If asked for salary history, list your base salary (or add commission and bonuses), omitting benefits.

✔ Give a complete employment history in months and years, including trivial three-month jobs that you left off the resume. When you don't tell the whole story, you leave a loophole of withholding information that later can be used against you to deny unemployment benefits if you're let go.

✔ Unless you have a condition directly affecting your ability to do the job for which you're applying, you need not elaborate on any disability.

Become a fountain of knowledge about disability rights; start with such specialty Web sites as the National Organization on Disability (`www.nod.org`) and Abilities Inc. (`www.abilitiesonline.org`).

✔ Divulge any criminal record (misdemeanor or felony) unless your records are sealed; consult a lawyer about the possibility of expungement before job hunting.

In certain instances, a job seeker can legally and ethically answer "no" on a question about a past offense; for information, visit Privacy Rights Clearinghouse (`www.privacyrights.org/ar/rosencrim.htm`).

✔ Be honest about having collected unemployment benefits (but remember that repeaters are frowned on). If you're caught lying about it later, practice your farewell speech.

Content to Omit: Your Salary Story

Never mention salary on your resume. Period.

Sometimes a job ad asks for your salary history (past) or salary requirements (future). Realize that revealing dollar figures in advance puts you at a disadvantage. This is especially true if you've been working for low pay — or if you've been paid above market.

In addition to job ads, profile forms on job sites and online personal agent programs almost always ask for your salary information. If you decide to participate, state your expectations in a range, and include the value of all benefits, bonuses, and perks in your salary history, not just cash.

When you choose to disclose your salary history or requirements online, make a distinction between general information forms and formal signed applications (legal documents). Include benefits (total compensation) on general information forms, but omit benefits on formal signed applications that ask for salary history.

Make sure you do these two things before you provide salary requirements:

✔ Research the market rate for someone with your skills and experience. Start with the Web sites Salary.com (www.salary.com), Salary Expert (www.salaryexpert.com), and PayScale (www.payscale.com).

✔ Find out why the smart money advises against being too quick to pipe up with hard figures on the money you've made and the money you want. What can you expect in return for revealing salary information, job unseen? You get a chance to name your price and hope you find takers, many of whom will want to talk your price down. (See Chapter 3 for salary advice.)

Exception to salary silence advice: Tell recruiters with whom you have a serious interest in working how much you've earned and how much it will cost an employer to hire you. Otherwise, know that recruiters don't want to waste time playing games and are likely to fold up their interest and move on.

Accomplishments Are Your Content Aces

The next chapter (Chapter 9) speaks of selling, not telling, your worth. Citing your earned accomplishments is how you make that happen.

Focus on your most marketable content — you made or saved money for an employer, for example. Don't rush the construction of your resume: If you build it right, the interviews will come.

Putting your content in online resume builders

How much do the free online resume builders offered at virtually all substantial job boards and some company Web sites help you "sell it rather than tell it?"

Many automated resume builders benefit the recruiting side of the employment industry, not the job-seeking side. Their builder software, aiming for efficiency, tries to standardize data — to compare apples to apples. Such builder software limits you to a synopsis of bare bones information. That is, they offer space for the essentials — your contact information, last three jobs, and education, for example. But they may not provide space for humanizing experiences, such as volunteerism, honors, and awards.

If you use specific resume builder software program to construct your online resume, notice whether it (a) favors the recruiter, or (b) favors the job seeker.

If you want to use an online resume builder with a job board or a company Web site, remember to think for yourself and not assume the technology will bring to light your most marketable qualities, which this book shows you how to emphasize.

Part III
Resume Basics That Wow 'Em Every Time

The 5th Wave
By Rich Tennant

RICHTENNANT

FULLER BELL & WHISTLE Co

"It's a pretty good resume, but I would have liked to see more bells and whistles."

In this part . . .

How do you show off your strengths and shine the best light on your not-so-strengths? This part of the book shows you how to handle a slew of less than ideal work histories or situations, from too much experience to too little. In this part, I also explain how to give your content the zing it needs and how to make sure your resume's a looker.

Chapter 9

Creating Your Best Resume

· ·

In This Chapter

▶ Selling your value to people you want to work for

▶ Focusing your resume like a high-powered laser

▶ Selecting the format that flatters your image

▶ Comparing the good and the bad for each format

▶ Sampling superb but uncommon formats

· ·

How much are you worth to employers? Are you a top pick, a maybe pick, or . . . gulp, a no-hire pick? Your resume inspires their first best guess, so make sure it's a compelling portrait of how your strengths and skills benefit the enterprise that you're hoping will write your next paycheck.

No matter the platform, you need to show your value via a well-constructed resume. Construct a crisp and shorter new version for the smaller screens of smartphones, e-readers, and tablets, as well as the larger screens of desktop computers, laptops, and paper. The principles are the same: It's not the size of the stage on which your resume appears that counts; it's how much of your value it communicates.

Begin any resume construction by making foundation decisions about how to best present your value. That is, determine to use a persuasive messaging voice and a strong focus, housed in your most favorable format. This chapter reveals the nuts and bolts of how to mount a successful marketing campaign when the product is *you*.

"Telling It" Mutes; "Selling It" Sings

Pretend you're in the market for replacement windows in your home. Which of the following two messages would better pique your interest in taking a closer look at the company?

The Turner Group has been in existence replacing windows for 30+ years at the same easy-to-find showroom. We offer 25 different models and window sizes — a choice to fit every home and budget.

The Turner Group has been assisting homeowners to protect their home values with 25 models of high-quality replacement windows at discount prices — and in all sizes — since the mid-1970s.

The first statement is an example of telling it; the message is "look at us!" The second statement is an example of selling it, and its message is "here's what we can do for you."

OnTarget resumes don't tell it — they sell it! Dry, dull descriptions of what you did on a job are as boring as video of a friend's childhood birthday party.

Instill excitement! List your background facts but make sure you position them as end-user (employer) benefits.

One way to sell your value and your benefits to an employer who has the power to hire you is to get specific. Communicate the importance of what you've done by using details — numbers, names, achievements, outcomes, volume of sales or savings, and size of contracts, for example.

Remember, when you sell it, you breathe life into a rigid, dreary, boring, and generally coma-inducing document. Here are several examples of the sell-it strategy for resumes.

Tell it	*Sell it*
Supervisor of HR generalist and recruiting functions for 10 years at company headquarters.	Supervisor with 10 years' successful management of 6 HR generalists and 3 recruiters for regional company with 3 administrative offices and 8 manufacturing plants.
Worked as network administrator with responsibility for administration and troubleshooting.	As network administrator, created in excess of 750 user scripts, installed 16 workstations, administered security codes to 350 clients, supervised installation of company-wide Microsoft XP Pro, and regularly solved stress-causing malfunctions in operating system and software.
Leading sales rep for new homes in prestigious development in year when housing market began to cool.	In a cooling housing market (off 11% from previous year), became number-one sales rep, selling $7,800,000 in 12 months — 13 homes at $600,000 floor.

For really tiny screens suitable only for 10-year-old eyes, consider preserving your sell-it statements with a hyperlink to a free resume-hosting site, such as Yola.com (`www.yola.com`). One click allows small-screen readers to see your entire resume.

Help employers see not only what you were responsible for but how well you did it — and why it mattered.

Focus Your Resume

Too many jobs in your background threaten your focus. *Unfocused* is an ugly word in job-search circles, one that indicates you lack commitment, that you're perpetually at a fork in the road. It's a reason *not* to hire you.

When your resume looks as though it will collapse under the weight of a mishmash of jobs unconnected to your present target, eliminate previous trivial pursuits. Group the consequential jobs under a heading that says *Relevant Work Experience Summary*. What if this approach solves one problem — the busy resume — but creates another, such as a huge, gaping hole where you removed inconsequential jobs? Create a second work history section that covers those gaps, labeling it *Other Experience*. Figure 9-1 shows an example.

Dealing with an unfocused career pattern is easier when it's under the banner of a temporary service company. The treatment in this case lists the temporary services company as the employer. You choose one job title that covers most of your assignments. Under that umbrella title, identify specific assignments. Give the dates in years next to the temporary services firm, skipping dates for each assignment. Figure 9-2 shows an example.

What if you work for several temporary services at the same time? The simple answer is that you use the same technique of dating your work history for the temporary service firms, not for the individual assignments. This dating technique is a statement of fact; you legally are an employee of the temporary services firm, not of the company that pays for your temporary services.

Impacted Resume with Focus

Professional Experience

UNITECH, Hamburg, Germany
Computer Laboratory Assistant, [dates]
> Manage and troubleshoot hardware and software systems. Recover data, create programming architecture, and install parts and software. Assist a team of 18 engineers.

TECHNIK TECH, Hamburg, Germany
Assistant to System Analysts, [dates]
> Participated in construction, repair, and installation of systems at local businesses. Diagnosed faulty systems and reported to senior analysts, decreasing their workload by 25%.

TRADE NET, Berlin, Germany
Applications and Network Specialist, [dates]
> Set up and monitored a Windows-based BBS, including installation, structure, security, and graphics. Authored installation scripts for Trade Net, licensing U.S. software use in Europe.

Other Experience

AMERICAN TOY STORE, Berlin, Germany, Sales Representative, [dates]
Arranged and inventoried merchandise, directed sales and customer relations. Developed strong interpersonal skills and gained knowledge of retail industry.

CAMP INTERNATIONAL, Oslo, Germany, Activities Director, [dates]
Organized daily activities for more than 300 children from English-speaking countries, including sports, recreation, and day classes. Supervised 10 counselors and kitchen staff of five, developing responsible and effective management skills.

Figure 9-1: Solving the gap problem in a jobs-impacted resume by creating a focus plus a second work history section.

Focusing with Temp Jobs

Professional Experience

Relia-Temps   [dates]

Executive Secretary

- North Western Banking Group
Perform all clerical and administrative responsibilities for 10-partner investment and loan firm, assisting each partner in drafting contracts, reviewing proposals, and desiging various financial programs. Supervise 7 staff members. Introduced 50% more efficient filing system, reducing client reviews from 4 to 3 hours.

Administrative Assistant

- Mosaic Advertising
Supervised 3 receptionists and 4 clerical specialists, reporting directly to president. Administered daily operations of all accounting and communication transactions. Using extensive computer savvy, upgraded company computer networks withWindows 98.

- Blakeslee Environmental, Inc.
Assisted 8 attorneys at interstate environmental protection agency, scheduling meetings and conferences, maintaining files, and updating database records. Redesigned office procedures and methods of communication, superior organizational skills.

Figure 9-2: Listing your temporary job assignments without looking unfocused.

Resume Formats Make a Difference

Resume format refers not to the design or look of your resume but to how you organize and emphasize your information. Different format styles flatter different histories.

At root, formats come in three family trees:

> ✔ The *reverse chronological* lists all employment and education, beginning with the most recent and working backward.

> ✔ The *skills-based functional* shouts what you can do instead of relaying what you've done and where you did it.
>
> ✔ The *hybrid* or *combination* is a marriage of both formats.

The narrative format is an outdated chronological format that starts with the oldest facts and works forward to the newest facts. A pretentious variation of the narrative format uses the third person as though you were writing a biography. I strongly suggest that you don't use either of these formats.

These basic styles have spawned a variety of other formats, each of which I discuss in this chapter. The best-known formats are these:

> ✔ Professional
>
> ✔ Academic curriculum vitae
>
> ✔ International curriculum vitae

Subcategories of formats, which I also discuss later in this chapter, include accomplishment, linear, and keyword resumes.

Table 9-1 gives you a breakdown of which of the above formats enhances your personal curb appeal.

Table 9-1	Your Best Resume Formats at a Glance
Your Situation	*Suggested Formats*
Perfect career pattern	Reverse Chronological
Rookie or ex-military	Functional, Hybrid
Seasoned ace	Functional, Hybrid
Business	Reverse Chronological, Hybrid
Technical	Reverse Chronological, Hybrid
Professional	Professional, Academic Curriculum Vitae, Portfolio
Government	Reverse Chronological, Professional, Hybrid
Arts/teaching	Professional, Portfolio, Academic Curriculum Vitae
Job history gaps	Functional, Hybrid
Multitrack job history	Functional, Hybrid
Career change	Functional
International job seeker	International Curriculum Vitae
Special issues	Functional, Hybrid

The following sections explore each type of resume format so that you can choose the style best for you and your skills.

Reverse Chronological Format

The *reverse chronological* (RC) format, shown in Figure 9-3, is straightforward: It cites your employments from the most recent back, showing dates as well as employers and educational institutions (college, vocational-technical schools, and career-oriented programs and courses). You accent a steady work history with a clear pattern of upward or lateral mobility.

Strengths and weaknesses

Check to see whether the reverse chronological resume's strengths work for you:

- ✔ This upfront format is by far the most popular with employers and recruiters because it is so, well, upfront.

- ✔ RC links employment dates, underscoring continuity. The weight of your experience confirms that you're a specialist in a specific career field (social service or technology, for example).

- ✔ RC positions you for the next upward career step.

- ✔ As the most traditional of formats, RC is a good fit for traditional industries (such as banking, education, and accounting).

Take the weaknesses of the reverse chronological format into account:

- ✔ When your previous job titles are substantially different from your target position, this format doesn't support your objective. Without careful management, the RC reveals everything, including inconsequential jobs and negative factors.

- ✔ RC can spotlight periods of unemployment or brief job tenure.

- ✔ Without careful management, RC reveals your age.

- ✔ Without careful management, RC may suggest that you hit a plateau but stayed in a job too long.

Reverse Chronological Format

YOUR NAME
City, State
Home and Cell Phones
E-mail

Objective:
A position that uses your skills.

SUMMARY
- Years of work experience, paid and unpaid, relevant to target position's requirements
- Achievement that proves you can handle the target
- Another achievement that proves you can handle the target
- Skills, competencies, characteristics — facts that further your ability to handle target job
- Education and training relating to the target (if unrelated, bury in resume body)

PROFESSIONAL EXPERIENCE AND ACCOMPLISHMENTS

[dates]   **Job Title**   Employer, Employer's Location
A brief synopsis of your purpose in the company, detailing essential functions, products
and customer base you managed.
- An achievement in this position relevant to objective (do not repeat summary)
- A second achievement in this position relevant to current objective
- More accomplishments, i.e., awards, recognition, promotion, raise, praise, training

[dates]   **Job Title**   Employer, Employer's Location
Detailed as above.

[dates]   **Job Title**   Employer, Employer's Location
A briefer synopsis of your purpose in the company, overviewing functions, products,
customer base.
- An achievement made during this position relevant to current objective
- More accomplishments, i.e., awards, recognition, promotion, raise, praise, training

[dates]   **Job Title**   Employer, Employer's Location
An even briefer synopsis of your purpose in the company, overviewing functions,
products, customer base.
- An achievement made during this position that's relevant to current objective

EDUCATION AND PROFESSIONAL TRAINING

Degree(s), classes, seminars, educational awards and honors
Credentials, clearances, licenses

Figure 9-3: The tried-and-true, basic reverse chronological format.

Who should use this format and who should think twice

Use the reverse chronological if you fall into any of these categories:

- ✔ You have a steady school and work record reflecting constant growth or lateral movement.

- ✔ Your most recent employer is a respected name in the industry, and the name may ease your entry into a new position.

- ✔ Your most recent job titles are impressive stepping stones.

- ✔ You're a savvy writer who knows how to manage potential negative factors, such as inconsequential jobs, too few jobs, too many temporary jobs, too many years at the same job, or too many years of age.

Think twice about using the RC under these circumstances:

- ✔ You have a lean employment history. Listing a stray student job or two is not persuasive, even when you open with superb educational credentials enhanced with internships and co-op experiences.

  With careful attention, you can do a credible job on an RC by extracting from your extracurricular activities every shred of skills, which you present as abilities to do work with extraordinary commitment and a head for quick learning.

- ✔ You have work-history or employability problems — gaps, demotions, stagnation in a single position, job hopping (four jobs in three years, for example), reentering the workforce after a break to raise a family.

  Exercise very careful management to truthfully modify stark realities. However, you may find that other formats can serve you better.

Creating a reverse chronological resume

To create an OnTarget RC resume, remember to focus on areas of specific relevance to your target position. List all pertinent places you've worked. Include for each the name of the employer and the city in which you worked, the years you were there, your title, your key responsibilities, and your measurable accomplishments.

To handle problems such as unrelated experience, you can group unrelated jobs in a second work history section under a heading of Other Experience, Previous Experience, or Related Experience. I tell you more about handling a variety of special circumstances in Chapter 13.

Functional Format

The functional format (see Figure 9-4) is a resume of ability-focused topics — portable skills or functional areas. It ignores chronological order. In its purest form, the functional style omits dates, employers, and job titles. But employers don't like it when you leave out the particulars, so contemporary functional resumes list employers, job titles, and sometimes even dates — but still downplay this information by briefly listing it at the bottom of the resume.

The functional format is oriented toward what the job seeker can do for the employer, instead of narrating history.

Strengths and weaknesses

The following are the strengths of the functional format:

- A functional resume directs a reader's eyes to what you want him or her to notice. It helps a reader visualize what you can do instead of when and where you learned to do it. Functional resumes salute the future rather than embalm the past.

- The functional format — written after researching the target company — serves up the precise functions or skills that the employer wants. It's like saying, "You want budget control and turnaround skills — I offer budget control and turnaround skills." The skills sell is a magnet to reader eyes!

- It uses unpaid and nonwork experience to your best advantage.

- The functional format allows you to eliminate or subordinate work history that doesn't support your current objective.

The weaknesses of the functional format include the following:

- Recruiters and employers are more accustomed to RC formats than other types. Departing from the norm may raise suspicion that you're not the cream of the crop of applicants. Readers may assume that you're trying to hide inadequate experience, educational deficits, or who knows what.

- Functional styles may leave unclear which skills grew from which jobs or experiences.

- This format doesn't make a clear career path obvious.

Functional Format

YOUR NAME
City, State
Home and Cell Phones
E-mail

Job Title You Desire

More than (# years paid and unpaid) work experience, in target area, contributing to an (achievement/result/high ranking in industry/top 5% of performance reviews). Add accomplishments, strengths, proficiencies, characteristics, education, brief testimonial — anything that supports your target job title.

PROFESSIONAL EXPERIENCE AND ACCOMPLISHMENTS

A TOP SKILL (Pertinent to objective and job requirements)
• An achievement illustrating this skill, and the location/employer of this skill*
• A second achievement illustrating this skill, and the location/employer of this skill*

A SECOND TOP SKILL (Pertinent to objective and job requirements)
• An achievement illustrating this skill, and the location/employer of this skill*
• A second achievement illustrating this skill, and the location/employer of this skill*

A THIRD TOP SKILL (Pertinent to objective and job requirements)
• An achievement illustrating this skill, and the location/employer of this skill*
• A second achievement illustrating this skill, and the location/employer of this skill*

A FOURTH SKILL (Optional — must relate to objective and job requirements)
• Detailed as above

A UNIQUE AREA OF PROFICIENCY (Pertinent to objective and job requirements)
• An achievement testifying to this proficiency, including the location/employer*
• A list of equipment, processes, software, or terms you know that reflect your familiarity with this area of proficiency
• A list of training experiences that document your qualifications and proficiency

EMPLOYMENT HISTORY

[dates]	**Job Title**	Employer, Location
[dates]	**Job Title**	Employer, Location
[dates]	**Job Title**	Employer, Location
[dates]	**Job Title**	Employer, Location

PROFESSIONAL TRAINING AND EDUCATION
Degrees, credentials, clearances, licenses, classes, seminars, training

* Omit locations/employers if your work history is obviously lacking in lockstep upward mobility

Figure 9-4: No experience? Use the functional resume format.

Who should use this format and who should think twice

The functional resume is heaven-sent for career changers, contract workers, new graduates, ex-military personnel, seasoned aces, and individuals with multitrack job histories, work-history gaps, or special-issue problems.

Job seekers with blue-ribbon backgrounds and managers and professionals who are often tapped by executive recruiters should avoid this format.

Creating a functional resume

Choose areas of expertise acquired during the course of your career, including education and unpaid activities. These areas become skill, competency, and functional headings, which vary by the target position or career field. Note accomplishments below each heading. A few examples of headings are: *Management, Sales, Budget Control, Cost Cutting, Project Implementation,* and *Turnaround Successes.*

List the headings in the order of importance and follow each heading with a series of short statements of your skills. Turn your statements into power hitters with measurable achievements.

Hybrid Format

The hybrid, a combination of reverse chronological and functional formats, satisfies demands for timelines as well as showcases your marketable skills and impressive accomplishments. Many people find the hybrid to be the most attractive of all formats.

Essentially, in a hybrid, a functional summary tops a reverse chronological presentation of dates, employers, and capsules of each position's duties. Figure 9-5 gives you a template for this format.

The hybrid style is similar to the contemporary functional format — so much so that making a case for distinction is sometimes difficult.

Hybrid Format

YOUR NAME
City, State
Home and Cell Phones
E-mail

Objective: Position as_____using your___ (#) years of experience in skills key to target.

SUMMARY OF QUALIFICATIONS
Number of years in area of target position
Related education, training and accreditation
An achievement pertinent to objective
Qualifications that reinforce your candidacy for this position
Other accomplishments, characteristics, proficiencies

SUMMARY OF SKILLS
• Technical skills   • Processes   • Computer software

ACCOMPLISHMENTS AND EXPERIENCE

Job Title, Top Qualifications Used   Employer, Location   [dates]

    A Top Skill (Pertinent to objective/requirements)
    • Accomplishments made while in this position
    • Several apt achievements from position, pertinent to this skill and the objective
    Another Skill (Pertinent to objective)
    • Several achievements pertinent to this skill and the objective

Job Title, Top Qualifications Used   Employer, Location   [dates]

    A Top Skill (Pertinent to objective/requirements)
    • Accomplishments made while in this position, even more detailed
    • Several apt achievements from this position, similar to above
    Another Skill (Pertinent to objective)
    • Several achievements pertinent to this skill and the objective

Job Title, Top Qualifications Used   Employer, Location   [dates]

    A Top Skill (Pertinent to objective/requirements)
    • Accomplishments made while in this position
    • Several apt achievements from position, pertinent to this skill and the objective
    Another Skill (Pertinent to objective)
    • Several achievements pertinent to this skill and the objective

PROFESSIONAL TRAINING AND EDUCATION
Degrees, accreditations, licenses, clearances, courses

Figure 9-5: The hybrid format — the best of both worlds.

Strengths and weaknesses

Hybrid resumes appear to be rapidly gaining in popularity. A hybrid format combines the strengths of both the reverse chronological and functional formats, so check out those earlier sections. Its weakness is that, like a functional resume, it departs from the straightforward reverse chronological format that a very conservative employer may prefer.

Who should use this format and who should think twice

The hybrid is a wise choice for rookies, ex-military personnel, seasoned aces, those with job history gaps or a multitrack job history, and individuals with special-issue problems. Additionally, job seekers who want to highlight their flexible qualifications for a variety of positions benefit with this format. Seekers of jobs requiring a security clearance or the handling of large sums of money should stick to the straightforward reverse chronological format.

Creating a hybrid resume

Build a functional format of ability-focused topics and add employment documentation — employers, locations, dates, and role duties.

Professional Format

A professional format, also called a *professional vitae* or *professional CV*, is slightly long winded (say, three to five pages), but factual. It emphasizes professional qualifications and activities. This format, shown in Figure 9-6, is essentially a shortened academic curriculum vitae.

Strengths and weaknesses

The professional resume is mandatory for certain kinds of positions; your choice is whether to send this type, or go all the way and send an academic curriculum vitae.

Professional Format

YOUR NAME
City, State
Home and Cell Phones
E-mail

EDUCATION AND PROFESSIONAL TRAINING

Degrees, credentials, awards, achievements, honors, seminars, clearances, licenses.

OBJECTIVE: A position that uses your talents, with an emphasis on your special skills.

SUMMARY

- Number of years of work experience, paid and unpaid, relevant to target

- Accomplishment(s) that prove your unique candidacy for this position

- Qualifications geared for the objective position or company requirements

- Other things the employer will like to know — proficiencies, characteristics, achievements, training, credentials and education

PROFESSIONAL EXPERIENCE AND ACCOMPLISHMENTS

[dates]   **Job Title**   Employer, Employer's Location

A brief synopsis of your purpose in the company, detailing essential functions and products you managed, and your customer base.

- An achievement made during position pertinent to target

- A second achievement made during position also pertinent to target

- More achievements — awards, recognition, promotion, raise, praise, training

[dates]   **Job Title**   Employer, Employer's Location

An even briefer synopsis of your purpose in the company, overviewing functions, products, customer base.

- An achievement made during this position that is applicable to target

- More achievements — awards, recognition, promotion, raise, praise, training

* *List three previous jobs with the same detail as above; divide jobs according to job*

Figure 9-6: The long but effective professional format is perfect for certain careers.

But be aware that professional resumes are reviewed under a microscope; every deficiency stands out. Adding a portfolio that shows your experience-based work skills may compensate for missing chunks of formal requirements. Just make sure that any unsolicited samples you send are high quality and need no explanation.

Who should use this format and who should think twice

Professionals in medicine, science, and law should use this format. Also use it when common sense or convention makes it the logical choice, as when you're applying for a leadership civil service appointment in government.

For most nonprofessionals, especially managers, the professional format is tedious.

Creating a professional resume

Begin with education, professional training, and an objective. Follow with a summary of the main points you want the reader to absorb. Follow that information with details of your professional experience and accomplishments.

Follow the template in Figure 9-6, paying attention to accomplishments. Just because you present yourself in a low-key, authoritative manner doesn't mean that you can forget to say how good you are.

Academic Curriculum Vitae

The academic *curriculum vitae* (CV) is a comprehensive biographical statement, typically three to ten pages, emphasizing professional qualifications and activities. A CV of six to eight pages, ten at the most, is recommended for a veteran professional; two to four pages is appropriate for a young professional just starting out (see the "Professional Format" section earlier in this chapter).

If your CV is more than four pages long, show mercy and save eyesight by attaching an *executive summary* page to the top. An executive summary gives a brief overview of your qualifications and experience.

Among various possible organizations, the template in Figure 9-7 (a variation of the hybrid format but with exhaustive coverage) illustrates a lineup of your contact information, objective, qualifications summary, skills summary, and professional background.

Academic Curriculum Vitae Format

YOUR NAME
Curriculum Vitae
City, State
Home and Cell Phones
E-mail

Objective (optional): Position as_____(title of position employer offers) using ___ (#) years of experience in _____ (qualifications essential and specialized to the position).

SUMMARY OF QUALIFICATIONS

- A summary of your education, proficiencies, and career pertinent to target
- Number of years in objective area, explaining similarities to job and its responsibilities
- Related education, training, and accreditation, reflecting employer's goals/priorities
- An achievement directly related to target
- Traits reinforcing your candidacy for this position, specifically those asked for by the employer and those generally in demand in the field
- Other accomplishments, characteristics, knowledge either rare or prized in the field

SUMMARY OF SKILLS

•Topics of specialty or innovation within field •Areas of particular familiarity
•Software equipment •Processes •Terminology relevant to target •Languages

PROFESSIONAL BACKGROUND

EDUCATION
Degrees:
    Ph.D., institution, date of degree (or anticipated date), specialization
    M.A./M.S., institution, date of degree, major, minor, emphasis, concentration
    B.A./B.S., institution, date of degree, major, minor
Courses: Those taken, honors, seminars, number of units, G.P.A. (if a recent graduate)
Other Accreditations: Licenses, clearances
Academic Achievements: Appointments, nominations, leaderships, scholarships, grants,
    awards, praise, scores, recognitions, accomplishments
Affiliations: Societies, associations, clubs, fraternities, sororities, leagues, memberships

PH.D. DISSERTATION
    Title, advisor, director
    Abstract summary (4-5 sentences) discussing content and methodology

HONORS, AWARDS, AND ACHIEVEMENTS
Appointments, nominations, leaderships, awards, praise, scores, recognitions,
accomplishments, high scores, grades, G.P.A.s, fellowships, scholarships, grants,
(including B.A./B.S.)

Figure 9-7: Brevity definitely isn't a feature of the academic CV.

TEACHING EXPERIENCE

Job Title, Top Qualifications Used   Employer, Location   **[dates]**

A Top Responsibility (Relevant to objective)
• Accomplishments made in this position targeting the employer's priorities/mission
• Several other achievements from this position, pertinent to objective
Another Skill (Appropriate to objective)
• Several achievements from this position, pertinent to objective

*   *Repeat above pattern for each position.*

RESEARCH EXPERIENCE
Positions, locations, dates, descriptions of research in pertinence to target position

TEACHING INTERESTS
Discipline, certification

RESEARCH INTERESTS
Areas of inquiry

PUBLICATIONS
*   List all those you are willing to show the search committee
*   Include work in progress or pending
*   Cite works as follows:

•**"Title of work,"** Name of publication/publisher (*Newsletter, Newspaper, Magazine, Journal, Book*), location of publisher (state & city or major city), date of publication, volume number (v.##), issue number (#.#), series number (#.#.#), page numbers (# - #) (type quotes around the title of your article).

PRESENTATIONS AND PUBLIC APPEARANCES
*   Include conference papers and research reports
*   List as follows:

•**"Title of presentation,"** location of presentation (City, State), [dates]; optional synopsis of content and/or purpose of presentation, audience, results, etc.

PROFESSIONAL AFFILIATIONS
A society, association, league, or club with which you associate, position held, [dates]
A society, association, league, or club with which you associate, position held, [dates]
A society, association, league, or club with which you associate, position held, [dates]

RECOMMENDATIONS
Names and contact information of 3-4 references willing to write recommendation letters

CREDENTIALS

Strengths and weaknesses

A CV presents all the best of you, which is good, but for people with aging eyes, a CV may be too reading-intensive. More important, weaknesses in any area of your professional credentials are relatively easy to spot.

Who should use this format and who should think twice

Anyone working in a PhD-driven environment, such as higher education, think tanks, science, and elite research and development groups needs to use this format.

Anyone who can avoid using it should do so.

Creating an academic curriculum vitae

Create a comprehensive summary of your professional employment and accomplishments: education, positions, affiliations, honors, memberships, credentials, dissertation title, fields in which comprehensive examinations were passed, full citations of publications and presentations, awards, discoveries, inventions, patents, seminar leadership, foreign languages, courses taught — whatever is valued in your field.

International Curriculum Vitae Format

The international CV is *not* the same document as an academic CV. Think of an international CV as a six- to eight-page excruciatingly detailed resume (Figure 9-8 gives you a template). Although it solicits private information that's outlawed in the United States, such as your health status, the international CV is favored in some nations as a kind of global ticket to employment.

International Curriculum Vitae Format

YOUR NAME
Curriculum Vitae
City, State, Country, Province
Include international codes:
Home and Cell Phones
E-mail
Objective (optional): Position as_____(title of position employer offers) using
your____ (#) years of experience in _____ (skills essential and specialized to the position).

SUMMARY OF QUALIFICATIONS

• A summary of your education, proficiencies, and career pertinent to target
• Number of years in area of objective, explaining similarities to it/its responsibilities
• Related education, training, and accreditation, reflecting employer's goals/priorities
• An achievement directly related to target, that the employer needs
• Traits reinforcing your candidacy for this position, specifically those asked for by the
  employer and those generally in demand in the field
• Other accomplishments, characteristics, knowledge either rare or prized in the field
• Traveling in field, countries visited, improvements made, distinctions, and so forth

SUMMARY OF SKILLS

• Topics of specialty or innovation within field   • Areas of particular familiarity
• Software equipment   • Processes   • Terminology relevant to target   • Languages

PROFESSIONAL BACKGROUND

EMPLOYMENT

Job Title   Employer, Location   **[dates]**
Present
A Top Responsibility (Relevant to objective)
   • Accomplishments made in this position targeting the employer's
     priorities/mission
   • Several other achievements from this position, pertinent to objective
Another Skill (Appropriate to objective)
   • Several achievements from this position, pertinent to objective

   * *Repeat above pattern for all jobs.*

PROFESSIONAL HONORS
All honorary positions, awards, recognitions, or titles, with locations, [dates]

PUBLICATIONS
•**"Title of work,"** Name of publication/publisher (*Newsletter, Newspaper, Magazine,
   Journal*), location of publisher (country, languages, state & city or major city), date of
   publication, volume number (v.##), issue number (#.#), series number (#.#.#), page
   numbers (# - #)

   * *Repeat above citation for all publications.*

Figure 9-8: The international CV is an option when applying for jobs outside your home country.

PRESENTATIONS AND PUBLIC APPEARANCES
•**"Title of presentation,"** location of presentation (Country, City, State, Province, Language), Date; optional synopsis of content and/or purpose of presentation, audience, results, etc.

    * *Repeat above citation for all presentations.*

PROFESSIONAL AFFILIATIONS
    All societies, associations, leagues, or clubs, positions held, locations, [dates]

EDUCATION

Degrees: Ph.D., institution, date of degree (or anticipated date), specialization
                M.A./M.S., institution, date of degree, major, minor, concentration
                B.A./B.S., institution, date of degree, major, minor
                * *Give equivalents of these degrees in other countries*
Courses: Those taken, honors, seminars, number of units, G.P.A. (if a recent graduate)
Other Accreditations: Licenses, clearances
Academic Achievements: Appointments, nominations, leaderships, scholarships, grants,
                    awards, praise, scores, recognitions, accomplishments
Affiliations: Societies, associations, clubs, fraternities, sororities, leagues, memberships

DOCTORAL DISSERTATION
Title, advisor, director
Abstract summary (4-5 sentences) discussing content and methodology

HONORS, AWARDS AND ACHIEVEMENTS
Appointments, nominations, leaderships, awards, praise, scores, recognitions, accomplishments, high scores, grades, G.P.A.s, fellowships, scholarships, grants, (including B.A./B.S/equivalents)

PERSONAL INFORMATION
• A sentence or so that describes personal attributes pertinent to employer's interests. Think positively, omit negatives, and highlight goal-oriented, functional characteristics that promise of a good worker-employer relationship and reliably good work product. Present specific work-related examples of these personality highlights and explain how they are significant to the employer. Without exaggerating, accentuate the positive, and include all favorable quotes from employers and co-workers, members of the clergy, and public service, volunteer organization, nonprofit organization and political officials
• Age, Marital Status (Single, Engaged, Married)
• Hobbies and leisure activities (travel, clubs, sports, athletics, collections, subscriptions)
• Volunteer service, public service

The international CV is usually a reverse chronological format that includes your contact information, qualifications summary, professional background, education, and personal information. Some European countries prefer the chronological format, which lists education and work experience from the farthest back to the present.

Americans should remember that when working overseas for a native employer, they are not protected by Equal Employment Opportunity laws.

Strengths and weaknesses

International employment experts say that if you don't use this format, foreign recruiters may think you're hiding something. But keep in mind that the international CV format intrudes into private areas of your life.

Who should use this format and who should think twice

Use this format if you're seeking an overseas job and don't object to revealing information that may subject you to discriminatory hiring practices.

Individuals who feel strongly about invasions of privacy or fear identity theft, or who aren't willing to be rejected out of hand because of gender, religion, race, age, or marital status should avoid this format.

Of course, if you want an overseas job and you don't use this format, you may be out of luck unless you're working through an American recruiter. The recruiter can interpret your concerns and negotiate for a bare minimum of personal information. Nationals of countries other than the United States can also use this technique.

Creating an international curriculum vitae

Formality prevails with the international CV. England has a suggested CV form, which is more like the American resume than not.

- If you're applying in a non-English-speaking country, have your CV translated into the appropriate foreign language. Send employers and recruiters both the English and the native-language version.

- Unless it's untrue, mention in the personal section that you have excellent health.

> ✔ Suggest by appropriate hobbies and personal interests that you'll easily adapt to an overseas environment.
>
> ✔ In the unlikely case that you're submitting your international CV on paper, handwrite the cover letter that goes with it — Europeans use handwriting analysis as a screening device. If your handwriting is iffy, enclose a word-processed version as well. If you want to send hand-written e-mail, search online for technical tips about how to do it.

In addition, make sure that your cover letter shows a sincere desire to be in the country of choice.

Other Resume Presentations

A few adventuresome job seekers are using innovative resume formats. Here's a quick look at two possibilities that can't be classified as mainstream methods but may be just the vehicle you need to find the job that seems beyond your grasp.

Resume letters

In a targeted postal mailing campaign, a resume letter attracts attention because it reads more like a story than a document. The resume letter is a combination of cover letter and resume; often it is two pages. It typically opens with a variation of the question: "Are you looking for a professional who can leap high buildings in a single bound?" A resume letter opening might look a little something like this:

> *Should you be in the market for an accomplished, congenial senior human resources specialist who has earned an excellent reputation for successful HR technology acquisition analysis and management, this letter will be of interest to you.*

The resume letter continues to give a basic overview of a job seeker's strengths, including previous employers, achievements, skills and competencies, as they would apply to the recipient company.

Take extra care to discover the key qualifications most often required for the position you seek. Targeting is a no-lose strategy even for cold mailings.

Your strengths message may be in paragraph form or in bulleted statements. The resume letter format can be especially useful for a professional with an abundance of experience. But don't substitute a resume letter when you're responding to a job advertisement that asks for a resume. The employer calls the shots.

One of the most amazing placements I've ever heard about was the case of the chemist who at age 50 left the profession to take a fling dealing cards at a casino. Five years later, at age 55, he wanted to return to the chemistry workplace. A cold mailing of a well-written resume letter to owners of small chemical companies turned up a caretaker CEO job while the owner took an extended two-year trip out of the country. Would the resume letter and broadcast mailing approach work as well with e-mail? I have no data on this question. The trick would be to bypass spam filters.

Portfolios

Hard-copy samples of your work, gathered in a portfolio, have long been valuable to fields such as design, graphics, photography, architecture, advertising, public relations, marketing, education, and contracting.

Often, you deliver your portfolio as part of the job interview. Some highly motivated job seekers include a brief version of a career portfolio when sending their resumes, although recruiters say that they want fewer, not more, resume parts to deal with. If you must include work samples to back up your claims, send only a few of your very best.

The portfolio is a showcase for documenting a far more complete picture of what you offer employers than is possible with a resume of one or two pages. Getting recruiters to read it is the problem. When you determine that a portfolio is your best bet, take it to job interviews. Put your portfolio in a three-ring binder with a table of contents and tabs separating its various parts. Mix and match the following categories:

- ✔ **Career goals** (if you're a new graduate or career changer): A brief statement of less than one page is plenty.

- ✔ **Your resume:** Use a fully formatted version in MS Word.

- ✔ **Samples of your work:** Include easily understandable examples of problem solving and competencies.

- ✔ **Proof of performance:** Insert awards, honors, testimonials and letters of commendation, and flattering performance reviews. Don't forget to add praise from employers, people who reported to you, and customers.

- ✔ **Proof of recognition:** Here's where you attach certifications, transcripts, degrees, licenses, and printed material listing you as the leader of seminars and workshops. Omit those that you merely attended unless the attendance proves something.

- ✔ **Military connections:** The U.S. military provides exceptionally good training, and many employers know it. List military records, awards, and badges.

Make at least two copies of your hard-copy portfolio in case potential employers decide to hold on to your samples or fail to return them.

Your portfolio should document only the skills that you want to apply on a job. Begin by identifying those skills, and then determine which materials prove your claims of competency.

Choose What Works for You

The big closing question to ask yourself when you've settled on a format is:

Does this format maximize my qualifications for the job I want?

If the format you've chosen doesn't promote your top qualifications, take another look at the choices in this chapter to select a format that does help you present your top-pick value.

Chapter 10

Wow Words Work Wonders

. . . .

In This Chapter

▶ Wow words: Action verbs that sell you

▶ Keywords: Nouns that sell you

▶ Resume grammar: Simple rules that sell you

▶ Resume spelling: Simple tips that sell you

. . . .

Words: How powerful they are. It doesn't take many of them to change the world: The Lord's Prayer has 66 words, Lincoln's Gettysburg address numbers just 286 words, and the U.S. Declaration of Independence contains but 1,322 words.

Winston Churchill needed only two words to bind Russia to the *Iron Curtain*. A brief four words memorialized Martin Luther King's vision: *I have a dream*. And in a single sentence, John F. Kennedy set the challenge for a generation: *Ask not what your country can do for you, but what you can do for your country*.

Words are powerful — big words like *motherland* and *environmentalism* and small words like *peace* and *war* or *dawn, family, hope, love,* and *home*. Words are pegs to hang your qualifications on. Words are the power that lifts you above the faceless crowd and sets you in Good Fortune's way. The right words can change your life.

Begin your hunt for the right words to build an OnTarget resume, from action verbs and keyword nouns, to grammar and spelling tips.

 Wow words are action verbs describing your strengths: *improve, upgrade, schedule*. Keywords are usually nouns demonstrating essential skills: *technology transfers, PhD organic chemistry, multinational marketing*. A smattering of both can make your resume stand up and sing. An absence of either can make your resume sit down and shut up.

Wow Words Can Bring Good News

Use lively, energetic verbs to communicate your abilities and accomplishments. The important thing is to choose words of substance and power that zero in on what you're selling.

Try not to use the same word twice on your resume — an online thesaurus, such as Thesaurus.com, can give you a range of possibilities.

Take a look at the Wow words that follow and check off those words that are authentic for you:

Wow words for administration and management

advised	initiated	prioritized
approved	inspired	processed
authorized	installed	promoted
chaired	instituted	recommended
consolidated	instructed	redirected
counseled	integrated	referred
delegated	launched	reorganized
determined	lectured	represented
developed	listened	responded
diagnosed	managed	reviewed
directed	mediated	revitalized
disseminated	mentored	routed
enforced	moderated	sponsored
ensured	monitored	streamlined
examined	motivated	strengthened
explained	negotiated	supervised
governed	originated	taught
guided	oversaw	trained
headed	pioneered	trimmed
influenced	presided	validated

Wow words for communications and creativity

acted	edited	proofread
addressed	enabled	publicized
arranged	facilitated	published
assessed	fashioned	realized
authored	formulated	reconciled
briefed	influenced	recruited
built	initiated	rectified
clarified	interpreted	remodeled
composed	interviewed	reported
conducted	introduced	revitalized
constructed	invented	scheduled
corresponded	launched	screened
costumed	lectured	shaped
created	modernized	stimulated
critiqued	performed	summarized
demonstrated	planned	taught
designed	presented	trained
developed	produced	translated
directed	projected	wrote

Wow words for sales and persuasion

arbitrated	judged	purchased
catalogued	launched	realized
centralized	lectured	recruited
consulted	led	reduced
dissuaded	liaised	reported
documented	maintained	repositioned
educated	manipulated	researched
established	marketed	resolved

expedited	mediated	restored
familiarized	moderated	reviewed
identified	negotiated	routed
implemented	obtained	saved
improved	ordered	served
increased	performed	set goals
influenced	planned	sold
inspired	processed	solved
installed	produced	stimulated
integrated	promoted	summarized
interpreted	proposed	surveyed
investigated	publicized	translated

Wow words for technical ability

analyzed	expedited	operated
broadened	fabricated	packaged
charted	facilitated	pioneered
classified	forecast	prepared
communicated	formed	processed
compiled	generated	programmed
computed	improved	published
conceived	increased	reconstructed
conducted	inspected	networked
coordinated	installed	reduced
designed	instituted	researched
detected	integrated	restored
developed	interfaced	revamped
devised	launched	streamlined
drafted	lectured	supplemented
edited	maintained	surveyed
educated	marketed	systematized
eliminated	mastered	trained

excelled   modified   upgraded

expanded   molded   wrote

Wow words for office support

adhered	distributed	managed
administered	documented	operated
allocated	drafted	ordered
applied	enacted	organized
appropriated	enlarged	packaged
assisted	evaluated	planned
assured	examined	prepared
attained	executed	prescribed
awarded	followed up	processed
balanced	formalized	provided
budgeted	formulated	recorded
built	hired	repaired
charted	identified	reshaped
completed	implemented	resolved
contributed	improved	scheduled
coordinated	installed	screened
cut	instituted	searched
defined	justified	secured
determined	liaised	solved
dispensed	maintained	started

Wow words for teaching

acquainted	designed	influenced
adapted	developed	informed
advised	directed	initiated
answered	dispensed	innovated
apprised	distributed	installed
augmented	educated	instituted

briefed
built
certified
chaired
charted
clarified
coached
collaborated
communicated
conducted
coordinated
delegated
delivered
demonstrated

effected
empowered
enabled
enacted
enlarged
expanded
facilitated
fomented
formulated
generated
grouped
guided
harmonized
implemented

instructed
integrated
lectured
listened
originated
persuaded
presented
responded
revolutionized
set goals
stimulated
summarized
trained
translated

Wow words for research and analysis

administered
amplified
analyzed
applied
articulated
assessed
audited
augmented
balanced
calculated
charted
collected
compared
compiled
composed
concentrated

detected
determined
discovered
documented
drafted
edited
evaluated
examined
exhibited
experimented
explored
extracted
focused
forecast
found
generated

interviewed
invented
investigated
located
measured
obtained
organized
pinpointed
planned
prepared
processed
proofread
researched
reviewed
riveted
screened

conducted	grouped	summarized
constructed	identified	surveyed
consulted	integrated	systematized
critiqued	interpreted	unearthed

Wow words for helping and caregiving

advanced	encouraged	reassured
advised	expedited	reclaimed
aided	facilitated	rectified
arbitrated	familiarized	redeemed
assisted	fostered	reeducated
attended	furthered	referred
augmented	guided	reformed
backed	helped	rehabilitated
balanced	instilled	repaired
boosted	liaised	represented
braced	mentored	served
clarified	ministered	settled
collaborated	negotiated	supplied
comforted	nourished	supported
consoled	nursed	stabilized
consulted	nurtured	streamlined
contributed	obliged	translated
counseled	optimized	treated
demonstrated	promoted	tutored
diagnosed	provided	unified

Wow words for financial management

adjusted	economized	reported
administered	eliminated	researched
allocated	exceeded	reshaped
analyzed	financed	retailed

appraised

audited

balanced

bought

budgeted

calculated

computed

conciliated

cut

decreased

developed

disbursed

dispensed

distributed

doubled

downsized

forecast

funded

gained

generated

increased

invested

maintained

managed

marketed

merchandised

planned

projected

purchased

quadrupled

reconciled

reduced

returned

saved

shopped

secured

sold

solicited

sourced

specified

supplemented

systematized

tested

tripled

underwrote

upgraded

upsized

vended

Wow words for many skills

accomplished

achieved

adapted

adhered

allocated

appraised

arbitrated

arranged

articulated

assured

augmented

collected

communicated

composed

evaluated

executed

facilitated

forecast

founded

governed

guided

illustrated

improved

increased

initiated

integrated

interpreted

invented

overhauled

performed

prioritized

promoted

proposed

reconciled

rectified

remodeled

repaired

reshaped

retrieved

solved

stimulated

streamlined

conceptualized	launched	strengthened
conserved	led	trained
contributed	navigated	upgraded
coordinated	optimized	validated
demonstrated	organized	won
dispensed	originated	wrote

The last word on Wow words: Little words never devalue a big idea.

Keywords Are Recruiters' Key to Finding You

In the long-ago 1990s, recruiters and employers used keywords to search computer databases for qualified candidates. Today they type keywords into search engines to scour the entire Internet for the best people to select for a candidate pool.

That's why, when you're looking for a job, you can't afford to ignore the search engines which seem to grow and grow. Take pains to feed those woolly-mammoth software creatures with effective keywords that shoot your resume to the top of recruiting search results. (In techie talk, the concept is called search engine optimization, or SEO.)

So, what are keywords as used in the job market? "Keywords are what employers search for when trying to fill a position: the essential hard skills and knowledge needed to do the job," explains this book's technical reviewer, James M. Lemke.

Keywords are chiefly nouns and short phrases. That's your take-home message. But once in a while, just to confuse everyone, keywords can be adjectives and action verbs.

Is there one comprehensive dictionary of keywords? No, Lemke explains. "Employers choose their own list of keywords — that's why no list is universal."

In computerized job searches, keywords describe not only your knowledge base and skills but also such things as well-known companies, big-name colleges and universities, degrees, licensure, and professional affiliations.

Keywords identify your experience and education in these categories:

- Skills
- Technical and professional areas of expertise
- Accomplishments and achievements
- Professional licenses and certifications
- Other distinguishing features of your work history
- Prestigious schools or former employers

Employers identify keywords, often including industry jargon, that they think represent essential qualifications necessary for high performance in a given position. They specify those keywords when they search for resumes.

Keywords are arbitrary and specific to the employer and each employer search. So the keywords (qualifications) — starting with the job title — in each job ad are the place to start as you customize your resume for the position. Make educated guesses when you're responding not to advertised jobs but are merely warehousing your resume online in a Web site database. The following lists provide a few examples of keywords for selected career fields and industries.

Action verbs are a prelude for keywords in stating your accomplishments. You managed *what?* You organized *what?* You developed *what?* Applicant software looks for the *whats,* and the whats are usually nouns.

Keywords for administration and management

administrative processes	facilities management
bachelor's degree	front office operations
back office operations	office manager
benchmarking	operations manager
budget administration	policy and procedure
change management	production schedule
crisis communications	project planning
data analysis	records management
document management	regulatory reporting

Keywords for banking

branch manager	loan management
branch operations	loan recovery
commercial banking	portfolio management
construction loans	retail lending
credit guidelines	ROE (Return On Equity)
debt financing	ROI (Return On Investment)
FILO (First In, Last Out)	trust services
financial management	turnaround management
investment management	Uniform Commercial Code Filing
investor relations	workout

Keywords for customer service

account representative	Help desk
call center	key account manager
customer communications	order fulfillment
customer focus groups	order processing
customer loyalty	product response clerk
customer needs assessment	records management
customer retention	sales administration
customer retention innovations	sales support administrator
customer service manager	service quality
customer surveys	telemarketing operations
field service operation	telemarketing representative

Keywords for information technology

automated voice response (AVR)	global systems support
chief information officer	Help desk
client/server architecture	multimedia technology

cross-functional team

data center manager

director of end-user computing

disaster recovery

end-user support

network development analyst

project lifecycle

systems configuration

technology rightsizing

vendor partnerships

Keywords for manufacturing

asset management

assistant operations manager

automated manufacturing

capacity planning

cell manufacturing

cost reductions

distribution management

environmental health and safety

inventory control

just-in-time (JIT)

logistics manager

manufacturing engineer

materials coordinator

on-time delivery

outsourcing

shipping and receiving operation

spares and repairs management

union negotiations

warehousing operations

workflow optimization

Keywords for human resources

Bachelor of Science, Business Administration (BSBA)

college recruitment

compensation surveys

cross-cultural communications

diversity training

grievance proceedings

job task analysis

labor contract negotiations

leadership development

organizational development (OD)

recruiter

regulatory affairs

sourcing

staffing

succession planning

team leadership

training specialist

wage and salary administration

Keywords are the magnets that draw junior screeners and nonhuman eyes to your talents.

Where to Find Keywords

How can you find keywords for your occupation or career field? Use a high-lighter to pluck keywords from these resources.

- ✔ **Online and printed help-wanted posts and ads:** Highlight the job skills, competencies, experience, education, and other nouns that employers request.

- ✔ **Job descriptions:** Ask employers for them, check at libraries for books or software with job descriptions, or search online. To find them online, just enter such terms as "job descriptions" or "job descriptions trainer" or "job descriptions electrical engineer" on a search engine.

- ✔ **The *Occupational Outlook Handbook,*** published by the U.S. Department of Labor: Read free online at bls.gov/oco.

- ✔ **Your core resume:** (See Chapter 6) Look through to highlight nouns that identify job skills, competencies, experience, and education.

- ✔ **Trade Web site news stories:** News about your career field or occupation should be ripe with keywords. Don't overlook Wikipedia, as well as blogs written by industry and company insiders.

- ✔ **Annual reports of companies in your field:** The company descriptions of key personnel and departmental achievements should offer strong keyword clues.

- ✔ **Programs for industry conferences and events:** Speaker topics address current industry issues, a rich source of keywords.

- ✔ **Internet search engine:** Plug in a targeted company's name and search the site that comes up. Look closely at the careers portal and read current press releases.

You can also use Internet search engines to scout industry-specific directories, glossaries, and dictionaries.

Mining for keywords in job descriptions

The excerpts below of two job descriptions posted on Business.com (www.business.com; search for job descriptions) illustrate how you can find keywords almost everywhere. In these examples, the keywords are italicized.

Auto Dismantler:

- ✔ Knowledge of proper operation of *lifts, forklifts, torches, power wrenches,* and so on.

- ✔ Knowledge of *warehouse, core,* and *stack locations.*

(continued)

(continued)

> ✔ Skill to move *vehicles* without damaging vehicle, other vehicles or personnel.
>
> ✔ Skill to remove *body* and *mechanical parts* without damage to part, self, or others.
>
> ✔ Ability to read a *Dismantler report* and assess *stock levels*.
>
> ✔ Ability to accurately assess condition of *parts* to be inventoried.
>
> Budget Assistant:
>
> ✔ Reviews *monthly expense statements,* monitors *monthly expenditures,* and
>
> gathers supporting *documentation* for supervisor review and approval.
>
> ✔ Performs basic *arithmetic operations* to calculate and/or verify *expense totals* and *account balances.*
>
> ✔ Operates *computer* to enter data into *spreadsheet* and/or *database.* Types routine *correspondence* and *reports.*
>
> ✔ Operates older office equipment such as *photocopier, fax machine,* and *calculator.*

How to Use Keywords

Who reads the first pass of your resume? In many HR departments, resumes are screened by junior workers who lack the experience to read between the lines but work on a verbatim basis. That's why nearly matching word for word — rather than liberally paraphrasing — at least a portion of a job's requirements — is the way to go.

If the job requirements state:

> *Ability to lead the development of staffing strategies and implementation plans and programs that identify talent internally and externally through the effective use of external sources.*

You write:

> *Developed and implemented staffing strategies that identified talent internally and externally though the effective use of external sources.*

By incorporating some of the employer's language, you strongly increase your odds of surviving the first cut. Your resume lives to fight for you another round when senior screeners look you over.

Get a Grip on Grammar

Resume language differs from normal speech in several ways. In general, keep the language tight and the tone professional, avoiding the following:

✔ **First-person pronouns (I, we):** Your name is at the top of each resume page, so the recruiter knows it's about *you*. Eliminate first-person pronouns. Also, don't use third-person pronouns (he, she) when referring to yourself — the narrative technique makes you seem pompous. Simply start with a verb.

✔ **Articles (the, a, an):** Articles crowd sentences and don't clarify meaning. Substitute *retrained staff* for *retrained the staff*.

✔ **Helping verbs (have, had, may, might):** For professionals and managers, helping verbs weaken claims and credibility — implying that your time has passed and portraying you as a job-hunting weakling. Say *managed* instead of *have managed*.

✔ **"Being" verbs (am, is, are, was, were):** Being verbs suggest a state of existence rather than a state of motion. Try *monitored requisitions* instead of *requisitions were monitored*. The active voice gives a stronger, more confident delivery.

✔ **Shifts in tense:** Use the present tense for a job you're still in and the past tense for jobs you've left. But, among the jobs you've left, don't switch back and forth between tenses. Another big mistake: dating a job as though you're still employed (2008–Present) and then describing it in the past tense.

✔ **Complex sentences:** Unless you keep your sentences lean and clean, readers won't take time to decipher them. Process this mind-stumper:

Reduced hospital costs by 67% by creating a patient-independence program, where they make their own beds, and as noted by hospital finance department, costs of nails and wood totaled $300 less per patient than work hours of maintenance staff.

Eliminate complex sentences by dividing ideas into sentences of their own and getting rid of extraneous details:

Reduced hospital costs by 67%. Originated patient independence program that decreased per-patient expense by $300 each.

✔ **Overwriting:** Use your own voice; don't say *expeditious* when you want to say *swift*.

✔ **Abbreviations:** Abbreviations are informal and not universal — even when they're career-specific. Use *Internet* instead of *Net*.

The exception is industry jargon — use it, especially in digital resumes. Knowledge and use of industry jargon adds to your credibility to be able to correctly and casually use terms common to the industry in which you're seeking employment.

A Few Words about Spelling

What is the name of a resume self-defense manual for job seekers? The dictionary!

Of all the reasons causing recruiters and hiring managers to shoot down resumes, carelessness with spelling, grammar, and choice of words ranks close to the top. Even when the real reason for rejection is bias or something else entirely, as in "I just don't like that dude," the use of misspelled words is a convenient justification. Who can quarrel with the adage "Garbage in, garbage out"?

Employers especially recoil from impaired spelling when the job seeker botches the interviewer's or the organization's name. (You can Google your way to the company's Web site to spell the organization's name; you can call to confirm the spelling of the interviewer's name.) Here's the take-away message:

Goofy spelling

You don't have to win a spelling bee but, if you're like me (someone who has been known to make some *humongus spelling miztakes*), you need to be on Code Red alert when you're putting words down for the world to read. Here is a sampling of frequently misspelled words. Add your personal goofy spellings to the list.

accommodate	guarantee	personnel
address	immediate	recommend
all right	independent	referred
bureau	its/it's	reference
calendar	judgment	relevant
category	maintenance	schedule
column	millennium	sergeant
committed	miscellaneous	their/they're/there
conscientious	misspell	truly
definitely	nuclear	until
experience	occasionally	your/you're
government	occurrence	weather/whether

Know thy computer spell checker. Know thy online dictionary. And know a human being who can carefully proofread your resumes to pick up grammar mistakes or misused words.

Words Sell Your Story

Remember, when your words speak for you, you need to be sure to use words that everyone can understand and that relate to the job at hand. Value your words. Each one is a tool to your future.

Avoid poison words

Recruiters advise staying away from the following words on your resume:

✔ **Responsibilities included:** Make your resume accomplishment-driven, not responsibilities-driven. Job-descriptions language tells, not sells, in a resume.

✔ **Salary:** Money talk doesn't belong on a resume, period. Spilling your financial beans limits your options because you may be priced too high or too low. If you absolutely must deal with salary history or salary requirements before the interview, discuss dollars in a cover letter.

✔ **Fired:** Don't let this word slip into your resume if you want it to escape being lost in a database. *Laid-off* or *reduction in force* generally aren't good terms either, but you can use them when circumstances make it sound as though you were fired. A *layoff* or a *reduction in force* implies the action was no fault of yours, but *fired* suggests that you screwed up. The basic rule: Don't state why you left a position; save the explanation for an interview.

✔ **References available upon request:** References are assumed. Save the space for more important information.

✔ **Social Security number:** Never make yourself vulnerable in this era of identity theft. The exception to this rule is when you apply for a federal government position; in that case, you may be required to submit your SSN if the agency uses an older system, but the newer federal systems no longer ask for a SSN.

✔ **Assisted with, worked with, helped with:** Did you really just assist or help someone else? Were you standing by watching someone else do the work? Use action verbs to describe how you contributed to each achievement.

✔ **Also:** The word is unnecessary. (For example, Manage budget of $1 million. *Also* interface with consultants.) Write tightly. Eliminate *also, an, the,* and *and* wherever you can. Use the saved space to pack more punch, and the resume won't lose meaning.

Chapter 11

Refine Your Design for Great Looks

. . . .

In This Chapter

▶ Considering design factors in digital resumes

▶ Recognizing that small things mean a lot

▶ Giving your qualifications room to breathe

▶ Choosing an overall look for your resume

. . . .

*G*ood design is about more than simply looking good. Good resume design means making your document appealing and accessible for prospective employers. Making it relevant for the job you seek. Making it appropriate for someone in your shoes.

There's no reason why handsome physical design cannot be — and every reason why it should be — applied to the resume information so important to your journey ahead.

As I explain in Chapter 7, the *full-design resume* can be a blue-ribbon winner at any resume show, conveying a visual message along with information expressed in typographic text. The graphic elements of a full-design resume — such as bullets, columns, graphs, and a generous use of white space — make human reading easier and more inviting.

Modern recruiting software usually can handle fully formatted resumes in a word-processing attachment (typically MS Word). All the design tips I describe in this chapter work on paper and attached online resumes.

By contrast, the *plain-text resume* is constructed without formatting and reads like a one-paragraph page in a book. But, because online resume databases usually accept only documents submitted in plain text, you're often stuck with the style.

The *hyperlinked resume* refers to a plain-text resume sent online that includes a link to a full-design resume stored on a Web site, whether it's a resume-hosting site, or your own personal site. A *resume synopsis* (or resume brief) is a couple of summary paragraphs that include a hyperlink to a full-design resume.

Crafting Resumes That Resonate

Although the job market has moved to digital resumes — and away from paper resumes — tree-and-ink products will be around for the foreseeable future. Paper resumes are the medium of choice in the following situations:

- ✔ When you're making the rounds of booths at career fairs, hand out your paper resumes. (Yes, some employers, for legal reasons, won't accept paper resumes at fairs, but they're in the minority.)

- ✔ When you're calling on your personal network to assist your job search, circulate paper resumes. People are more likely to remember you and your search with a piece of paper to remind them than they are to recall that your resume is hanging out somewhere on the Internet.

- ✔ When you meet an employer or recruiter in a job interview, bring along several copies of your paper resume. An attractive resume makes a good impression and can jump-start questions that you want to answer.

Here are suggestions on how to make the first cut in the employment screening process.

Typewritten copies carbon date you back before Zeus. Use a computer and a high-quality printer to produce your resume. Today's standard is a sharp-looking resume printed on a laser or inkjet printer. Old-fashioned dot matrix printers just can't crank out the good-looking product recruiters expect.

Paper selection

In a digital era, how good should your paper be? Although you're using paper only for hand-to-hand delivery, the standards haven't changed. For professional, technical, managerial, and executive jobs, the stock for a paper resume should be quality paper that contains rag content of perhaps 25 percent, as well as a watermark (a faint image ingrained in the paper). For lower-level positions, any decent-looking paper will do.

What color should you choose? Stick to white or off-white, eggshell, or the palest of gray. Print on only one side of the sheet.

What about theme papers — musical notes for musicians, tree leaves for environmental jobs, and the like? Although the use of theme paper for resumes has grown over the past decade, my preference is for plain stock unless you're in a highly creative field. Most employers still prefer the no-frills look in paper.

Consistency, consistency, consistency

Make reading easy on employers by deciding on a style and sticking to it. You detract from your words — and your image — when you

- ✔ Mix differently spaced tabs and indentations.
- ✔ Make a habit of mixing bullet styles without thought. You can mix bullets and checkmarks if the result is tasteful and doesn't look cluttered.
- ✔ Use different spacing between lines. Keep your line spaces the same between headings and the body text for each data point. You're going for a finished look, which means no careless placement of content.

When three's not a crowd

Certain groupings are just more pleasing to the eye, so many resume pros use the rule of threes: three skills groups, three accomplishments, three sentences on a topic, and so forth. A grouping of five is also attractive.

But avoiding even numbers is not a hard-and-fast rule — groups of two and four are equally acceptable. Look for examples of odd-number groupings in the sample resumes in Part IV. Ask a friend with artistic good taste to look at your final draft and give you an honest opinion of your design technique.

Come on, break it up!

How often have you tried to read a solid block of text and given up because it makes you want to run for the eye drops? Employers and recruiters reading resume after resume also space out on dense text, especially in small type. The answer is to break it up, to segment your data points in related groups.

Too blocky and dense

Great Eastern Bank, Princeton, NJ
2003-2008
Second Vice President – Global Markets Project Manager
* Developed, outlined, and scheduled 98 conferences covering spectrum of
  financial risk management issues
* Launched 53-page quarterly newsletter on new products and fluctuations
  Researched and edited copy from technical specialists and regulatory agencies
* Expanded circulation of client newsletter more than 500% in three years
* Managed $1.2 million budget and monitored department expenses
* Provided marketing management support for Senior Vice President
* Traveled to Hong Kong, Singapore, and London delivering educational
  seminars on derivative products and uses
* Administered 17 bank personnel policies for seven staff members
* Directed office closure due to outsourcing.

Just right

Great Eastern Bank, Princeton, NJ
2003-2008
Second Vice President –Global Markets Project Manager

Communicator:
* Developed, outlined, and scheduled 98 conferences covering spectrum of
  financial risk management issues
* Launched 3-page quarterly newsletter on new products and fluctuations
* Researched and edited copy from technical specialists and regulatory agencies
* Expanded circulation of client newsletter more than 500% in three years

Manager:
* Managed $1.2 million budget and monitored department expenses
* Provided marketing management support for Senior Vice President
* Administered 17 bank personnel policies for seven staff members
* Directed office closure due to outsourcing

Business Traveler:
* Traveled to Hong Kong, Singapore, and London delivering educational
  seminars on derivative products and uses

Open spaces

White space is the master graphic attention-getter; it makes recruiters want to read a resume. Too often, job seekers hearing that they must not exceed one page (Untrue!) try to cram too much information in too little space.

Although some resume pros advise that you right-justify the text (align it down the right side of the page), you're not hurting your chances if you use a ragged right-hand margin. Right justification creates wasted white spaces that add nothing to an impression of a document's openness.

In addition to margins and white space between parts of a resume, consider the vital issue of line spacing — the space between lines in a paragraph and the space between paragraphs. Thoughtful line spacing is very important because it impacts a document's overall look.

Whatever you choose, be clear that an overcrowded page almost guarantees your resume won't be read by younger recruiters and hiring managers who grew up in an age of television and quick-reading stories in newspapers, magazines, and Web content. And older eyes won't take the wear and tear of too many words jammed into a small space.

When you're concerned that your resume is overstuffed, it probably is too hard to read. A ratio of one-quarter white space to text is about right.

Typefaces and fonts

A *typeface* is a family of characters — letters, numbers, and symbols. A *font* is a specific size of a typeface. For example, Helvetica is a typeface; Helvetica 10-point, Helvetica 12-point, and Helvetica 14-point are three different fonts.

No more than two typefaces should appear on one resume, but if you don't have an eye for good design, stick to one typeface. Times New Roman, Arial, Verdana, or Helvetica used alone is a fine choice for your resume.

If you want to mix two typefaces, I like Helvetica for headings and Times New Roman for text and lesser headings. Printing your name in small capital letters can be pleasing. Use italics sparingly; italicized words lose readability in blocks of text.

Professional resume writers use many tricks of the trade to put more information in a resume without making it seem packed to the rafters. They condense type, use a smaller-size font, and manipulate vertical spacing. Most amateur resume writers don't want to get into this depth of detail. Doing so is a time-consuming learning experience and risks readability, something you can't afford to lose.

A few more tips on appearance

When wrapping up the fair face of your resume, bear these factors in mind:

- ✔ Your name and contact information can be flush left, centered, or flush right.

- ✔ Important information jumps in the recruiter's face when set off by bullets, asterisks, and dashes.

- ✔ Typos and spelling errors are attention killers. They come across as carelessness or lack of professionalism. Even when your resume is a customized point-by-point match for the available job, a spelling mistake or poor grammar blemishes its overall impression and may sink your chances.

  Use your computer's spell-check feature, read your finished resume carefully, and ask a friend who is a good proofreader to read it.

- ✔ Don't staple together a two- or three-page resume or put it in a folder or plastic insert. The resume may be photocopied and distributed, or it may be — *gasp,* shades of ancient technology! — scanned into a database.

  To minimize the risk of a page becoming an orphan, put a simple heading or footer atop each page after the first with your name and page number. In a multiple-page resume, you may want to indicate the total number of pages (for example, Page 1 of 2).

Checking out a resume makeover

Using an easily read layout is fundamental. Take a look at what I mean: Figure 11-1 shows you the *before* version of the resume of Bruce Begovic, who holds a new master's degree in biology. It's nothing but a "design dump" in which Bruce's data is merely unloaded onto a single page without giving thought to layout refinements. Pass the eyewash! Figure 11-2 shows the spruced-up version.

Which version would you rather read — the dense, eye-crossing one-pager, or the roomier, eye-pleasing two-pager?

Bruce Begovic
* 760-431-9999 *
* 9999 Veranda Ct. Carlsbad CA 92010 * bbegovic@gmail.com *

Offering solid competencies and proven track record documented by Master's degree in Biology and targeted Bachelor's degree, paired with eight years' part time work experience in biotech, communications and teaching/tutoring fields

Education

Master of Science, Biology -California State University San Marcos, [date]
- Graduate thesis project entailed locating and classifying full length-retrotransposable element through probing of genomic library and PCR-mediated genome walking

Bachelor of Science, Biology with Cellular and Molecular Biology Concentration
California State University, San Marcos, [date]
- Coursework: Molecular Cell Biology, Animal Physiology, Genetics, Microbiology, Immunology, Virology, Neurobiology, Viral Evasion, Biochemistry, Research Mathods
- Hazardous Communications and Laboratory Safety trained and certified, [date]
- Radioactive Materials Handling and Safety trained and certified, [date]
- Instructional qualifications include California Basic Education Skills Test certification

Skills

- RDA
- PCR, QPCR
- mass spectrometry
- gel electrophoresis
- SDS-PAGE
- Cloning
- restriction digests
- southern blotting
- plasmid prep
- cell culture
- bioinformatics
- probe design
- DNA extraction
- DNA, RNA isolation
- radiolabeling
- protein purification
- MS Word, Excel, PowerPoint

Work Experience

Graduate Lab Research Associate   [dates]
California State University, San Marcos
- Project leader in a representational difference analysis to determine somatic cell genomic rearrangements between healthy and virally infected species
- Responsible for training and supervision of undergraduate students

Teaching Associate   [dates]
California State University, San Marcos
- Supplemental Instruction course leader for Principles of Genetics class
- Instructor for Intro to Cell/Molecular Biology lab, General Education Science lab
- Teaching Assistant for Genetics Lab

Biology Department Lab Technician   [dates]
California State University, San Marcos
- Prepared graduate/undergraduate lab exercises for classes including: Genetics, Cellular Biotechnology, Microbiology, and Animal Physiology
- Responsible for media /solution preparation, cell culture and all other aspects of lab component preparation
- Supervised undergraduate assistants

Primary Science/Math Tutor   [dates]
Tutoring Pros Educational Services
- Tutored high school students in science and math, including Advanced Placement Biology, Chemistry, Calculus, Statistics and Physics courses

Editorial Associate   [dates]
Sun Features, Inc.
- Research online, copy edit and fact check a wide range of topics for nationally syndicated columnist Joyce Lain Kennedy
- Provided content evaluation and technical direction for several of Kennedy's *For Dummies* books

Accomplishments

- 3.9 GPA in graduate courses
- Presenter, Plant and Animal Genome Conference, [date]
- Presenter, Society for Molecular Biology and Evolution Conference, [date]
- Financed 100% of education through concurrent part-time employment and University grants

Figure 11-1: Bruce's initial thrown-together resume looks like he wrote it in 10 minutes on the fly. It's a snooze.

Bruce Begovic

760-431-9999
bbegovic@gmail.com

9999 Veranda Ct.
Carlsbad, CA 92010

Offering solid competencies and proven track record documented by Master's degree in Biology and targeted Bachelor's degree, paired with eight years' part time work experience in biotech, communications and teaching/tutoring fields

Education

Master of Science, Biology

California State University San Marcos, [date]

- Graduate thesis project entailed locating and classifying full length-retrotransposable element through probing of genomic library and PCR-mediated genome walking

Bachelor of Science, Biology with Cellular and Molecular Biology Concentration

California State University, San Marcos, [date]

- Coursework: Molecular Cell Biology, Animal Physiology, Genetics, Microbiology, Immunology, Virology, Neurobiology, Viral Evasion, Biochemistry, Research Methods
- Hazardous Communications and Laboratory Safety trained and certified, [date]
- Radioactive Materials Handling and Safety trained and certified, [date]
- Instructional qualifications include California Basic Education Skills Test certification

Skills

• RDA	• restriction digests	• DNA extraction
• PCR, QPCR	• Southern blotting	• DNA, RNA isolation
• mass spectrometry	• plasmid prep	• radiolabeling
• gel electrophoresis	• cell culture	• protein purification
• SDS-PAGE	• bioinformatics	• cell culture
• cloning	• probe design	• MS Word, Excel, PowerPoint

Work Experience

Graduate Lab Research Associate [dates]

California State University, San Marcos

- Project leader in a representational difference analysis to determine somatic cell genomic rearrangements between healthy and virally infected species
- Responsible for training and supervision of undergraduate students

Teaching Associate [dates]

California State University, San Marcos

- Supplemental Instruction course leader for Principles of Genetics class
- Instructor for Intro to Cell/Molecular Biology lab, General Education Science lab
- Teaching Assistant for Genetics Lab

Biology Department Lab Technician [dates]

California State University, San Marcos

- Prepared graduate/undergraduate lab exercises for classes including: Genetics, Cellular

(1 of 2)

Figure 11-2: Bruce's revised resume dramatically improves his resume's appearance and projects an image that reinforces his value.

Biotechnology, Microbiology, and Animal Physiology

- Responsible for media /solution preparation, cell culture and all other aspects of lab component preparation
- Supervised undergraduate assistants

Primary Science/Math Tutor   [dates]

Tutoring Pros Educational Services

- Tutored high school students in science and math, including Advanced Placement Biology, Chemistry, Calculus, Statistics and Physics courses

Editorial Associate   [dates]

Sun Features, Inc.

- Research online, copy edit and fact check a wide range of topics for nationally syndicated columnist Joyce Lain Kennedy
- Provided content evaluation and technical direction for several of Kennedy's For Dummies books

Accomplishments

- 3.9 GPA in graduate courses
- Presenter, Plant and Animal Genome Conference, [date]
- Presenter, Society for Molecular Biology and Evolution Conference, [date]
- Financed 100% of education through concurrent part-time employment and University grants

(Bruce Begovic 2 of 2)

Boost Visibility with Resume Architecture

Unless you're the sort of person who enjoys reading the fine print on credit card agreements, you'll agree with me that white space is one of the two most powerful design elements in today's search sweepstakes.

But there's a second potent design element to think about — a resume's overall look and feel.

Until recent years, the look and feel was pretty much plain vanilla. Now career marketing documents are evolving into a more distinctive look and feel. In today's marketplace you find forward-leaning job seekers stepping out with crisp, more dramatic resume architecture.

This time around, maybe your resume needs a design-lift. Why not think about how you can make your job information jump off the screen or page by framing it in vibrant architecture? To pull this off you need to use boldface type (but not too much of it), tasteful graphic highlights, and creative planning to allocate space gracefully.

The following four *template shells* (Figures 11-3 through 11-6) illustrate the concept of vibrant architecture. I named the examples template shells because I present only the design structure here; you fill in the text, and perhaps alter the headings, with your unique information.

The following four shells were created in my office by a 20-year-old college student using MS Word drawing tools. If you'd like to copy a shell but don't have a clue about using drawing tools, read the latest edition of *Word For Dummies* by Dan Gookin (Wiley). You can also beg a tech-savvy friend to do it for you or hire a teenager who probably learned Word drawing skills in middle school.

Template shell with modern appeal

This shell can work for most career fields but is especially cool for technical resumes. You can use the architecture in Figure 11-3 for resumes of one, two, or more pages.

In longer resumes, the headings in the left column vary. For example, an information technology resume can include such headings as Programming Languages, Development Environments, Web Environments, Platforms & Mobile, and other discrete areas of abilities and accomplishments.

Template shell for intern career fair

Peppy and preppy, the high-impact design in Figure 11-4 is a generic natural for college students dropping off resumes at campus career fairs where writing customized resumes for an anticipated company recruiter isn't feasible. (Companies can jump in or drop out of these fairs at the last minute.)

With a change of headings, the stylized architecture can also work for adult career fairs and, in fact, be a good choice in any environment where eye-catching attention is a necessity.

Template shell for dash without flash

A job seeker in virtually any career field can use the classy design that Figure 11-5 shows. It's a good choice for professional and managerial job seekers who lean toward the traditional presentation style but want to look up-to-date.

You can add any headings you like, such as achievements, honors and awards, skills, and competencies.

Template shell showing "it's a match!"

Use the resume architecture in Figure 11-6 to show an OnTarget matching of what the company says it wants and how you fill the bill. Of the several ways to show the connection between the employer's requirements and your qualifications, the direct comparison is a jackpot winner.

The "personal traits" in the heading should apply specifically to you, showing four different traits or branding terms (See Chapter 2). Examples for professional jobs: Analytical Thinker, Problem Solver, Strategic Leader, Proven Planner. Examples for non-professional jobs: Dedicated Worker, Reliable Researcher, Skillful Organizer, Budget Manager.

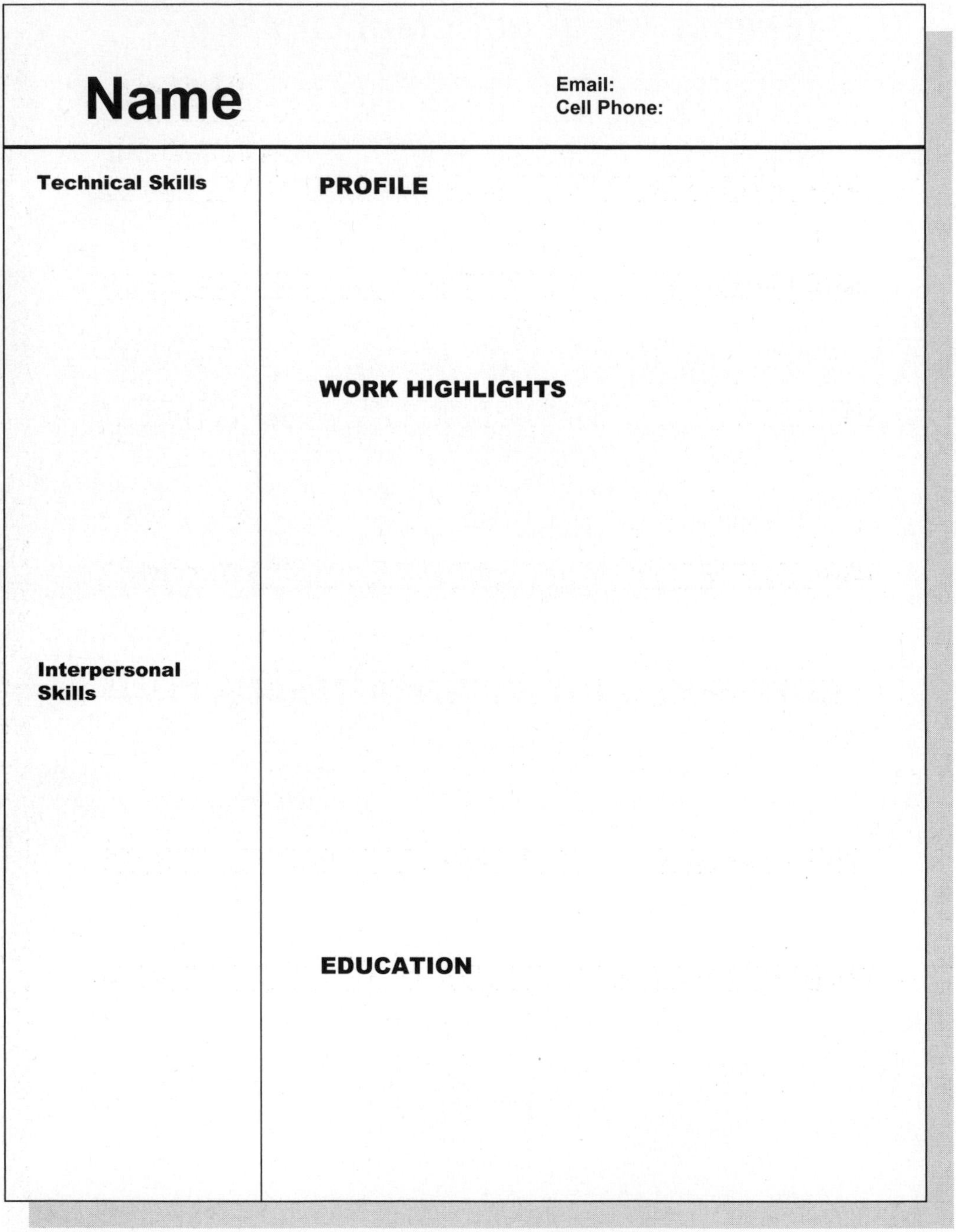

Name

Email:
Cell Phone:

Technical Skills

PROFILE

WORK HIGHLIGHTS

Interpersonal Skills

EDUCATION

Figure 11-3: This design presents an up-to-date image and is appropriate for most job seekers.

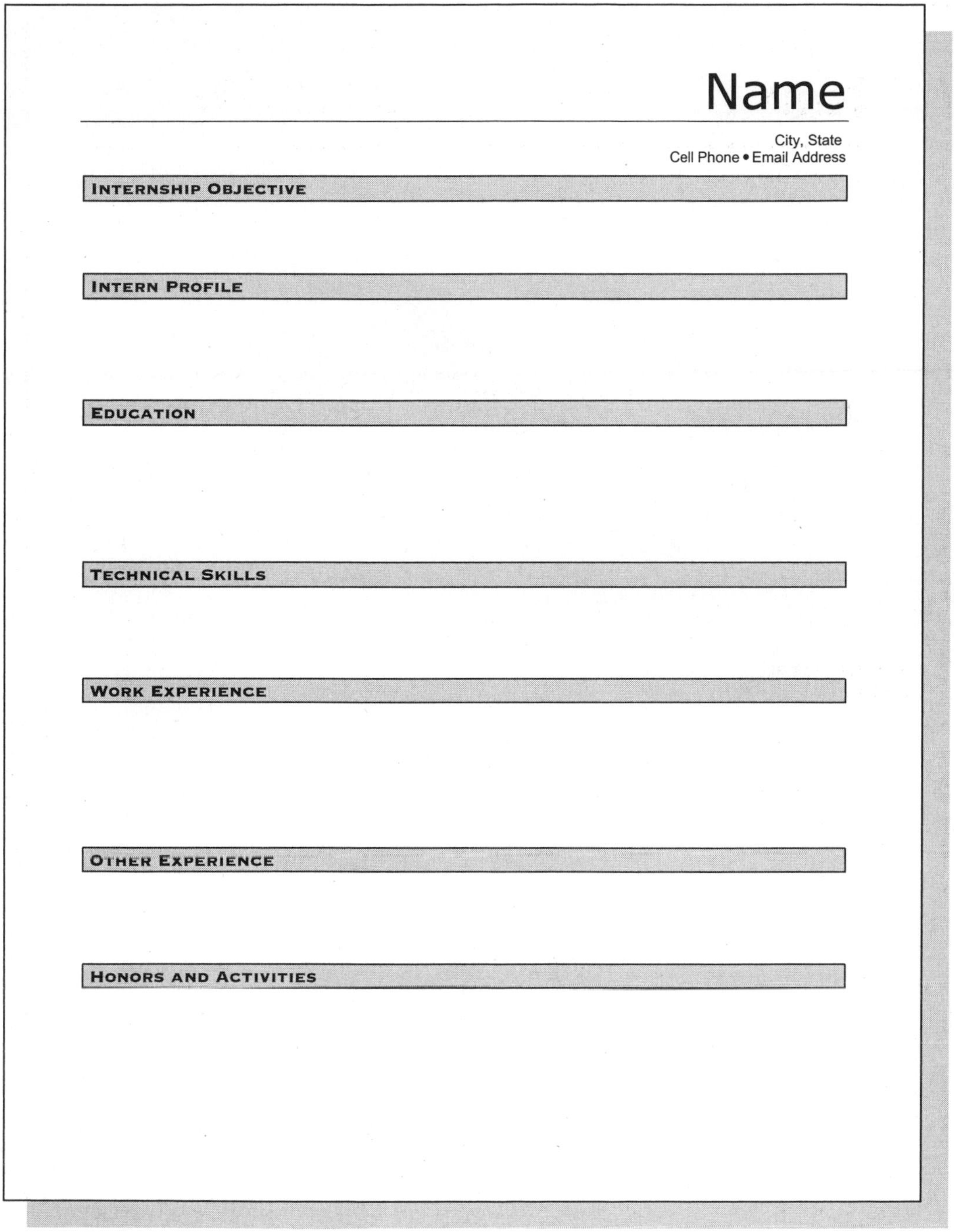

Name

City, State
Cell Phone • Email Address

INTERNSHIP OBJECTIVE

INTERN PROFILE

EDUCATION

TECHNICAL SKILLS

WORK EXPERIENCE

OTHER EXPERIENCE

HONORS AND ACTIVITIES

Figure 11-4: Be careful not to choose a screen color so dark that headings are difficult to read.

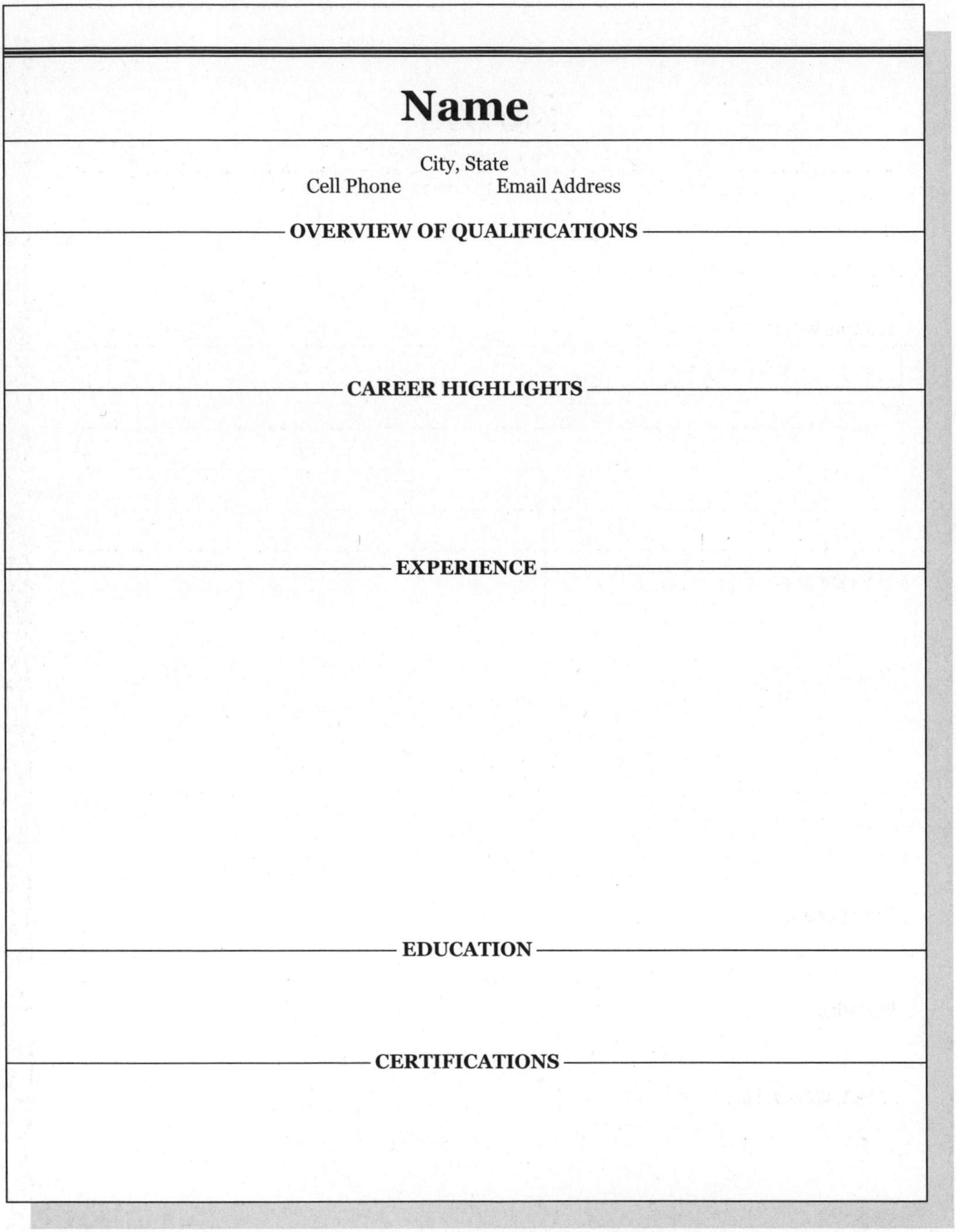

Name

City, State
Cell Phone   Email Address

———— **OVERVIEW OF QUALIFICATIONS** ————

———— **CAREER HIGHLIGHTS** ————

———— **EXPERIENCE** ————

———— **EDUCATION** ————

———— **CERTIFICATIONS** ————

Figure 11-5: This design features a prominent display of certification(s) for your occupation, which may be critical in today's market.

Name

Cell Phone ❖ Email Address

Personal Trait | Personal Trait | Personal Trait | Personal Trait

Seeking (Job Title) at (Name of Company)

Offering (Two or three lines of relevant top skills and accomplishments)

Position Requirements

(Company) Asks For	*I Deliver*
❖	✓
❖	✓
❖	✓
❖	✓

Technical Skills

Work Experience

Other Experience

Education

Honors and Activities

Figure 11-6: This design highlights a "benefits bringer," rather than a "skills slinger." It is very effective.

Design That Showcases Your Words

This chapter's takeaway: Pay plenty of attention to your resume's appearance in presenting your targeted content. Well-chosen resume architecture and design are like a guided tour — an employer's eyes are directed to the factual tip-offs that answer these three essential questions:

- ✔ Why are you contacting me?
- ✔ What can you do for me?
- ✔ How do I know you can do this?

Beware Web sites offering free resume templates

The four template shells (Figures 11-3 through 11-6) here are far from the only layout possibilities open to you. Web search for "free resume templates" and you find a head-spinning 50,000 of such sites as Sample Words (sample words.com) and Resume Help (resume-help.org). Microsoft Office (office.microsoft.com) offers scores of free resume templates. But not all free resume template sites are created equal. Take care.

In fact, hang on to your wallet, advises resume expert Michael Speas, NRWA, PAWRCC, and president of the San Francisco-based resume writing service, AlphaDogResumes.com.

After noticing a consumer alert Speas posted on his own site about resume firms that offer questionable job "guarantees," I hoped he might know how template Web sites stay in business. He does. Here's what Speas told me:

"Some free resume template Web sites are legitimate sources of great free resume help. Others use free resume samples as bait to get you to click on advertisement after advertisement.

"Remember that 'free' may not really mean what you think. If you're not careful, you're likely to end up paying a lot of money for so-called free advice. Be wary of sites that ask for your credit card number. You could be charged a one-time fee for their services and information, or worse, a recurring subscription fee that takes real effort to cancel."

"Read all the fine print carefully, looking for 'Terms of Use' and 'Privacy Statements.' The devil is in the contract details."

Chapter 12

Passages: Resumes for Your Life's Changing Phases

In This Chapter

▶ Jumpstart your career right out of the gate

▶ Successfully continue your career no matter what

▶ Hop from the military into a civilian career

The economy is marked by passages — from schoolwork to adult work, from old work to new work, and from military work to civilian work. In the swirling pool of life, transitional passages occur when the lily pad you're standing on sinks. At those times, you must take your destiny in hand and leap to another lily pad, preferably without drowning.

That's why, metaphorically speaking, this chapter is dedicated to the swimming lessons that keep your head above water and ease your transition when you're racing to a new lily pad. Within it you discover how

✔ Employers are inclined to view you

✔ You can manage their perceptions

✔ You land upright at your new workplace destination

Pay rapt attention when you belong to one of the three groups of job seekers featured here:

✔ Recent graduates

✔ Baby boomers

✔ Returning military members

Even if you're not in the new-lily-pad market, you may pick up some really useful tips in this chapter. Ready, aim, swim!

Scoring Big as a Recent Graduate

When you've just walked the cap-and-gown line, you can sidestep "no experience" potholes by impressing employers with your vim and vigor, accomplishments, and up-to-date knowledge. Here's a primer on newbie strengths and weaknesses.

Quick take: Rookie strengths

As a recent graduate, you have three main selling points and various minor ones:

- ✔ You're energetic and fired up to tackle assigned tasks. With no kids, you're more likely to smile when asked to work long hours than are older employees who have family obligations.
- ✔ You're more current in technical skills than older competitors.
- ✔ You're available for the right price. You cost much less than an older, experienced person. Maybe half as much.

Throw in assertions that you're a fast learner, are untarnished by earlier workplace habits that may be anathema to new employers, and that, as a rookie, you're prime material to be developed in concert with a prospective employer's viewpoints. Provide real-life examples of each claim or you risk coming off as a windbag who merely memorized slick talking points.

Quick take: Rookie soft spots

Weaknesses you have to wrestle include the stereotyping by employers of recent graduates as inept greenhorns who can't find their butts with both hands. In fact, multiple and recent surveys raise the decibel level on what many employers have long suspected or complained about: Most college students lack marketable skills. What can you do to offset this image of incompetence?

If you have a grade point average (GPA) above 3.5 or have worked as a tutor, emphasize that fact on your resume and at the top of job interviews. You're trying to create the *halo effect;* that is, if you lead with an attention-grabbing accomplishment, potential employers swayed by that first great impression apply it to the rest of your qualifications.

If your GPA is poor or marginal, omit it from your resume but bring it up midway in a job interview. Comment that you had to work to pay for your school and living expenses. And, for jobs working with people, explain that you devoted much time to "real life" experiences, such as leadership in campus organizations. Ideally, you also can show that your grades in your major are excellent, and that your GPA rose as you learned better study habits.

As a recent graduate, you can build a rewarding career in federal service, an especially appealing option in downturns when private companies aren't breaking speed records to hire you. See USAJobs (www.usajobs.gov).

Tips for recent graduates

Times and resumes have changed since your older pals graduated. As I explain in Chapter 6, your first step is writing a multiple-page core resume that includes familiar requirements for your career field. If popular requirements in your target field include A, B, C, and D, be sure your core resume reflects your qualifications in A, B, C, and D.

Your core source document is the wellspring for cranking out shorter and targeted marketing communications, whether in resumes or social media profiles. Customize your spinoff resumes when you reply to specific job ads. You can also customize your spinoff resumes for posting in resume databases maintained by different industries, like chemical and healthcare.

Take care to match requirements with your qualifications in your opening skills summary (Chapter 8) and throughout your resume. Keep the following resume boosters in mind, as well.

Amp up your sales pitch

Thicken your work experience by including all unpaid positions — internships, special projects, and volunteer jobs. List them in reverse chronological order in your Work Experience section. Statements like these are powerful agents on your resume:

> *Sales: Sold $1,200 worth of tickets to college arts festival*
>
> *Counseling: Advised 16 freshman students as peer counselor*
>
> *Public Policy Coordination: Coordinator for student petition drive to save California Cougar from sports hunting, gaining 2,000 signatures in 35 days*

Highlight the work experience most relevant to your intended future. If you have at least one year of full-time professional experience, place education after experience — unless your education is changing your career path.

Clarify your aim

If you use an objective statement, make sure it's clear. Don't use a lofty statement of the absurd, like this one:

> *Seeking a challenging position that will allow me to actualize my talents in saving the world, with good potential for professional growth and pay commensurate with my ability.*

Instead, cut to the chase, like this:

> *Research position in urban planning field in Chicago area.*

You can add a summary, too, as I show you in Chapter 8.

Dump unhelpful information

Don't fatten your Web portfolio with work-irrelevant data or pictures. And don't enclose your paper resume in a report cover or bulky package or attach school transcripts or letters of recommendation, unless they're requested.

Include an activity only if it reveals skills, competencies, accomplishments, results, or other qualification to support your intended job. Omit high school data unless it adds a unique fact to the total impression that you're creating.

What about the laundry list of your college courses — do they earn their keep on your resume? No, unless the course work is unusual or you have little to say without them.

Data-mine your college experience

Need a job? Get experience! Need experience? Get a job! This predicament has frustrated new graduates since the Industrial Revolution.

You have a difficult resume challenge when you have nothing but education to work with. Only dedicated job research and customizing each resume gives you a chance of producing a persuasive product. Perhaps you overlooked something; even child-sitting or pet-sitting offers experience in accepting responsibility and demonstrates reliability.

Consider the following factors to identify the experience and skills you garnered in college and match your information with the job you hope to land:

- ✔ **Work:** Internships, summer jobs, part-time jobs, campus jobs, entrepreneurial jobs, temporary work, and volunteer work.
- ✔ **Sports:** Proven ability to achieve goals in a team environment.
- ✔ **Awards and honors**
- ✔ **Research papers and projects**
- ✔ **Campus leadership**
- ✔ **Grade Point Average (GPA):** If it's 3.0 or above; otherwise, omit it (some advisers set the GPA floor at 3.5).
- ✔ **Technical skills and software facility**

Concerning student jobs, one technique to make the most of your experience is to separate your jobs into fragments and explain them. For example, don't say that your job title was "office help" or "office clerk" and stop there. Instead, do this:

1. **Divide your job into functions.**

   Some examples: telephone reception, telephone sales, social media sales, contract negotiations, purchasing, inventory, staff training, computer application training, Web design, public speaking, and written communications.

2. **Describe each function in terms of your accomplishments and their outcomes.**

If an exhaustive search of your hobbies, campus activities, or community service turns up absolutely nothing worth putting on your resume, your education must carry the entire weight of candidacy for employment. Milk it dry, as the example in Figure 12-1 suggests.

New Graduate — Little Experience

Deanna R. McNealy
(111) 213-1415

1234 University Drive,#56B
Irvine, California 78910

Seek retail management trainee position. Offer more than three years' intensive study of public communication. Completed Bachelor's degree, developing strong research, language, interpersonal, computer, and disciplinary skills. Proven interactive skills with groups and individuals. Energetic, adaptive, fast learner.

BACKGROUND & EDUCATION

- **Bachelor of Arts, University of California at Irvine (UCI), May, 20##, Literature & Social Studies**

Self-Directed Studies [date] - Present
Focusing on mainstream culture and trends, study merchandising and population demographics of individuals between the ages of 18 and 49. Browse media and advertising extensively, developing an in-depth understanding of material consumption in U.S. culture.

University Studies
[dates]   Literary Philosophy, Graduate, UCI, Irvine, California
Accumulated skills in prioritizing, self-management and discipline, accomplishing over 90 pages of commentary on the subject of philosophical thought.

[dates]   Social Text and Context, UCI, Irvine, California
Developed in-depth understanding of public consensus and modern value systems.Concentration: the relationship between ideals and historical and economic patterns.

[dates]   Critical Thinking, UCI, Irvine, California
60 hours of self-directed research and lecture attendance, studying essential elements of critical thought. Developed skills in argumentative dialogue, logic, analysis, and approaching perception from an educated and diverse persepctive. Focus: anatomy of critical thought.

[dates]   Public Communication, UCI, Irvine, California
Intensive study of the psychological and social techniques of speech and communication. Developed comprehensive understanding of debate, physical language, formal and informal delivery, subliminal communication, and advertising. Focus: written and visual advertising techniques.

Other Experience [date] - Present, UCI, Irvine, California
15th and 16th Century Rhetoric, French Poetry, Literature in Music, Women, Words & Wisdom, FilmTheory, Shakespeare, British Fiction, U.S. Fiction, World Literature.

SKILLS
Computer: All word processing applications on Macintosh and PC, Internet savvy.
Interpersonal: Experienced in working with groups and individuals using teamwork and collaboration, setting goals, delegating and communicating effectively.

Figure 12-1: The resume of a graduate with marketable skills but little experience.

Gaffes common to new graduates

New graduates are more likely than experienced job seekers to make the following mistakes.

Falling short of image standards

If you present an online resume blemished with the type of shorthand used for tweets and texting, or a paper resume flawed with typos, or a persona degraded with whoopee pictures or a goofy profile on a social media site, you flunk.

Omitting heavy-hitter points

You distinguish yourself by creating an opening summary that calls to mind an image of your brand, as I describe in Chapter 2. For example:

> As team captain, used strong influencing skills and tremendous personal energy. Got marketplace experience through multiple internships and 6 student jobs, including tutoring. GPA 3.8 despite heavy course load.

Keep your summary brief — three to four accomplishments is plenty.

Overcompensating with gimmicky language

Don't tart up your resume to compensate for a lack of qualifications. Avoid using exotically original language, such as "eyelinered genius," a term used by a business graduate applying for an entry-level marketing position in the cosmetics industry. The term may be colorful, but charm communicates better in the interview.

Making employers guess

Employers hate being asked to decipher your intent. Merely presenting your declared major and transcript excerpts is not enough to kick off a productive job search. Add either an objective to your resume and/or a skills summary directed at a specific career field.

Leveling the experience field

Your resume is no place to give every job equal billing. Many rookie resumes are little more than rote listings of previous jobs — subpoena server, TV satellite dish sales representative, waiter, landscape helper, and computer coach, for example.

Separate your jobs into an A list and a B list. The A list contains the jobs that relate to what you want to do next, even if you have to stretch their importance to make a connection. Briefly mention jobs on the B list in a section called *Other Experience* or *Other Jobs*.

Stopping with bare bones

Some rookies look at a sheet of paper and then at their embarrassing, bedraggled collection of jobs in their paid-experience stew. Desperate to get *anything* written, they settle for name, rank, and serial number (employer, job title, and dates of employment).

The solution is to pull together *all* experience, including volunteer and part-time gigs. Sit, think, think some more, and add all your relevant competencies and skills pointing in the direction in which you hope to thumb a ride. One strategy is to sign up for a postgraduate internship. Speak with your college's career counselors or internship counselors about this possibility.

Still stymied? Look online for sample resume ideas. Try a Web search for "new college graduate sample resumes."

Hiding hot information

Data entombed is data forgotten. Employers remember best the information you give first in a resume, not the data folded into the middle. The first page of your resume is prime real estate; determine your selling points and pack that punch up front.

Ask three friends to read your resume and immediately tell you what they remember about it.

Highlighting the immaterial

Many first-time resume writers feature the wrong skills and knowledge acquired on each job.

Suppose you want to be a Web producer and one of your work experience citations is your three years of effort for campus student theatrical productions. You painted scenery, sold tickets, and designed sets. It's the experience in designing sets that helps qualify you for Web producer, not painting scenery or selling tickets.

Wrap yourself in the skills that help employers imagine you playing a role for their benefit in their company.

Ignoring employers' needs

Even the smartest new graduates, who may have survived research challenges as rigorous as uncovering the body language of ancient French cave dwellers, make this mistake: They forget to find out what employers want from new hires.

At this moment in time, no one cares what you want — the only thing that matters is the value-pack you bring to the employer. Your college career center can sprinkle your search path with gems of wisdom in reading employers' wish lists.

Writing boastfully

Appearing too arrogant about your talents can cause employers to question your ability to learn and function as a junior team member. Even when you're just trying to compensate for your inexperience, avoid terminology that comes across as contrived or blatantly self-important.

When you're not sure whether you sound too full of yourself, ask older friends to describe the kind of person they think your resume represents.

Grabbing Good Jobs as a Baby Boomer

If you're on the shady side of 50 (or even 40 in some occupations), don't bother wondering whether job-market age discrimination lives. It does.

Joblessness for Americans 55 and older surged a whopping 331 percent over the 2000–2009 decade, according to AARP. Frustrated job hunters in their 50s say they've hit the "gray wall" and decry the toothless enforcement of age discrimination law.

In this section, I don't discuss legal remedies or self-employment. Instead, I show you how to do all within your power to beat pesky bias and display your excellent qualifications for employment on your resume.

Quick take: Boomer strengths

You have at least six main selling points and a slew of minor ones:

- ✔ **Road-tested.** You have more knowledge and greater wisdom than you did when you were half your age. Your judgment is a valuable commodity. You can easily save an employer substantial "mistake dollars" because you've seen most situations play out in some form over the course of your learning lifetime. You have the common sense that comes with experiencing life. You won't rush into hasty decisions.

- ✔ **Reliable.** You won't take off for frivolous reasons. Employers can count on you showing up and doing the job as expected. You're more grateful for a good job than younger workers and show your appreciation with a strong work ethic. Your work history shows that your word is your bond.

- ✔ **Flexible.** You're motivated to be adaptable. You may value working less than a full-time schedule. You can adapt to the changing needs of a business.

✔ **Financially viable.** You may be able to work for less money than your competition. Your kids are grown and your expenses are down.

✔ **Collaborative.** You've perfected a talent for team playing because you've seen how all hands can work collectively for the good of a business.

✔ **Big-picture vision.** You take a 360-degree view when dealing with people. You've had years to discover what makes them tick. You know from firsthand experience the quality of customer service consumers expect and appreciate. You've learned to look around corners before making decisions that may come back to bite an employer.

Your brain is better than ever between ages 40 and 65, say researchers. Leading science writer Barbara Strauch, author of *The Surprising Talents of the Middle-Aged Mind* (Viking), says that baby boomers are better at all sorts of things than they were at age 20, including problem solving and making financial judgments. Middle-aged brains, according to studies, are primed to navigate the world better because they've been navigating the world better longer.

Quick take: Boomer soft spots

The notion that older people have had their day and should make room for the next generation is deeply ingrained, say researchers. The stereotype is that you can't teach an old dog new tricks and that all mature workers are alike in their abilities to learn, perform, energize, remember, and deal with change in a new kind of world.

Here is a selection of prevalent myths about workers of a certain age, followed by the defense realities to reflect in your resume:

✔ **Older workers can't or won't learn new skills.**

A smart, well-executed resume proves this bit of conventional wisdom wrong, as it certainly is: The over-50 crowd is the fastest growing group of Internet and social media users. Use technical terms on your resume if appropriate. Mention new skills recently acquired. Cite recent coursework, degrees, and certifications.

✔ **Training older workers is a lost investment because they won't be around for long.**

Boomers are just not retiring like they used to. Studies repeatedly report that workers are extending their careers, either by choice or because their retirement funding has suffered a huge hit in recent years. Find ways to tell employers that you

• Are committed to doing quality work

• Get along with coworkers and younger bosses

- Have strong skills in reading, writing, and math

- Are someone they can count on in a crisis

- Are cheerful about multiple hats and tasks

- Can work weekends if needed

✔ **Benefit and accident costs are higher for older workers.**

Skyrocketing health insurance costs have become a third rail for hiring workers of the boomer generation. Employers pay a higher premium for employees between ages 50 and 65 (65 being the magic number when Medicare starts paying the medical bills).

Small employers in particular, pressing to keep their health insurance expense to a minimum and stay in business, may prefer to hire workers in a younger demographic — unless you change their minds.

Play your ace-in-the-hole: offsets. Certain characteristics even out generational cost differences. For example, a study by the AARP shows that older workers take fewer sick days per year than do other age groups because they have fewer acute illnesses and sporadic sick days. What's more, older workers take fewer risks in accident-prone situations and statistically have lower accident rates than other age groups.

Overall, employee benefit costs stay the same as a percentage of salary for all age groups. Handling this on a resume is tricky but, if true, you can say: "Robust health; physically active; no dependents other than spouse."

As new health insurance provisions roll out, generational differences in health insurance costs will become less important, and perhaps even moot. Be on the lookout for developments that level the playing field for job-hunting boomers and use them to your advantage.

As a baby boomer, you're somewhat less likely to be clobbered by age bias in government (federal, state, local) work and more likely to be appreciated for your proven talents. Look for opportunities at USAJobs.com.

Tips for baby boomers

To fight the age bias that keeps you out of job interviews, start with a clean, contemporary-looking resume design (revisit Chapter 11) and stock it with accomplishments, skills, and experience that make you look younger than springtime by taking to heart the following tips.

Match your target job description

Find or write job descriptions of your target occupations. If you like your current field and are leaving involuntarily because it's disappearing from under your feet like the world's biggest sinkhole, start with job descriptions in closely related jobs. Compare requirements of related jobs with your transferable (crossover) skills profile. If you don't like your current field, forget I mentioned it.

To identify occupations closely related to your current field, check out *Occupational Outlook Handbook* published by the U.S. Department of Labor. Read it online at www.bls.gov/oco.

Knowing what you have to offer gets you up off your knees, out of the past, and into the future; it enables you to write a resume that readers respect, by, in effect, saying, "This is what I can do for you that will add to your productivity, efficiency, or effectiveness. And, of course, a little bump on the bottom line."

Shorten your resume

The general guideline is "Go back no more than 10 or 15 years." But if that doesn't work for the job you seek, one answer is to create a functional or hybrid resume (Chapter 9), in which you emphasize your relevant skills in detail toward the top of the resume and downplay overly impressive titles that might intimidate younger employers. For example, *Senior Vice President, Sales* becomes *Sales Executive*.

Focus your resume

For emphasis, I'll repeat that: Focus your resume. (See Chapter 9.) Concentrate on highlighting your two most recent or most relevant jobs. Don't attempt to give equal attention to each of your past jobs, especially if the experience is irrelevant to what you want to do now.

When your job experience has been overly diverse, your resume probably looks like a job-hopping tale of unrelated job after unrelated job. (If that's your problem, see Chapter 13.)

Show that you're a tower of strength

Give examples of how you solved problems, recovered expenses, and learned to compensate for weaknesses in your working environment. Emphasize how quickly such adjustments occurred. Gray heads who've survived a few fallen skies are valuable assets in difficult times.

Demonstrate political correctness

Show that you're familiar with contemporary values by using politically correct terms wherever appropriate. Examples include *diversity, cross-cultural, mainstream, multiethnic,* and *people with disabilities* (never *handicapped*), and *women* (not *girls* or *gals*). Sensitivity is especially important for positions that have contact with the public.

Send your resume online

Doing so helps dispel any ideas that you're over the hill and haven't the vaguest idea that you live in a digital age. If you want to be seen as a hub of hip, tweet about your resume. See Part I for more on digital resumes and using social media.

Murder ancient education dates

Of course, the absence of dates sends a signal: This is a geezer who read a resume book. But at least your awareness shows that you have sufficient faculties to read the book and play the game.

Trim your resume to fighting weight

For very experienced professionals, sorting out the most powerful resume points can be difficult. It's like being a gifted child — so many choices, and you're good at all of them! Ask a couple of smart friends to help you decide what information stays and what information goes.

Employ appropriate headings

When you're relying on freelance or non-paid work — hobby or volunteer — as the substance for your experience statement, use the heading *Work Experience* and list it first.

But when you've changed your career focus through education, list *Education* before *Experience*. To refine the education heading, you can substitute target-job-related learning, such as *Accounting Education* or *Healthcare Education*. Your employment history follows.

What can you do with all the experience that was great in your old job but means zero where you want to go? Lump it together at the end of your resume under *Other Relevant Experience* or *Earlier Experience*. Shrink it to positions, titles, employers, and/or degrees and educational institutions. If extraneous experience is older than five years, boot it entirely.

Taking a lower-level job

When you're willing to step down from your previous level of work, don't try to do it with a resume. Go directly to the hiring manager in a personal meeting where you have a chance to color your positioning in the best hue. For instance, avoid the classic mistake of saying you no longer want to be the "point person."

Show skills as they apply to new position

Making a career change? As you list your skills, competencies, education, and experience, lead with the information relevant to the new position and then list the other data. You have to quickly convince the employer that you have the ability to handle the position.

Assume an engineer wants to move into sales. The resume should mention things like "client liaison," "preparing presentations for meetings," and "strong communications skills" — and accomplishments that back up the claims.

You may begin by writing: "Used a strong technical background and excellent communications skills in a sales role." Then continue to speak of your ability to provide good technical advice in a business relationship.

Writing that you "enjoy learning" is, in some cases, a coin with two sides: The employer may see you as admirable in your desire to further your education, or, conversely, make a negative judgment that you don't have the skills right now to hit the ground running.

Instead, here's your best positioning slant: You certainly are not a burned-out manager looking to bail by settling for a much less responsible job. You're a career changer exploring new fields:

> *In the past decade, I've put in very long hours and exceeded expectations in jobs in the same industry. I realized I'm a doer who needs new mountains to climb. I have too much to give to the business world to ride on autopilot the rest of my life. I want to check out other ways I can make a contribution in a different career field, hopefully at your company.*

Explain your reasoned willingness to accept lower compensation:

> *I have a great work attitude and excellent judgment. Show me a new task, and I get it right away. I understand, of course, that the trade-off in moving into your industry is less pay and responsibility.*

When you've opened the door, it's time to hand over your hybrid resume (described in Chapter 9). You need breathing room to shape your resume in a way that spotlights your crossover skills as they pertain to the job you seek, such as talent for working with numbers, reliability, and good attendance record, as well as fast learning ability.

When you're a major seeking a minor position, emphasize that sometimes the best workers need new chapters in their lives.

Gaffes common to boomers

When you have a long job history, you're more likely to need updates on the following issues.

Choosing the wrong focus

Choosing the wrong focus is a problem shared with new graduates who fail to elaborate on those jobs that best address the hoped-for next job. (Review "Tips for Recent Graduates" earlier in this chapter.) Like the real estate adage that the operating principle is location, location, location, the operating principle for better jobs is target, target, target.

Using old resume standards

Many baby boomers, still working on last century's calendar, have an outdated concept of what a resume should be. An office neighbor recently expressed surprise when I told him to leave out his personal information, which once was standard fare on resumes.

"Oh, I thought personal information was supposed to humanize you," the seasoned ace said. Busy employers and resume-processing computers don't care that you're a par golfer or play impressive tennis; this kind of personal bonding information comes out at the interview. For more information on resume content, cast your eyes on Chapter 8.

Lacking a summary

Because of the extensiveness of your experience, your resume may be a grab bag without a summary. Suppose you're an auditor who yearns for the country life. You can write: *Internal Auditor: Farm Equipment Industry,* followed by a one- or two-paragraph summary of why you're qualified. Think of a summary as a salesperson's hook. It describes some of your special skills, your familiarity with the target industry, and your top accomplishments (see Chapter 8).

TIP

Presenting short-term work on your resume

Boomers who find that they're doing work for a specific company but are being paid through a staffing firm or other intermediary, may be unsure about how to report the information on their resumes. You don't have to list the middle-man firm. Note only the companies for which the work was performed, as the following sketch illustrates:

Company A, Company B, Company C [date] to present

For **Company A,** Name of Department/Division

As **job title,** performed:

✔ accomplishment

✔ accomplishment

✔ accomplishment

In the same format as I show for Company A, offer the company, department/division, job title, and accomplishment information for Companies B and C.

P.S. If your job titles are extreme — insignificant or overly exalted — don't bold them.

Not supplementing a high school education

If your highest education attainment is high school, don't forget to mention any continuing education, including seminars and workshops related to your work — if those studies apply to what you want to do next.

Winning Interviews As a New Civilian

If you're trading military life for your first civilian gig, be sure to sign up for the federal government's invaluable Transition Assistance Program. TAP offers a three-day class to help active-duty personnel write resumes and prepare for interviews.

Transition coaches say that a lot of young military retirees overlook TAP — perhaps the very ones who need it the most. As one TAP coach wryly observed: "Some of those we don't see here think they're gun fighters who will go out into the world and do great things and just aren't interested in resumes."

That attitude is dead wrong and self-defeating, as you see in the following gem of a section that has been impressively refreshed in this edition by Don Orlando, a retired Air Force full colonel. He is one of America's leading career coaches, as well as one of its very best resume writers.

(Full disclosure: I persuaded Don Orlando to take message control command for this section because the last uniform I wore was green and had a Girl Scouts of the USA insignia on it.)

Orlando has directed the prestigious Executive Transition Assistance Program at the Air Force's Air University for years. He is the military-to-civilian blogger for the Career Thought Leaders' Consortium (www.career thoughtleaders.com/blog).

Quick take: Transitioning military strengths

With a chest full of selling points, you've got six super marks of merit:

✔ You have exceptionally good training. And military bosses required you to master dozens of new, complex skills quickly and well. You're trainable.

✔ As you relate your substantial problem-solving experience, always go beyond *what* you did to show *how* you did it. Some brief stories show how you improved lives; others draw a straight line between what you did and why it made a difference to the mission.

✔ You know how to be a team player, and you show up on time. You perform well under pressure. You know how to accomplish assignments in a structured organization.

✔ You may have experience with a direct fit to the civilian job market: operations management, supply chain procurement, human resource management, systems administration, or financial planning.

✔ You have a strong work ethic to get it right the first time.

✔ You're flexible and able to quickly adapt to changing situations.

Quick take: Transitioning military soft spots

Communication is the biggest reason recruiters or hiring managers overlook well-qualified military candidates, say career coaches who specialize in transitioning from military to civilian jobs. They just don't get what your resume says when you speak military-ese instead of civilian-ese.

The military-talk habit is hard to shake. A news report describes an incident involving a former soldier named Perkins who was transitioning to civilian life after a 20-year hitch. Applying to a staffing company, Perkins spelled out his last name in military alphabetic code: Papa-Echo-Romeo-Kilo-India-November-Sierra.

Debunk four worst military myths

Because the United States has had an all-volunteer force for about 40 years, many hiring decision makers have developed wildly inaccurate stereotypes about your life on active duty. Ace career coach Don Orlando reveals how to dispel the worst job search sinkers:

✔ **"Military people don't have to think; they need only give and take orders."** Counter this by focusing on success stories that reflect true leadership and mentoring.

✔ **"Military people are inflexible."** You can easily destroy this myth by relating how you frequently got uncertain jobs done with

incomplete guidance and less-than-perfect information.

✔ **"Military people don't understand profit and loss."** Most people have no idea the military competes for goods and services in a "market place." Relate how you got the most value for the taxpayers' buck and you'll beat this red herring.

✔ **"Military services always have unlimited resources of every kind."** You can deflate this old fiction as you explain how you got the mission done even though you were undermanned and underfunded.

I discuss in more detail the problems resulting from noncommunication when you use military-ese (also called *milspeak*) on your resume later in the section "Get the message about milspeak."

When finished writing your resume, put it through the civilian translation wringer by asking friends and neighbors who know not a whit about things military to read it and see whether they understand what you're talking about.

Admittedly, some employers do hold a stigmatized stereotype of military service members as being rough, tough, rigid, and hard-headed types whose idea of leadership is command and control. Don't expect a resume to alter that perception, but a well-built resume helps get you inside an interview room where your pleasing personality can reverse false, preconceived notions.

Tips for new civilians

Many employers appreciate vets as employees and give you preference above a comparable nonvet competitor. The federal government awards 5 to 10 extra points (beyond a passing score of 70 points) to a veteran's application — good news if you're applying for a federal position.

Government contractors hire big numbers of former military members. That's why it's especially important when preparing your resume to factor in federal requirements in online recruiting processes designed to promote equal employment procedures. Federal contractors must play by the rules set by the Office of Federal Contract Compliance (OFCCP). Read more about OFCCP rules on the U.S. Department of Labor site (www.dol.gov).

Here are other resume pointers to keep you moving ahead.

Advertise what you're selling

Avoid building your resume around your military rank or title. Employers and recruiters may not really understand what you did while in the military and fail to comprehend why you should be hired. Instead, emphasize the qualifications you bring to the employer.

Consider your best format

A hybrid resume (Chapter 9) is a good choice, say many career coaches who work with transitioning military, because it features competencies and skills in professional categories, rather than chronological history by rank or job title. But this doesn't mean a reverse chronological resume format can't be used to your advantage.

If you're working with a third-party recruiter, use the format that the recruiter — who is carrying your immediate future in his or her hands — advises.

Quantify, quantify, quantify

Measure your results in numbers, percentages, and dollars whenever you can (see Chapter 18). In the civilian job market, the candidate who wins the numbers game often wins the job.

For example, if you were an executive leader assigned to collect contributions to the United Way campaign, did you exceed your goal and by how much? Were your results better than any in the past? Here's how your accomplishment might look in your resume:

> *Results: Led our United Way campaign to bring in 110% of the goal — the best results in the last decade. Our organization topped all 10 competitors at the next highest management level.*

Place your accomplishment in context

Context is a powerful platform on which to display your outstanding performance and accomplishments. For example, in citing an impressive performance, was the task remarkable because you did it with no experience in that area? Did you accomplish the task in three days instead of five days? How many members in your unit scored as well as you in producing the accomplishment?

Here's how this information might look in your resume:

> *Payoffs: Brought senior leadership complete information concerning 6,000 assets critical to our mission — even though I had never done this complex task before. Delivered in just 24 hours, one-fifth the normal time.*

Promote your promotions

Were you sought out by a senior officer for a specific job? If so, do you know how many others could have been considered for that position? Imagine an entry like this in your job history:

> *Sought out personally by a four-star general (civilian CEO equivalent) from more than 500 eligibles to serve as Director of Operations.*

Not all promotions are formal. Maybe you received a de facto promotion by being given an assignment tagged as one to be filled by a higher rank. Similarly, perhaps you were promoted "below the zone" (before you normally would be considered for advancement), which doesn't happen often and recognizes talent you can use to impress employers, writing something like this:

> *Selected by a panel of senior executives as one of only 13 (from 15,000 eligibles) to be promoted exceptionally early — a rare feat in the history of our service.*

Web browse for "below-the-zone promotions" and call the personnel resource manager for your career field and service at the Pentagon to quantify how rare an honor you received.

Use "expert" testimony

Search for quotes from letters, e-mails, or performance reports that compliment your work *in specific terms*. Avoid those composed entirely of well-intentioned, but general words that could apply to anybody. Be sure you indicate what level the compliment came from. Here's how it might look in your resume:

> *I've seen Jack's work at first hand. He handled our relocation so well, I told my counterparts he should be their "go-to" guy whenever they have similar challenges. — General Two-Star*

Zero in on job fairs

Job fairs are potent employment avenues for service members and veterans to meet employers, network, and even be interviewed on the spot. Also called career fairs, some events are aimed at attracting transitioning military, especially individuals who have current top-secret clearances. (Find job fairs by checking the classified pages of your Sunday newspapers or by searching the Internet.)

Others are *virtual job fairs* — online versions of events at which employers and job seekers find each other. Virtual fairs may include videos, downloadable materials, animations, Webinars, live chat, and more technologies geared to the hiring process.

When planning to attend an on-site job fair, get a jump on your competition and make life easier for the fair organizer by calling the organizer well in advance. Say you want to make the day as effective as possible for company team members who will man the booths.

Ask for any available job postings. (If the fair is for federal government jobs, ask for available job announcements that interest you.) Also ask for the name of company reps who will man the relevant booths, but don't be surprised if, for competitive reasons, the organizer won't share that information.

You know the saying, "If you don't ask, you don't get." You can use every bit of competitive advantage when competing with hundreds of candidates for the same position.

Before the fair, print copies of your resume and put the name of the company and its rep in pencil at the top of the first page. Bring a lot of extra copies.

After you arrive, take a moment to locate the booths you want to visit. (The organizer almost always has a map with that information.) Imagine the confidence you'll project when you walk up to the booth, greet the company rep by name, and readily show how you meet the needs spelled out in the job posting or announcement you read before you came through the door.

Job fairs are noisy, informal affairs, but treat every conversation you have with a company employee as an interview.

Protect your identity from theft

Your Social Security number is the combination to the vault for identity thieves. Unless you're applying for a federal job, which sometimes does require your Social Security number, keep it off your resume, cover letter, or application form. As the federal government updates its hiring process, fewer agencies are requiring SS numbers.

Be a resource collector

You deserve entire books dedicated to your special needs when transitioning from military to civilian life. Luckily, a number of winners are at your beck and credit card. Here are five great picks and one comprehensive catalog:

- *Military-to-Civilian Resumes and Letters,* by Carl S. Savino and Ronald L. Krannich, PhD. (Impact Publications)

- *Expert Resumes for Military-to-Civilian Transitions,* 2nd Edition, by Wendy S. Enelow and Louise M. Kursmark (JIST Publishing)

- *Military to Federal Career Guide,* 2nd Edition, by Kathryn Kraemer Troutman (The Resume-Place, 2010), and *Ten Steps to a Federal Job, 3rd Edition,* by Kathryn Kraemer Troutman (The Resume-Place)

- *Job Search: Marketing Your Military Experience,* by David G. Henderson (Stackpole Books)

- *Veterans World* (www.veteransworld.com), an online book catalog of transition resources

Visit key Web sites

Dozens of useful Web sites offer help for transitioning military personnel. Start with the following resources, which may link to other Web sites you'll want to know about:

- TAOnline (www.taoline.com)

- VetJobs.com (www.vetjobs.com)

- Corporate Gray (www.corporategray.com)

- Military Officers Association of America (www.moaa.org)

- Non Commissioned Officers Association (www.ncoausa.org)

Get the message about milspeak

Bill Gaul, a former military officer and placement specialist, popular media commentator, and acknowledged expert on the military transitioning job market, answers questions about demilitarizing your resume.

Q: Can you give an example of what you call *milspeak?*

A: An Army officer's resume read: "As commanding officer of a 500-person organization, I was responsible for the health, morale, and welfare of all personnel." Health, morale and welfare? Just think of the incredible range of skills and experience completely overlooked in that milspeak phrase. Far-reaching accomplishments and important responsibilities are whitewashed into boilerplate terms that mean nothing to a civilian hiring manager.

For example, digging into "health, morale, and welfare," we found "policy development, human resource management, budget planning and administration, process improvement, operations management, and staff development."

Q: What's the deal with job titles?

A: Some military job titles are ambiguous, some misleading. For example, a Navy fire control technician does not put out fires but operates and maintains electronic weapons targeting systems.

Translate your job title without misleading the employer:

- Mess cook (food service specialist)
- Fire control technician (electronic weapons systems technician)
- Motor pool specialist (automotive maintenance technician)
- Provost marshal (law enforcement officer)
- Quartermaster (supply clerk)
- Base commander (mayor of a small city)

When in doubt about the ethics or clarity of "civilianizing" your job title, you can list it like this: Functional Job Title: Mayor of Small City.

When you need a tool to help you translate military job titles to their civilian counterparts, find the Military Occupational Classification Crosswalk at the O*NET Resource Center (www.onetcenter.org), a free Department of Labor Web site.

Q: What can you do in situations where your specific work experience doesn't closely relate to the job you're applying for?

A: You can communicate your organizational position instead of your job title. An E-5 Marine Corps embassy guard applying for a management position in the security industry listed his job title as "facility supervisor." He added the details of his experience within the body of his resume. This drew readers because it represented more of a fit than someone who kept people in proper lines applying for visas.

Q: Aren't most military members in combat-related jobs?

A: Yes, and that can be a problem, trying to relate the job you've had to the job you want, unless you're applying for law enforcement positions. But for the straight combat MOS (military occupational specialty) — infantry, tank gunner, reconnaissance Marine, and the like — there are several options.

List your relative position in an organization — "unit supervisor" instead of "platoon sergeant" as your title. Your work in collateral duties may be the key. A platoon sergeant seeking a position in staff development and training, based on duty as a training NCO (noncommissioned officer), can list "training supervisor" as her title.

The dates listed must accurately reflect the time you spent in the specific collateral duties, of course. As you know, it is often the case that you will have more than one collateral duty while performing a key role for an organization.

Q: How should you list your level of authority?

A: Omit references to rank or grade like "NCO, "petty officer," and "sergeant." Unless an employer has military experience, these terms won't communicate your relative position within an organization. Instead, list civilianized equivalents appropriate to your level of authority:

- ✔ Safety Warrant Officer OSHA (coordinator)
- ✔ Training NCO (training supervisor)
- ✔ Barracks sergeant (property manager)

Q: What about education and training?

A: Many courses and schools leave recruiters wondering exactly what you trained for because the course titles can be esoteric and arcane. The rule is this: List your training in a way that will provide immediately apparent support for your job objective.

If the name of a school or course doesn't communicate exactly what you were able to do after the course that you couldn't do before, show that value because you are trying to inform, not mystify. You are trying to demilitarize the language to help resume reviewers understand the nature of your military training. Some examples:

- ✔ SNAP II Maintenance School (Honeywell Computer Server Maintenance School)
- ✔ NALCOMIS Training (Automated Maintenance and Material Control System Training)

> ✔ Mess Management School (Food Service Management School)
>
> ✔ NCO Leadership Training (Leadership and Management Training)

Q: Is that all there is to civilianizing a military background?

A: Not quite. To help resume reviewers understand the depth of your training, list the number of classroom hours you studied. To determine the number of hours, multiply the number of course days by 8, or the number of weeks by 40. If you completed the course within the past 10 years, list the competition date. If the course is older, leave off the date. Here are two examples:

Leadership and Management Training, 3/07 (160 hours)

Leadership and Management Training (160 hours)

Look for an edge in marketing your military education and training. Did you have to compete to win a slot in the training program or school? Were you a distinguished graduate with honors? Did you finish in the top 10 percent of your class? Call the school to get the figures on how many students achieved your distinctions. Don't forget to use civilian language to describe your edge.

Changing Course with an OnTarget Resume

Whether you're exhaling after your last college final, struggling with an abundance of birthdays, or leaving a uniform behind, as you race in your passage to a new lily pad, you make better time with better traveling papers.

Chapter 6 illustrates easy ways to create a core resume (which, kitchen sink that it is, thankfully, only you see). Your core resume is the factory for whipping out as many OnTarget resumes as you need when you need them — and that's before someone else snags the job you want.

Chapter 13

Successful Solutions to Resume Problems

Chances are that not everything in your career history is a plus. Minuses — either fact or perception — like your age (be it a little or a big number) and experience (whether too much or not enough) need special care to keep them from setting off alarm bells. It's always better to anticipate factors in your background that can screen you out of the running and do what you can to minimize them.

Nobody's perfect. But rarely are we jammed up against problems so severe that they cannot be solved in some way. Careful resume management is a good start.

Here are some ideas on how to turn lemons into lemonade.

Too Much Experience

Not only is inappropriate experience — too much or too little — often the real reason that you're turned down, but it's also too frequently a cover story for rejections that are really based on any factor from bias to bad breath.

Too many qualifications or ageism?

A reader writes that his qualifications for a training position are superior but too ample. He explains:

> *Preoccupation with age seems to be the pattern. I'm rarely called for an interview; when I call after sending a resume in response to an ad or a networking contact, I'm told I'm too experienced for the position — that I seem to be overqualified. How can I keep my resume from looking like lavender and old lace?*

Ageism often is the subtext in the *overqualified* objection. Deal with it by limiting your work history to the most recent positions you've held that target the job opening. To avoid seeming too old or too highly paid, limit your related experience to about 15 years for a managerial job and to about 10 years for a technical job.

What about all your other experience? Leave it in your memory bank. Or if you believe that the older work history adds to your value as a candidate, you can describe it under a heading of *Other Experience* and briefly present it without dates. Figure 13-1 is an example of a resume that shows recent experience only.

The recent-experience-only treatment doesn't work every time, but give it a try — it shows that you're not stuck in a time warp, and it's a better tactic than advertising your age as one that qualifies you for carbon dating.

If the employer is notorious for hiring only young draft horses, rethink your direction. Try to submit your resume to employers who can take advantage of your expertise, such as a new or expanding company operating in unfamiliar territory.

What if the overqualified objection is just that and not a veil for age discrimination? The employer legitimately may be concerned that when something better comes along, you'll set a sprint record for shortest time on the job.

On the other hand, another version of rejection based on too many qualifications or ageism occurs when a candidate who qualifies for AARP membership wants to kick back a bit and work at less demanding, lower-paying work. The employer questions the applicant's true intent — why would an older engineer want a technician's job? — and consequently doesn't bother to interview a candidate she suspects of seeking any port in a storm.

Recent Experience Only

Work Experience.

FEIN AND SONS – Operates continuously in Long Beach, Calif. **Sole Proprietor, Broker.** Real estate brokerage, development, asset management, and consulting. In-house brokerage company, specializing in eight- and nine-figure acquisitions, shopping centers, and commercial space, obtaining entitlements and economic analysis. Personal volume: over $100 million.

SONNHAARD INC. – Solana Beach, Calif. [dates]. **Marketing Manager.** Real estate development corporation. Primary project: Le Chateau Village, a French-theme 100-lot residential development in Del Mar. Sourced architect, designers, and contractors. Limited liability company built 60 upscale custom homes by architect Jacques Donnaeu of Toulouse. Supervised 10 sales representatives. Sales gross exceeded $40 million, selling 58 homes ahead of project schedule by six months.

WEST COAST ASSOCIATION – Los Angeles, Calif. [dates]. **Executive Vice President**. International trade association with 190 firms holding annual fairs, from 25 states and all of Canada, including two theme amusement parks, 15 affiliated breed organizations and 300 service members who provide goods and services to members. Annual convention attended by over 2,000 executives. Acted as legislative advocate for California district and county fairs, nine of which have horse racing and pari-mutuel wagering. Increased membership by 200%, administering seven-figure budget, with staff of five professionals.

Other Experience.

• BBH & Co., d.b.a. ENVIRONMENT AFFILIATED, **Executive Vice President.** Administered six-figure budget and supervised 27 managers. Directed recruitment and marketing activities.

• CSU Long Beach, **Development Director.** Managed 40-million-dollar project to expand campus grounds 30%. Maintained lowest campus construction budget in state, including contracting and materials.

• TRADE ALTERNATIVE, **Commercial Properties Manager.** Marketed, leased, and acquired $900,000 in commercial property. Catered to such upscale clientele as high-end law firms.

Figure 13-1: Focusing on recent experiences is an effort to avoid the problem of being seen as too old.

When you really prefer to take life easier physically or to have more time to yourself, spell it out in your resume's objective. Writing this kind of statement is tricky. You risk coming across as worn-out goods, ready to relax and listen to babbling brooks while you collect a paycheck. When you explain your desire to back off an overly stressful workload, balance your words with a counterstatement reflecting your energy and commitment:

> *Energetic and work-focused but no longer enjoy frenzied managerial responsibility; seek a challenging nonmanagerial position.*

Too much experience in one job

A reader writes:

> *I've stayed in my current and only job too long. When my company cut thousands of workers, we received outplacement classes. I was told that job overstayers are perceived as lacking ambition, uninterested in learning new things, and too narrowly focused. What can I do about this?*

Here are several strategies for meeting this issue head-on.

Divide your job into modules

Show that you successfully moved up and up, meeting new challenges and accepting ever more responsibility. Divide your job into realistic segments, which you label as Level 1, Level 2, Level 3, and so on. Describe each level as a separate position, just as you would if the levels had been different positions within the same company or with different employers. If your job titles changed as you moved up, your writing task is a lot easier.

Deal honestly with job titles

If your job title never changed, should you just make up job titles? *No.* The only truthful way to inaugurate fictional job titles is to parenthetically introduce them as "equivalent to . . . ." Suppose that you're an accountant and have been in the same job for 25 years. Your segments might be titled like this:

- Level 3 (equivalent to supervising accountant)
- Level 2 (equivalent to senior accountant)
- Level 1 (equivalent to accountant)

To mitigate the lack of being knighted with increasingly senior job titles, fill your resume with references to your continuous salary increases and bonuses and the range of job skills you mastered.

Tackle deadly perceptions head-on

Diminish a perception that you became fat and lazy while staying in the same job too long by specifically describing clockless workdays: "Worked from 8 a.m. past 5 p.m. at least once a week throughout employment."

Derail a perception that you don't want to learn new things by being specific in describing learning adventures: "Attended six semesters of word-processing technologies; currently enrolled in adult education program to master latest software."

Discount a perception that you're too narrowly focused by explaining that although your employment address didn't change, professionally speaking, you're widely traveled in outside seminars, workshops, professional associations, and reading.

Highlight the issue

In a departure from the normal practice of omitting from your resumes reasons for leaving a job, consider indicating why you're making a change after all this time.

Neutralize the issue burning in every employer's mind: "Why now? Why after all these years are you on the market? Downsized out? Kicked out? Burned out?" If the question isn't asked, that doesn't mean it isn't hanging out in the employer's mind. Even though you may be seen as a moss-backed antique, present yourself as interested in current developments by adding this kind of phrase in your objective:

Focusing on companies and organizations with contemporary viewpoints

In an even more pioneering move to solve the same problem, create a whole new section at the tail of your resume headed "Bright Future," with a statement along the lines of this one:

Layoffs springing from a new management structure give me the welcomed opportunity to accept new challenges and freshen my work life.

Don't let too little experience kick you to the curb

When a job posting calls for a specific number of years of experience — say, three years' experience and you come up short with only two years' experience — but you know you can do the job, the basic technique is to work with what you've got. Dissect your two years' experience, and then add a statement in parentheses that says: (skills acquired equivalent to three years' experience). The expansion technique won't work every time, but it's worth the gamble.

Too Long Gone: For Women Only

The "on-ramping" woman still has an uphill climb. After taking a career break to care for her family, trying to re-enter the workforce — whether by choice or economic necessity — may make her feel as though she's been living on another planet. A reader writes:

> *Employers don't want to hire women if they've been mothers and out of the market for more than a year or two. Hey, ya know, for the last ten years, I've worked my tail off! Don't they understand that? Doesn't intelligence, willingness to work hard, creativity, attention to detail, drive, efficiency, grace under pressure, initiative, leadership, persistence, resourcefulness, responsibility, teamwork, and a sense of humor mean anything these days?*

Every characteristic that this reader mentions is still a hot ticket in the job market, but the burden is on Mom to interpret these virtues as marketable skills:

- Grace under pressure, for example, translates to *crisis manager,* a valuable person when the electricity fails in a computer-driven office.

- Resourcefulness translates to *office manager,* who is able to ward off crank calls from credit collection agencies.

- A sense of humor translates to *data communications manager,* who joshes a sleepy technical whiz into reporting for work at 2 a.m. for emergency repair of a busted satellite hovering over Europe.

You can't, of course, claim those job titles on your resume, but you can make equivalency statements: Like a crisis manager, I've had front-lines experience handling such problems as electrical failures, including computer crashes.

If you're a returning woman, use the tips in the following sections to develop a great resume that connects what you can do with what an employer wants done. Figure 13-2 gives you an example of how it might come together.

Sifting through your past

Identify transferable skills that you gained in volunteer, civic, hobby, and domestic work. Scout for adult and continuing education experiences, both on campus and in nontraditional settings.

Reexamine the informative Web sites you've used, the educational television programs that you've watched, and the news magazines that you've monitored. Go to the library and read business magazines and trade journals that require subscriptions, or read them online if the ones you want are available without subscription.

Reentry

JOY R. NGUYEN

12 Watt Road, Palmira, Florida 34567   (321) 654-9876

SUMMARY OF EXPERIENCE

More than five years' experience in event-planning, fundraising, administration and publicity. More than nine years' experience in administration for retail and manufacturing firms. B.A. in Business. Florida Teaching Certificate.

NONPROFIT/VOLUNTEER SERVICE

[dates]   **Palmira Optimists' Association, Palmira, Florida Membership Committee Chair**

Planning, organizing programs, exhibits and events to recruit association members. Coordinated annual new member events.

[dates]   **Okeefenokee County Y.M.C.A., Okeefenokee, Florida Member, Board of Directors and Executive Committee**

Spearheaded first Y.M.C.A. organization in county. Designed programs, procedures, and policies, monitoring trustees in the construction of $3 million facility. Led $2.5 million fundraising campaign.

> • **Fundraising Chair**, [dates] Raised funds for entire construction project, establishing hundreds of donors and supervising project. Sourced contractors and directed fundraising activities, using strong interpersonal and networking skills.

HOME MANAGEMENT EXPERIENCE

• **Scheduling:** Assisted business executive and two children in the scheduling of travel and 160,000 miles of transportation. Arranged ticketing, negotiated finances of $12,000 in travel expenses.
• **Conflict Resolution:** Arbitrated personal, business issues. Effective interpersonal skills.
• **Relocation:** Launched inter state relocation of entire family, coordinating moving services, trucks, and packing schedules.
• **Budget & Purchasing:** Managed family finances, including budgeting, medical, dental, insurance packages, two home purchases, three auto purchases, expenses, and taxes. Developed finance and math skills.

ADDITIONAL PROFESSIONAL EXPERIENCE

[dates]   **Sunrise Books, Cabana, Florida**
                   Assistant Manager, Sales Representative

Managed daily operations of coffee house and bookstore, directing staff of 35. Supervised entire floor of merchandise and stock. Purchased all sideline goods.

• Spearheaded store's first sales campaign, resulting in tripled sales.
• Designed system for inventory analysis, streamlining purchasing. and display control.
• Redirected staff duties for more effective work hours.
• Promoted from sales to supervisor in 38 days; three months later to asst. mgr.

EDUCATION

• **Bachelor of Science in Business,** [year], University of Miami, Miami, G.P.A.: 3.75
• **Florida Teaching Certificate,** Business and English, 2001, Florida State, Palmira

Figure 13-2: A sample resume showcasing the skills of a family caregiver re-entering the work place.

Using professional terms

In recounting civic and volunteer work, avoid the weak verbs: *worked with* or *did this or that.* Instead say *collaborated with* or *implemented.* The use of professional words can help de-emphasize informal training or work experience. Chapter 10 lists words to jog your memory.

Professionalizing your domestic experience is a tightrope walk: Ignoring it leaves you looking like a missing person, and yet you can't be pretentious or naive. *Housewife* dates you; *family caretaker* sounds more modern and better describes your role. Refer to *home management* to minimize gaps in time spent as a homemaker.

Fill the home-management period with crossover (transferable) skills relevant to the targeted position. Examples range from time management (developing the ability to do more with less time) to budgeting experience (developing a sophisticated understanding of priority allocation of financial resources). Other examples include using a cellphone in drumming up support for a favorite charity (developing confidence and a businesslike telephone technique) and leadership positions in the PTA (developing a sense of authority and the ability to guide others).

Selected home-based skills

Don't overlook skills that you may have acquired inside the home. Here are a few examples of occupations in which they can be used. This illustration assumes that you lack formal credentials for professional-level work. If you do have the credentials, upgrade the examples to the appropriate job level.

✔ **Juggling schedules:** Paraprofessional assistant to business executives or physicians, small service business operator, dispatching staff of technicians

✔ **Peer counseling:** Human resources department employee benefits assistant, substance abuse program manager

✔ **Arranging social events:** Party shop manager, nonprofit organization fundraiser, art gallery employee

✔ **Conflict resolution:** Administrative assistant, customer service representative, school secretary

✔ **Problem-solving:** Any job

✔ **Decorating:** Interior decorator, fabric shop salesperson

✔ **Nursing:** Medical or dental office assistant

✔ **Solid purchasing judgment:** Purchasing agent, merchandiser

✔ **Planning trips, relocations:** Travel agent, corporate employee relocation coordinator

✔ **Communicating:** Any job

✔ **Shaping budgets:** Office manager, department head, accounting clerk

✔ **Maximizing interior spaces:** Commercial-office real estate agent, business furniture store operator

Knowing the score

Omit all information that the employer isn't entitled to, including your age, marital status, physical condition, number and ages of children, and husband's name. Even though the law is on your side, why drag in facts on your resume that can stir up bias? Your resume's job is to open interview doors.

To help in your quest, seek out seminars, workshops and services offered to on-ramping women. Discover such Web sites as Ladies Who Launch (`www.ladieswholaunch.com`), which covers creating your own job.

Job Seekers with Disabilities

Millions of job seekers are protected by the *Americans with Disabilities Act* (ADA), which makes it illegal for an employer to refuse to hire (or to discriminate against) a person simply because that person has one or more disabilities.

ADA protection covers a wide spectrum of disabilities, including acquired immunodeficiency syndrome (AIDS) and human immunodeficiency virus (HIV), alcoholism, cancer, cerebral palsy, diabetes, emotional illness, epilepsy, hearing and speech disorders, heart disorders, learning disabilities (such as dyslexia), mental retardation, muscular dystrophy, and visual impairments. The Act does not cover conditions that impose short-term limitations, such as pregnancy or broken bones.

Generally, the ADA forbids employers that have more than 15 employees from doing the following:

✔ Discriminating on the basis of any physical or mental disability

✔ Asking job applicants questions about their past or current medical conditions

✔ Requiring applicants to take pre-employment medical exams

The ADA requires that an employer make reasonable accommodations for qualified individuals who have disabilities, unless doing so would cause the employer "undue hardship." The undue hardship provision is still open to interpretation by the courts.

If you have a disability that you believe is covered by the ADA, familiarize yourself with the law's specifics. The U.S. Department of Justice's ADA home page can be found at `www.ada.gov`. For even more information, call your member of Congress, visit your library, or obtain free comprehensive ADA guides and supporting materials from the splendid Web site maintained by the Job Accommodation Network (`http://askjan.org`).

Deciding whether to disclose a disability

Do not disclose your disability on your resume. Remember, your objective is to get an interview. Save disclosure until a better time, if at all. Here are a couple of guidelines for deciding when and whether to disclose a disability:

- ✔ If your disability is visible, the best time to disclose it is after the interview has been set and you telephone to confirm the arrangements. Pass the message in an offhanded manner: "Because I use a wheelchair for mobility, can you suggest which entrance to your building would be the most convenient?" Alternatively, you may want to reserve disclosure for the interview.

- ✔ If your disability is not visible, such as mental illness or epilepsy, you need not disclose it unless you'll need special accommodations. Even then, you can hold the disclosure until the negotiating stage after you've received a potential job offer.

No matter what you decide to do, be confident, unapologetic, unimpaired, and attitude-positive.

Explaining gaps in work history

What can you do about gaps in your work history caused by disability? In years past, you may have been able to obscure the issue. No longer. New computer databases make it easy for suspicious employers to research your medical history. And with health insurance costs so high, they may do exactly that.

If your illness-related job history has so many gaps that it looks like a hockey player's teeth, I've never heard a better suggestion than writing "Illness and Recovery" next to the dates. It's honest, and the "recovery" part says, "I'm back and ready to work!"

If you have too many episodes of "missing teeth," your work history will look less shaky in a functional or hybrid format, which I discuss in Chapter 9. Online resume discussion groups, which you can find through the Job Accommodation Network (http://askjan.org), can serve as further sources of guidance on this difficult issue.

Asking for special equipment

If you need adaptive equipment, such as a special kind of telephone, I wouldn't mention it — even if the equipment is inexpensive or you're willing to buy it yourself. Instead, stick with the "time-release capsule" method of sharing information: Dribble out revelations that may stifle interest in hiring you only when necessary. Never lose sight of your objective: to get an interview.

When Demotion Strikes

Kevin Allen (not his real name) was the district manager of five stores in a chain when he was demoted to manager of a single store. The higher-ups were sending him a message — they hoped he'd quit so that they could avoid awarding a severance package of benefits. Kevin ignored the message, retained a lawyer, kept his job, and started a job hunt after work hours.

He finessed his resume by listing all the positions he had held in the chain, leaving out dates when each started and stopped:

> **Demoting Store Chain, Big City**
>
> District Manager, 5 stores
>
> Store Manager, Windy City
>
> Store Assistant Manager, Sunny City
>
> Store Clerk, Sunny City

Throwing all of Kevin's titles into one big pot seemed a clever idea, but it didn't work for him. After a year of searching, Kevin got interviews, yes, but at every single face-to-face meeting, he was nailed with the same question: "Why were you demoted?" The interviewers' attitudes seemed accusatory, as if they'd been misled. Kevin failed to answer the question satisfactorily and didn't receive a single offer during a year's search. How did all the potential employers find out the truth?

Among obvious explanations: (A) Kevin worked in a "village" industry where people know each other and gossip. (B) Employers ordered credit checks on him; credit checks may show employment details. (C) Employers authorized in-depth background checks.

No one knows what really happened, but in hindsight, Kevin may have done better had he accepted the message that the chain wanted him out, negotiated a favorable severance package that included good references, and quit immediately while his true title was that of district manager.

After two humiliating years of demotion status, Kevin took action by "crossing the Rubicon," an ancient Roman phrase that universities have adapted. It refers to those who seek a new beginning by returning to college for a law or business degree. Kevin enrolled in law school to make his happy ending.

In cases like Kevin's, a strategy that's forthright but doesn't flash your demotion in neon lights may work better than trying to cover up the demotion. Combine only two titles together, followed quickly by your accomplishments and strengths, as you see in Figure 13-3.

[dates] Demoting Company Name
Assistant Manager, Manager

As assistant manager, support the manager and carefully monitor detailed transactions with vendors, insuring maintenance of products and inventory; use skills in invoicing, billing, ordering, and purchasing. As manager, supervise all aspects of purchasing, display, and merchandise sales. Trained team of more than 30 employees in two-week period. Trained three assistant managers in essential functions of customers, employees, and finance. Increased sales revenues 25 percent in first six months.

Figure 13-3: Sample of combining a demotion with a higher position.

No matter how well you handle your resume entry, the reference of the demoting employer may ultimately end your chances of landing a new job that you want. In trying to mend fences, you may appeal to the demoting employer's fairness or go for guilt. Point out how hard you worked and how loyal you've been. Find reasons why your performance record was flawed. Ask for the commitment of a favorable reference and a downplaying of the demotion. If fairness or guilt appeals are denied, see an employment lawyer about sending the demoting employer, on law-firm letterhead, a warning against libel or slander.

The basic way to handle demotions throughout the job-hunting process is akin to how you handle being fired: by accentuating the positive contributions and results for which you are responsible. But being demoted is trickier to handle than being fired. Being let go no longer automatically suggests personal failure — but being demoted does.

Gaps in Your Record

Periods of unemployment leave hiccups in your work history. Should you (A) fill them with positive expressions such as *family obligations*, (B) fill them with less positive but true words such as *unemployed*, or (C) show the gap without comment?

Choosing B, *unemployed*, is dreary. Forget that! Choosing C, *leave-it-blank-and-say-nothing*, often works — you just hope that it isn't noticed. My choice, however, is A: Tell the truth about what you were doing but sugarcoat it in a dignified, positive way. A few examples: *independent study, foreign travel, career renewal through study and assessment.*

An info-blizzard of tips has been published on how to repair resume interruptions. Unless you were building an underground tunnel to smuggle drugs, the principles are simple:

- Present the time gap as a positive event.

- Detail why it made you a better worker — not a better *person*, but a better worker with more favorable characteristics, polished skills, and mature understanding, all of which you're dying to contribute to your new employer.

How can these principles be applied? Take the case of a student who dropped out of college to play in a band and do odd jobs for four years before coming back to finish his biology degree and look for a job. The student knows that employers may perceive him as uncommitted. In the resume, he should treat the band years like any other job: Describe the skills that were polished as a band leader. Identify instances of problem-solving, teamwork, leadership, and budgeting.

Do the real problem-solving in the cover letter that accompanies such a resume. You might say something like this:

> *After completing two years of undergraduate study, it was necessary for me to work to continue my education. Using my talents as a musician, I organized a band and after four years was able to continue my education. I matured and learned much about the real world and confirmed that an education is extremely important in fulfilling my career goals.*

The chief mistake people make is assuming that a positive explanation won't sell. Instead, they fudge dates from legitimate jobs to cover the gaps. You may get away with it in the beginning. But ultimately, you'll be asked to sign a formal application — a legal document. When a company wants to chop staff without paying severance benefits, the first thing that happens is an intense investigation of the company's database of application forms. People who lied on their applications can be sent out into the mean streets with nothing but their current paychecks on their backs.

Lying isn't worth the risk — it's a mistake.

Another method of papering-over glaring gaps is to include all your work under "Work History" and cite unpaid and volunteer work as well as paid jobs.

The consultant/entrepreneur gap

Professional and managerial job seekers are routinely advised to explain gaps by saying that they were consultants or that they owned small businesses. Not everyone can be a consultant, and there's substantial risk in the small-business explanation.

If it should happen to be true that you were a consultant, name your clients and give a glimmer of the contributions you made to each. If you really had a small business, remember: Employers worry that you'll be too independent to do things their way or that you'll stay just long enough to learn their business and go into competition against them.

Strategic antidotes: Search for a business owner who is within eyeshot of retirement and wouldn't mind your continuing the business and paying him or her a monthly pension.

Resume antidotes: Describe yourself as "manager," not "CEO" or "president," and if you have time, rename your business something other than your own name: "River's End Associates, Inc.," not "Theresa K. Bronz, Inc."

Suppose that you've been unemployed for the past year. That's a new timing problem to overcome. Even in a job-starved economy, some employers may wonder why you're still jobless if you're such a good worker. Some advisers suggest the old dodge of allowing the recruiter to misperceive the open-ended date of employment for your last job: "2008–" as though you meant "2008–Present." The open-ender solution often works — until you run into a recruiter who thinks that it's way too calculating.

Work history breaks are less obvious in a functional or hybrid format, which I discuss in Chapter 9. In the final analysis, if you can't find a positive explanation for a gap, say nothing.

If you possess a not-so-pristine past, stick with small employers who probably won't check every date on your resume.

Too Many Layoffs That Aren't Your Fault

Hard to believe, but good workers sometimes experience one layoff after another. One of my readers writes that he'd experienced four no-fault severances within seven years.

When you've been to the chopping block a few too many times, explain the circumstances after each listing of the company name:

Carol Interiors (company closed doors) . . . Salamander Furnishings (multirounds of downsizings) . . . Brandon Fine Furniture (company relocated out of town) . . . Kelly Fixture Co. (plant sold and moved overseas).

Offering brief explanations takes the blame from your shoulders — but I suppose that a cynic might think that you're a jinx.

Explaining Mergers and Acquisitions

A reader writes:

> *Upon graduating from college, I went to work for Company A. Several years later, Company A was acquired by Company B. More years passed, and Company B was acquired by Company C. Eventually, Company C merged with Company D, and as a result, after ten years with the four companies, I was laid off.*
>
> *My question is how best to handle this work history on my resume? I worked for four different corporate entities, with four different names, without ever changing jobs. Do I list all four on my resume? Or just the last one?*

Always try to show an upward track record — that you acquired new knowledge and skills, and just didn't just do the same thing over and over each year. And, you don't want the reader to assume that you worked for only one company that laid you off after a decade.

Taking these two factors into consideration, can you show correlation between your job titles and responsibilities with the changes in ownership? If yes, identify all four owners:

> *Job title, Company D (formerly Company C), years*
>
> *Job title, Company C (formerly Company B), years*
>
> *Job title, Company B (formerly Company A), years*
>
> *Job title, Company A, years*

If you can't show an upward track record that correlates with changes in ownership, just use the current owner name with a short explanation:

> *Job title, Company D, years*
> *(Through a series of mergers and acquisitions, the entities for which I have worked since college graduation were known as Company A, Company B, and Company C.)*

The reason for naming every entity is perception. Background and credit checks will turn up those company names, and if your resume doesn't mention them, it sends up a red flag for your potential employer!

Here a Job, There a Job, Everywhere a Job, Job

I once interviewed a man who had held 185 jobs over the course of his 20-year career, encompassing everything from dishwasher to circus clown and from truck driver to nursing aide. He wrote to me, not requesting resume advice, but to complain that a potential employer had the nerve to call him a *job hopper!*

Talk about an antiquated term: In the 21st century, the notion of job hopping is as far out of a reality circle as the concepts of job security, company loyalty, and a guaranteed company pension. The Great American Dumping Machine will continue to sack people who sometimes have to take virtually any job they can to survive.

Adding insult to injury, some employers cling to a double standard — hiring and firing employees like commodities, then looking with disfavor on applicants who have had a glut of jobs by circumstance, not by choice.

Overcoming a job-hopping image

Even when it wasn't at your initiative, holding five or more jobs in ten years can brand you as a job hopper. The fact that you're out of work now underscores that impression. Even employers who are guilty of round after round of employee dismissals instinctively flinch at candidates they perceive to be hopping around.

Take pains to reverse that disapproval. When you draft your resume, post a list of negative perceptions on your desk; when you're finished writing, compare your resume with the list. Offer information that changes negative perceptions of you as a job hopper. The following list identifies perceptions employers often have of a job hopper and ways to counter them.

Perception	*Counter*
Is disloyal and self-focused	Perfect attendance, volunteer office gift collector
Will split in a blink for a better offer and take company secrets along	Competition of projects
Doesn't know what he/she wants and is never satisfied	Diverse background that promoted impressive results

After checking for damage control, go back and review your resume for accomplishments that enhance your image, such as the following:

> ✔ **A fast learner:** Give examples of how your skills aren't company-specific and you rapidly adjust to new environments.

✔ **A high achiever:** Show favored skills much courted by headhunters, and at end of each job mention, put "Recruited for advanced position."

✔ **A quick adapter:** Mention examples of agreeable flexibility in adjusting to new ideas, technology, and position requirements.

✔ **A relationship builder:** List praise from co-workers for commitment to team success.

✔ **A determined worker:** Briefly mention your commitment to meeting standards of superior workplace performance despite the tough job market of recent years. Use terms such as "positive attitude" and "cheerful perspective."

Omit interview-killer data

The best way to handle some land mines on your resume is to ignore them. Generally, revealing negative information on a resume is a mistake. Save troublemaking information for the all-important job interview, where you have a fighting chance to explain your side of things.

Stay away from these topics when constructing a resume:

✔ Firings, demotions, forced resignations, and early termination of contracts

✔ Personal differences with co-workers or supervisors

✔ Bankruptcy, tax evasion, or credit problems

✔ Criminal convictions or lawsuits

✔ Homelessness

✔ Illnesses from which you have now recovered

✔ Disabilities that do not prevent you from performing the essential functions of the job, with or without some form of accommodation

Should you ever give reasons for leaving a job? Almost never. In most instances, resume silence in the face of interview-killing facts is still the strategy of choice. But the time has come to rethink at least one special issue: losing a job.

Now that jobs are shed like so many autumn leaves, losing a job is no longer viewed as a case of personal failure. It may be to your advantage to state on your resume why you left your last position, assuming that it was not because of poor work performance on your part. If you were downsized out, the recruiter may appreciate your straightforward statement, "Job eliminated in downsizing."

A related circumstance is when it may appear that you were fired (job tanked quickly, for instance) but you really were not fired, or the employer agreed to say you were laid off; it is acceptable to add "Layoff" after the date of employment — *3/2008 to 5/23/2009 (Layoff)*.

But remember, if you elect to say why you lost one job, for consistency, you have to say why you left all your jobs — such as for greater opportunity or advancement.

When your current joblessness comes after a background that a quick-change artist would admire, use your resume to prepare the way to acceptance. Emphasize project completion and career progression, using years not months. If you still have trouble landing interviews, include more positive statements in your cover letter to tackle your history. For ideas, read my book, *Cover Letters For Dummies,* 3rd Edition (Wiley).

Cleaning out your job closet

The harsh realities of business may force you to detour from a single career path to alternative tracks where you can acquire new skills and experiences, even if they're not skills and experiences of choice. If so, you need serious creative (but truthful) writing to keep your resume focused on the work history that is relevant for the next job sought.

Use these workarounds when you find that you have too many jobs in your history:

- ✔ Start by referring to your *diversified* or *skills-building* background.

- ✔ Use a functional or hybrid resume format (see Chapter 9) and present *only your experience relevant to the job you seek.*

- ✔ Alternatively, you can list jobs relating to the position you now seek first under "Relevant Work Experience" and cluster the nonrelevant jobs under "Other Work Experience."

- ✔ Express your work history in years, not months and years.

When Substance Abuse Is the Problem

Substance abuse is a disability under the Americans with Disabilities Act. If you're recovered from the addiction, you're entitled to all the Act's protections. If you're still abusing a substance, such as alcohol or illegal narcotics, you're not covered by the Act. Don't disclose previous substance abuse on your resume.

Cover gaps in your work history with the *Illness and Recovery* statement (see the "Job Seekers with Disabilities" section earlier in this chapter) or simply don't address the issue at all.

Be careful when deciding which information you put on a job application — remember that it's a legal form and that lies can come back to haunt you (see the "Gaps in Your Record" section earlier in this chapter).

If you were ever arrested for smoking pot or being intoxicated — even once in your life — the fact may surface to damage your employment chances. Asking about arrest records is illegal, but a few private database companies don't let that stop them — they compile electronic databases of such arrest information and sell them to any employer who will buy.

Avoid mentioning booze or drugs, be careful about application forms, and be honest at interviews — *if* you have recovered or *if* the experience was a brief fling or two.

If you're still held prisoner by a chronic, destructive, or debilitating overuse of a chemical substance that interferes with your life or employment, no resume tweaks will benefit you. Get help for your addiction.

A Bad Credit Rap

Job seekers who won't be handling money are surprised that employers may routinely check credit records. Credit histories — called *consumer reports* — hold much more than payment history. A consumer report contains data from names of previous employers and residential stability to divorces and estimated prior earnings.

Employers are wary of hiring people awash in debt because they fear that stress will impact job performance or that you have inadequate management skills or even that you may have sticky fingers with the company's funds.

Consumer reports have serious implications for students who graduate with sky-high education loans and credit card balances, especially if they or their families have missed payments. Divorced individuals may have interview-killing credit problems caused by the split-up and never know why their resumes aren't delivering interviews.

Among consumer protections against unfair credit treatment is the requirement that employers must get your permission in a stand-alone document to check your credit (Fair Credit Reporting Act) — no blending the request into fine print in the employment application.

After an employer receives a report on you — but before any adverse action is taken, such as rejecting your application for a job — the employer must give you a free copy of the report with related legal documents. Receiving a copy of the documents gives you a chance to correct mistakes and clean up your credit record if you can.

Background checks are even more invasive than credit reports. They include records for driving infractions, court and incarceration histories, workers' compensation, medical histories, drug testing, and more. For details, visit

The Privacy Rights Clearinghouse (`privacyrights.org` — search on Background Checks).

Ex-Offenders Job Hunting

Each year millions of offenders leave state and local prisons for the free world or circulate in and out of American jails and detention centers at the city and county levels. If you're one of these people, this book can help you — especially when it comes to meeting today's need to customize and send out your digital resume — but you need specialized help of the type that I describe at the end of this section.

Negative info kills your chances

Never forget that the purpose of your resume is to get a job interview. Period. Your resume is not the place to confess your sins, accentuate your weaknesses, or lie about yourself. Make sure your resume is future-oriented and employer-centered. Use your resume to clearly communicate to employers what it is that you can do for them. Issues concerning your criminal record are best dealt with during the job interview.

Avoid the chronological format

The reverse chronological format (Chapter 9) is not your friend. This format, with its emphasis on employers and dates, tends to point up the two major weaknesses of ex-offenders — limited work experience and major employment time gaps. Instead, choose a functional or hybrid combination format (Chapter 9) that emphasizes your qualifications as they relate to the job you seek — skills, competencies, and personal qualities.

Present prison experience in nonprison terms

If you acquired education, training, and work experience in prison, be careful how you list that experience on your resume. Instead of saying that you worked at "Kentucky State Prison," say you worked for the "State of Kentucky."

Both statements are truthful, but the first statement immediately raises a red flag that can prematurely screen you out before you get an interview.

Get help with job search moves

Unless you have strong analytical and writing skills, read specialized books and reach out for help from a local nonprofit group that functions to assist ex-offenders in writing resumes and finding jobs. Here are some resources:

- ✔ Find the best specialized books at www.exoffenderreentry.com.
- ✔ Discover re-entry resources in all 50 states at the National Hire Network (www.hirenetwork.org).
- ✔ Consider hiring a professional resume writer; see Chapter 20.

Look for Ways to Scoot Past Resume Blocks

You can't always move directly from start to finish of a successful job search with a single resume strategy. While suggesting solutions to difficult resume situations, I may not have addressed your specific concern. If not, use the illustrations here to inspire a creative solution to your difficulty that doesn't rely on telling lies. (Lies are time bombs!)

Need encouragement? Michael Jordan, widely considered to be the greatest player in the history of basketball, has a few words to say about the very kinds of obstacles you may face in creating a great resume on your way to a job interview:

> *Obstacles don't have to stop you. If you run into a wall, don't turn around and give up. Figure out how to climb it, go through it, or work around it.*

Part IV
Bringing It All Together: Sample Resumes

The 5th Wave — By Rich Tennant

"Well, I think we can do better than that. Let's think about it. You not only 'ring the bells,' but you 'jump on the bells,' you 'kick the bells,' you 'scream on the bells' ..."

In this part . . .

Nearly 50 sample resumes show you how to bring your most employable assets to the fore. You see samples of resumes by industry and experience level, and you find ways to work with special circumstances like a return to the workforce or career change. You also get to gander resume makeovers that I hope give you a soaring sense of what's possible for your own resume.

Chapter 14

A Sampling of OnTarget Resumes by Industry and Career Field

· ·

*N*o skeletons in your work history? No problems? If you're as perfect as they come, this is your kind of chapter. The sample resumes here reflect the job market by type of expertise and work skills being recruited or offered.

A text box atop each sample resume in this chapter contains a mission statement — that is, what the job seeker aims to accomplish, which usually is a better job. The mission statement also includes the requirements for a specific position — or a summary of the typically requested requirements for an occupation or career field.

Within the mission statement, each of the job's requirements has a number next to it. The same number also appears in the body of the resume next to the job seeker's matching qualification for that requirement.

The cross-matched numbers between a job's requirements and the candidate's qualifications shown here are for just for illustration, *not for your actual resumes.*

These samples are intended to laser your attention to requirement-and-qualification matching, the single most important factor in causing your candidacy to get noticed in an online swarm of resumes.

Sales. Sales Representative. Reverse chronological. College grad seeks Manufacturer's Representative position in home theater/electronics equipment industry. Requirements: Bachelor's Degree,[1] 3-5 years in consultative sales,[2] relationship development skills,[3] product knowledge,[4] and experience in sales management.[5]

CHARLES A. TRENTON   Cell: (555) 999-9999 • Email: catrenton@gmail.com • Detroit, MI

OBJECTIVE: SALES CONSULTANT – HOME THEATER/ELECTRONICS

SYSTEM EXPERTISE

Audio Formats[4]– Dolby Digital, Dolby Pro Logic II, and DTS; encoding surround sound.

Media Formats[4]– Introduce home theater systems with integrated video and audio sources such as HD (720p, 1080i, 1080p) and Standard (480p) video, DVD-Jukebox (Fireball) systems, Hard-Drive based (Kaleidoscope) systems and AV distribution including Cable, Satellite, WiFi, Bluetooth and Cat5e (Control-4, Elan).

Speaker Recommendations[4]– Satellite, center channel and subwoofers to achieve optimum sound. Advise on room placement to achieve maximum sound experience.

Sound Engineering License – Omega Studio, Detroit, Mich. [date]

SALES EXPERIENCE

Supreme Home Theater and Audio, Detroit, Mich.

SENIOR AUDIO VIDEO CONSULTANT – SYSTEM DESIGNER   [dates][2]

- Identify and analyze customer's home theater project interests and budget, understanding and anticipating needs and wants and recommending appropriate products and systems.[3] Discover unrealized music, home theater, and projection interests to grow sale.
- Build customer relationships based on trust;[3] personally manage sale and installation coordination.
- Develop innovative approaches to sales, such as demonstration CDs, to feature audio and visual equipment, resulting in increased enthusiasm and commitment to total quality system.
- Prepare and present sales proposals to decision makers and negotiate purchase agreement.

SYSTEM DESIGNER   [dates]

- Member, architect/interior design team, planning total installation of new and renovated homes.
- Conducted site inspections, including planning wiring, special construction and cabinetry.
- Designed whole-house audio and video networking solutions and home automation, including lighting, security, CCTV and HVAC control.
- Developed relationships with architects, general contractors, builders and interior designers.

SALES MANAGER, AUDIO VIDEO CONSULTANT – SYSTEM DESIGNER   [dates]

- Drove strategic business initiatives and managed daily operations.[5] Set standards and trained staff on customer assessments, product knowledge and introduction, sales techniques, relationship development and demo presentations.
- Motivated and mentored sales team on current technology and advanced applications.

Sales Accomplishments: Beat quota by 5-25% annually, increasing gross sales totals by $100,000+ per year for year-on-year growth. Top seller for [year] and [year]; Number 2 for [year].

Piano Town, Chicago, Ill.   [dates]
SALES CONSULTANT – RETAIL SALES. Achieved 105-135% of sales quota in keyboard department.

EDUCATION: B.A.,[1] Psychology, Wayne State University, Detroit, Mich., [date]

Healthcare. Medical Technologist. Reverse chronological. Medical Technologist I seeks level II position. Requirements: Bachelor's degree in Medical Technology, Biology, or Clinical Laboratory Sciences,[1] 2-4 years' experience in clinical laboratory setting,[2] and excellent computer, verbal and written communication skills.[3]

CELESTE PEREZ

9084 Robinson Road • San Francisco, CA 94107
Cellular: 777-222-5757 • Email: celesteperez@yahoo.com

PROFILE: Dedicated **Medical Technologist** with over 3 years' experience.[2] Skilled in clinical laboratory methodology and activities, including performing complex analyses using sophisticated instruments and good judgement. Strong computer proficiencies, with excellent communication skills.[3] Customer service focused, with polished interpersonal skills. Organized and detail-oriented; reliable and able to take the initiative. Energetic and hardworking; able to work well under pressure.

~ **B.S.,**[1] Medical Technology, San Francisco State University, San Francisco, Calif. [date] ~

Completed six-week rotation, performing all aspects of analytical testing within clinical laboratory sections, including Blood Bank, Hematology, Microbiology, and Chemistry.

PROFESSIONAL EXPERIENCE

Medical Technologist I
LabCenter, San Francisco, Calif.   [dates]

- Specimen Testing: Perform complex qualitative and quantitative immunochemistry analyses and testing; prepare detailed reports summarizing findings. Anticipate and plan work to complete assigned tasks in allotted time. Ensure compliance with company policies, as well as federal, state, and local regulations. (Also possess 2 years' experience conducting virology assays.)

- Quality Control/Troubleshooting: Perform and document all instrument checks and quality control tests. Conduct daily preventative maintenance and troubleshooting; recognize, analyze, and take corrective action to resolve instrument and clinical testing problems. Contact manufacturers' technical service departments to troubleshoot and correct equipment problems, as needed. Assist co-workers in resolving similar problems.

- Administration: Perform clerical functions associated with designated laboratory area. Review reports for clerical accuracy and clinical indications, help maintain files, and accurately input results into computer database. Track inventory and reagent use; request supplies from supervisor on weekly basis.

- Training: Attend and participate in regular department staff meetings and volunteer for cross-training. Train other laboratory personnel and students within designated area.

Accomplishments:

- Consistently receive highest rating on quarterly and annual reviews. Contributed to achievement of annual laboratory goals and objectives; awarded bonus.

- Volunteered to attend week-long new equipment training; upon return, trained select group of employees on new procedures and machinery.

- Routinely volunteer to work hard-to-cover shifts.

Project Management. Construction Project Manager. Reverse chronological. Seeks position with commercial building firm. Requirements: 5-7 years' construction experience,[1] B.S. degree in Construction Sciences or Engineering,[2] stable employment background[3] and proficiency in estimating and project management software.[4]

CASEY DAVIS

5050 Bellevue Circle   (888) 444-5656
Orlando, FL 32801   e-mail: davis_c@earthlink.net

CONSTRUCTION PROJECT MANAGER

- Project Scheduling
- Value Engineering
- Regulatory Compliance

- Historic Building Renovation
- Planning and Budgeting
- Contract Negotiation

OBJECTIVE: Project Manager – Commercial

SUMMARY OF QUALIFICATIONS

Over 7 years of success in managing multi-million dollar building construction and renovation projects from inception through occupancy.[1] Recent experience includes restorations and renovations of historic and public buildings, as well as new construction. Skilled in managing multiple projects simultaneously. Adept at working with engineers, architects, subcontractors, and field superintendents to coordinate activities and solve problems. Skilled in developing spreadsheet cost estimates, budgets, and project schedules using Master Builder, Primavera P3, MS Project, and MS Excel.[4] Supervisory experience includes functional supervision of subcontractors, field superintendents, and diverse workforce. Stable, upward job record.[3]

WORK EXPERIENCE

Construction Project Manager
Bauer Craig Becker Edwards, Inc., Tallahassee, Fl.   [dates]

Manage multi-million dollar building construction and renovation projects from inception through occupancy. Direct projects and ensure on-schedule completion within or below budget to meet contractual obligations.

- Define scope of work and review and interpret design specifications, and plans. Organize, plan, and conduct meetings with engineers, architects, and owners using tact and diplomacy.
- Forecast project costs and budget. Establish man-hour production rates, and crew requirements. Perform quantity take-off and material pricing.
- Solicit/review subcontractor proposals and ongoing project change orders with company executives and execute contractual agreements.
- Prepare job schedule for each phase of construction, order, and schedule material deliveries.
- Inspect workmanship for adherence to design specifications and quality standards. Ensure compliance with federal and state health and safety laws and regulations (OSHA), recognition/mitigation of HAZMAT, and company safety policies.
- Perform monthly project billing and final project closeout.

Recent Accomplishments:
- Tallahassee Community College Nursing School, $15M, 24-month project
- Leon County Public Parking Garage #5, $5M, 6-month project
- Florida State House of Delegates, $10M, 12-month project
- Florida State Central Services Facility, $12M, 18-month project

Facilities Construction Contract Compliance Inspector

Larmore County Government, Growth and Environmental Management, Tallahassee, Fl.   [dates]

With minimal direct supervision, monitored various facility contracts and vendors to ensure delivery of services and completion of tasks. Worked on a team to complete construction projects effectively.
- Evaluated scope and duration of work requests to produce legal agreements/permits. Reviewed blueprints to answer technical questions and produce takeoffs.
- Identified, researched, and resolved complex problems, and recommended and implemented solutions. Answered questions regarding bids, proposals, and contracts.
- Communicated effectively with the public, County Attorney, Structural Engineers, and other professional staff. Conducted pre-bid conferences; reviewed certificates of insurance and performance bonds. Inspected sites for completion of work and authorized release of bond documents.

Housing Inspector

Larmore County Government, Growth and Environmental Management, Tallahassee, Fl.   [dates]

Inspected privately-owned single and multi-family properties for HUD compliance.
- Determined fair market values. Estimated property damages in preparation for claims.
- Used effective interpersonal communications to defuse tense landlord/tenant situations.

Tradesworker II

Larmore County Government, Growth and Environmental Management, Tallahassee, Fl.   [dates]

Coordinated and instructed trades helpers on how and why of specific assignments.
- Estimated labor, equipment, and materials needed to accomplish structural renovations/repairs.
- Constructed, altered, and repaired structures where accuracy, space, and fit were essential, and structural soundness and appearance were meaningful.
- Read, interpreted, and applied complex building plans, specifications, blueprints, sketches, and building codes.

EDUCATION

B.S.,[2] Construction Engineering Technology, Florida A & M University, Tallahassee, Fl.   [date]

PROFESSIONAL TRAINING

Scaffold Training Institute, Scaffold User certification   [date]
Construction Specification Institute; Documents Technology certificate   [date]
American Management Association; Facilities Management certificate   [date]

Nursing. <u>Nurse R.N.</u> Reverse chronological. Healthcare professional seeks advancement. Requirements: current appropriate R.N. licensure,[1] graduate of accredited School of Nursing,[2] minimum of one-year medical-surgical nursing and hemodialysis experience,[3] ability to assist in lifting patients and equipment,[4] and ability to provide coverage at area facilities during times of short staffing.[5]

SOPHIE McCALL, R.N. [1]

St. Paul, MN • Cell: 333-444-1010 • Email: nursesophie@hotmail.com

PROFILE: Dedicated **Nurse R.N.** [1] with over 11 years' medical experience providing superior clinical care to broad-based patient populations. Skilled leader and team-member, able to maintain positive attitude and productive work environment.[5] Strong interpersonal, administrative and patient/family education skills. Demonstrated ability to establish trust, emote genuine patient caring, and manage crisis situations. Highly organized and able to efficiently prioritize multiple tasks. Able to lift 60 lbs.[4]

PROFESSIONAL EXPERIENCE

Charge Nurse/Clinical Nurse

Med-Surg/Renal Unit,[3] Medical Care North America, St. Paul, Minn.   [dates]

- Provide specialized care for renal patients on 32-bed unit on human dialysis floor. Rotate as charge nurse, overseeing staff members (LPNs, NAs, Nurse Extenders, and Unit Secretaries) and participating in team/unit meetings.
- Conduct patient assessments, and develop, implement, and evaluate individualized care plans. Provide appropriate care and achieve patient outcomes by combining patient involvement and education into total care plan. Adjust treatment plan as needed.
- Perform technical aspects of hemodialysis,[3] assessing and documenting response to therapy. Administer medications, monitor patient progress, develop discharge plans, provide health and nutrition education, and maintain charts and documentation.
- Key team member of unit study project to assess quality of patient care. Analyzed 12 months of patient records to review care, treatment plan, and outcome. Drafted revised policies to improve care and ensure best practices.

Staff Nurse/Charge Nurse

Medical Specialty Unit, Oakdale Rehabilitation Center, Oakdale, Minn.   [dates]

- On 28-bed subacute care unit, rotated as charge nurse. Scheduled and supervised staff.
- Provided primary nursing care and educated patients and family. Assessed patients; developed and implemented treatment plans. Performed variety of procedures and treatments including paritometrial dialysis, ventilator care, central lines and IV therapy.
- Administered medications and monitored patient response. Maintained charts and worked with other healthcare professionals to provide total quality care.

Charge Nurse

Valley Creek Convalescent Center, Woodbury, Minn.   [dates]

- Oversaw all phases of night shift clinical care on 46-bed specialized care unit. Scheduled and supervised LPNs and Nursing Assistants.

EDUCATION

B.S.,[2] Nursing, College of St. Catherine, School of Nursing, St. Paul, Minn.   [dates]

Accounting. <u>Civilian Pay Technician</u>. Reverse chronological. Candidate seeks more challenging accounting work. Requirements: 5+ years of accounting experience,[1] 1-2 years of business school or accounting training,[2] proficiency in Excel, Word, Outlook and PowerPoint,[3] strong analytical skills and attention to detail,[4] and verbal and written communication skills.[5]

SHANNON BRODY

Dayton, OH • (777) 683-5614 • shannonb@brody.net

OBJECTIVE: Staff Accountant

SKILLS SUMMARY: Customer-focused accounting professional with over 10 years of experience maintaining employee payroll accounts and managing billing and accounts receivables.[1] Effective troubleshooter and researcher with exceptional verbal and written communication skills.[5] Detail-oriented

with strong analytical skills [4] and ability to produce quality work under strict deadlines. Associate of Science, Accounting [2] The Ohio University, Athens, Ohio, [date].

COMPUTER SKILLS: SAP Business One, Exact Finances, and several other accounting and reporting systems. MS Word, Excel, Outlook, PowerPoint; [3] Remedy Problem Management Software.

PROFESSIONAL EXPERIENCE

Defense Finance Accounting Agency (DFAS), Dayton, Ohio   [dates]

Civilian Pay Technician   [dates]
- Managed payroll accounts under Defense Civilian Pay System for 200 employees; verified employee timesheet information was correctly entered on-time for bi-weekly payroll. Assured pay stubs and yearly tax information. Updated records and tax information.
- Determined validity of timekeeping debts and prepared letters to notify employees of indebtedness and mandatory involuntary deduction based on debt regulations. Complied and evaluated reports for data accuracy and made necessary adjustments.
- Responded to questions and provided payroll information to state taxing authorities, attorneys, family courts, employees and human resources staff. Assigned to call center for two years; effectively responded to numerous inbound customer service requests.

Accounting Technician   [dates]
- Received, sorted, processed and coded accounting documents, including invoices and checks. Prepared vouchers, invoices, checks, account statements, and reports for accounts receivable and payable. Produced batch control worksheets, processed voucher copies according to appropriation, and maintained monthly reports. Prepared financial statements, journal entries, month-end close, and collection vouchers.
- Matched hard copy accounting documents to automated system transmittals; identified and corrected erroneous transactions. Researched and reconciled incomplete accounting data and requested additional supporting documentation when needed; filed completed cases.
- Monitored budget activity, utilizing Merged Accountability Funds Reporting (MAFR) system and Excel spreadsheets to input and track billing information.

Supply Chain. Production/Logistics Manager. Reverse chronological. Seeking Supply Chain Manager Position. Requirements: 7-10 years' experience in Supply Chain Management: Distribution, Logistics, Transportation.[1] Previous experience in multi-site industrial or consumer products manufacturing,[2] solid track record of cost reduction and productivity improvement,[3] project management experience,[4] excellent leadership and communication and negotiating skills.[5] Degree required, MBA and/or Six Sigma Black Belt preferred.[6]

PAUL A. BUTLER

408 Grendel Road • Nashville, TN 37013
Residence: 111-777-1010 • Email: pabutler@verizon.net

SUPPLY CHAIN MANAGER

Distribution ~ Production Planning ~ Logistics Manager

PROFILE: Over 9 years' supervisory and managerial experience in **operations, warehouse, supply chain management** and **distribution** environments.[1] Proven track record of managing and improving operations and logistics for multi-million dollar entities, applying strong analytical skills and innovative and successful problem resolution expertise. Experienced in contract management and negotiations [5] and building vendor relationships. Outstanding budget management skills. Results-oriented leader with excellent communication and motivational skills.[5] Able to develop staff and build productive teams. Certified PMP;[4] Six Sigma Black Belt.[6] **B.S.,**[6] Business Administration, University of Tennessee, [date].

PRODUCTION & DISTRIBUTION EXPERIENCE

VITAMIN PRODUCTS, INC.   [dates]

Manage and coordinate complete production and delivery cycle for medical foods company,[2] *producing up to 10,000 cases of liquid and 500,000 units dry per cycle.*

Manager, Production & Logistics   Brentwood, Tenn. [dates]

- Production Planning: Track and analyze raw materials and finished goods inventory at third-party production facility and at local distribution warehouse. Coordinate production cycles. Assess vendors' proposals best value. Procure raw components from vendors.
- Vendor/Production Oversight: Assure vendors meet Good Manufacturing Practices. Conduct post-production review of product to ensure quality, as well as analyze production losses and causes. Assure labeling and packing integrity.
- Transportation/Logistics Management: Coordinate delivery of product to customers, distributors and local warehouse.

Key Accomplishments:
- Created significant cost reduction: reduced overall production costs by 8.5%, transportation costs by 4%, and packaging costs by 4.5%.[3]

BIG BOX ELECTRONICS, INC.   [dates]

Held a series of increasingly responsible positions at the nation's largest electronics retailer.[2]

General Manager   Mt. Juliet, Tenn. [dates]

- Managed 280,000 sq. ft. warehouse with full $18M P & L annual responsibility.
- Supervised 30+ employees. Trained management staff in procedures and policy implementation.
- Controlled costs by continually analyzing and streamlining operations procedures.
- Directed transportation contracts for replenishment carriers and home delivery service.
- Developed and maintained close working relationships with retail partners.

Key Accomplishments:
- Successfully managed $26M inventory by instituting audit processes.
- Consistently surpassed inventory budget expectations; facility-wide bonuses awarded.
- Increased productivity by 18% by instituting performance metrics to monitor activity.[3]
- Developed customer service standards with peer manager to create regional standards, improving customer services, resulting in increased customer loyalty.

General Manager   Deptford, N.J. [dates]

- Opened new market, third-party distribution facility; responsible for $10M annual P & L.
- Managed third-party logistics operations contract, including warehousing, store replenishment and home delivery; controlled contract costs.

Key Accomplishments:
- Developed and implemented audit processes to ensure accurate management of company's $17M inventory by third-party warehouse company.
- Consistently came in below budget on inventory; awarded bonuses.

Warehouse Supervisor   Madison, Tenn. [dates]

- Oversaw and directed daily warehouse operations, including preparation of shipments to 32 retail stores and 375 home delivery customers, with $26M inventory.
- Supervised warehouse staff of 20, in an 180,000 sq. ft. facility.

Key Accomplishment:
- Developed and instituted consistent procedures and policies to improve processes.

TENNESSEE COURIER SERVICE   Nashville, Tenn. [dates]

Distribution Coordinator

- Directed 30 carriers and routing of 300 packages and consignments for priority morning delivery. Trained couriers and drivers; participated in review and discipline process.

COMPUTER PROFICIENCIES: MS Word, Excel, Outlook, PowerPoint, Access, SAP

Banking. Bank Manager. Reverse Chronological. Career progression to bank manager; now seeks position as VP in larger bank or regional manager. Requirements: 5-7 years branch management experience,[1] extensive knowledge of operations and lending,[2] customer service managment,[3] staff development and training,[4] and business marketing and development.[5]

CLAUDIA RAMOS

Residence: 555-555-5555 • Cellular: 555-000-5050
Email: CRamos_7@hotmail.com • Twitter.com/ClaudiaRamos

BANK FINANCIAL/OPERATIONS MANAGER

Over 15 years' banking experience. Demonstrated competence in branch management,[1] staff recruitment and training, community relations, and business development.[4] Promoted 3 times in 4 years. Strong customer service and communications skills,[3] with keen ability to build relationships with diverse clients. Noted excellence in financial operations[2] and administration. Creative and resourceful in community relationships and marketing.[5] Grew new business portfolio 300% in 3 years. Professional and motivated, with strengths in problem resolution, team building, and research and analysis. Bilingual: English and Spanish. Over 300 hours of banking and management classes and 2 years' undergraduate studies. PC proficient.

PROFESSIONAL EXPERIENCE

PROVIDENT BANK, Highland Park, Ill.   [dates]
Branch Manager [dates];[1]
Customer Relations Manager [dates]; **Head Teller** [dates]

- *As Branch Manager,* direct operational, service, and administrative activities of branch. Lead staff of 20 in providing customer service and financial care.[3] Manage:
  - HR tasks, including hiring, coaching, training, and performance management.[4] Compliance with all policies and procedures; fraud control; loss prevention.
  - Procurement, service contract administration, and technology issues; action plans to improve controls, mitigate losses, and ensure superior client experience.
  - Overall branch performance and financial reports/analyses; sub-ledger, general ledger, and cash reconciliation.

- *As Customer Relations Manager,* opened new accounts, sold numerous bank services, resolved customer issues. Trained and supervised Customer Service Representatives.

- *As Head Teller,* interviewed, trained, and supervised daily functions of tellers. Ordered and received cash.

Recognition:
- Outstanding Performance Award, [date]; Employee of the Month Award, [date]; Outstanding Performance, [date]; Certificate of Excellence, [date]; Outstanding Performance Award,[date].

WACHOVIA BANK, Highwood, Ill.   [dates]
Financial Services Representative

- Opened retail and commercial accounts, including savings, checking, IRA, CDs, and Keoghs. Exceeded new account goals by 36%. Improved customer service satisfaction by 16%.

Office Work. <u>Administrative Assistant</u>. Hybrid. College graduate seeks Executive Assistant position in chemical industry. Requirements: Bachelor's Degree,[1] 3-5 years in responsible administrative role for chemical manufacturer,[2] strong computer skills,[3] excellent written and verbal communication skills.[4]

ERIN KINGSTON

Phone: 443.555.8989   Baltimore, MD   emkingston@aol.com

ADMINISTRATIVE/OPERATIONS ASSISTANT

Highly-motivated, personable Administrative Professional with over 3 years' experience in chemical industry.[2] Recognized for enhancing productivity through exemplary operational, client service, and sales support. Efficient with exceptional time management, problem-solving, and analytical skills. Very strong oral communication[4] and interpersonal skills. Flexible and adaptable to changing priorities.

CORE STRENGTHS
- **Administrative Operations:** Special event, meeting, and travel logistics; correspondence, file, records, and database management; project administration and executive-level support.
- **Sales Support:** Client service, accounts management, problem trouble-shooting and resolution; contract administration, order review, and shipping management; sales tracking and reporting.
- **Communications:** Polished telephone skills. Experienced business writer, proofreader, and editor.[4]
- **Financial/Budget Administration:** Budget oversight, invoice verification, and expense tracking; purchasing, supply, and inventory management.
- **Computer Expertise:** Skilled in creating reports, spreadsheets, presentations, and graphs. Proficient in MS Windows, Word, Excel, PowerPoint, and Outlook.[3]

PROFESSIONAL EXPERIENCE

ADMINISTRATIVE ASSISTANT, BioProducts, Inc. - Columbia, Maryland   [dates]

Provide high level of administrative, sales operations, and client service support for leading manufacturer and supplier of biopesticides and chemical pesticides. Directly support VP of Sales and Marketing and 19 regional sales managers and field development researchers. After 2 months, promoted to permanent position.
- **Administrative Support:** Effectively orchestrate a full range of strategic administrative functions, including correspondence and publications management; database and file management; travel, special events, and meeting planning; and general purchasing/budget oversight. Create scientific/technical PowerPoint presentations, spreadsheets, graphs, and reports for managers.
- **Sales, Operations & Customer Service:** Direct liaison between customers and sales. Field 20+ calls per day for product and order information. Input domestic sales orders into database, updating contracts, pricing information, and customer account data. Schedule and track shipments; troubleshoot problems. Conduct operations and management process analyses.

Accomplishments:
- Independently developed new sales report/pivot table, now company's primary tracking tool.
- Developed and implemented a linked paper-and-computer-based filing system, incorporating an Excel spreadsheet, to provide fast and easy access to new product and regulatory information.

ADDITIONAL WORK EXPERIENCE

Target, Ellicott City, Maryland - Backroom Stocker/Flow/Replenishment.   [dates]
Kohl's, Ellicott City, Maryland - Overnight Sales Floor Stocker.   [dates]

EDUCATION & TRAINING

B.A.,[1] History, University of Maryland Baltimore County, Baltimore, Maryland.   [date]

Information Technology. Information Technology Help Desk Analyst. Hybrid. Recent MBA graduate with sales and IT experience seeks Technical Sales Analyst position. Requirements: Bachelor's Degree,[1] 1-2 years IT experience and/or training,[2] excellent customer service skills, knowledge of Microsoft Access, Word, mail merge, Excel, Internet and graphic design,[3] and excellent oral and written communication skills.[4]

WILLIAM J. FRANKLIN, JR.

billjfranklin@comcast.net

Catonsville, MD   Cell: (888) 777-3434

OBJECTIVE: Technical Sales Analyst, Solimar Systems, Inc.

QUALIFICATIONS SUMMARY

Accomplished technical marketing and sales value for employer with over two years' progressively responsible experience in sales, customer support, and end-user training for telecommunications technologies and services.[2] Strong technical background with proven success building and managing customer relationships with major corporate and government clients. Keen problem solving, analytical, and negotiation skills. Excellent presentation and oral/written communications skills.[4] BS Marketing degree.[1]

Business, marketing, sales, & technology expertise:

➤ Business Development, Client Relationship Management, & Needs Assessment
➤ Competitive Product Positioning, Technical Support & Troubleshooting, Technology Training
➤ Strategic Alliances, Government & Corporate Partnerships
➤ Strategic Sales & Marketing Planning/Research, Presentations, & New Product Launch
➤ Managing Vendor/Supplier Relationships
➤ Statistical Analyses, Graphical Presentation of Data, & Competitive Benchmarking
➤ Wireless Voice and Data Communications, including Pagers, PDAs, and BlackBerry Products
➤ PC hardware, Software & Peripheral devices, including all Microsoft applications

PROFESSIONAL EXPERIENCE

Help Desk IT Analyst
NET SOLUTIONS, INC. International Unit, Washington, D.C.   [dates]

Provide first tier end-user technical support via telephone to over 8,000 staff. Assist and resolve complex technical issues and questions on Lotus Notes; MS Office XP; remote access; BlackBerry devices; and other internal software applications. Conduct remote diagnostics to troubleshoot and resolve desktop application issues.

Accomplishment:
➤ Currently facilitating seamless migration of windows 2000 Enterprise Desktop (ED3) to XP (ED4) and Lotus Notes R5 to Notes ND6 with virtually no interruption to workflow.

SPRINT COMMUNICATIONS, Vienna, Va.   [dates]

Fast-track promotion through positions of increasing challenge and responsibility, based on consistently strong performance in sales support, account management and technical support of multi-million dollar wireless technology contracts with Fortune 1000 companies and federal government agencies, including the Department of Defense, the CIA, and the Federal Energy Regulatory Commission.

William J. Franklin, Jr. ~ Cell: (888) 777-3434

National Account Sales Consultant [dates]

Established and fostered relationships with government and corporate clients to promote integrated wireless data and messaging services, including pagers, PDAs, and BlackBerry products. Directly supported four Account Executives.

➤ Expanded and strengthened sales and marketing efforts through new product and training presentations. Contributed to new product development of key accounts.
➤ Challenged to identify, evaluate, and capture opportunities for upgrade or expansion of contracts.
➤ Provided technical support and problem resolution and led end-user training.
  Accomplishments:
  ➤ Consistently achieved or surpassed team quota at 100% each month for 3 years.
  ➤ Coordinated and managed up to 30 strategic accounts simultaneously and provided direct customer support to 40-50 individual customers.
  ➤ Monitored, researched, and summarized market trends and competitor data and developed integrated product analyses for accounts executives that drove sales growth.

Team Customer Account Executive [dates]

Integral member of four-person account service team that developed and orchestrated multi-media presentations and on-site technical training sessions for clients nationwide. Fostered open communications with customers to gather vital feedback on products, pinpoint problems, and end-user issues. Resolved diverse range of technical, service, and billing problems.

  Accomplishments:
  ➤ Contributed sales support to government channel to reach over 137% of plan for [years].
  ➤ Improved customer satisfaction and retention by responding promptly to user and billing issues, staying alert to potential problem areas, and developing creative solutions.

Regional Implementation Specialist [dates]

Integral member of a seven-person team that supported pre-sales and closing presentations for federal and corporate accounts.

  Accomplishments:
  ➤ Successfully implemented over 60 accounts, improved customer satisfaction by 50%.
  ➤ Closed 20 new government and corporate accounts.

ADDITIONAL WORK EXPERIENCE

Credit Manager, MBNA, Baltimore, Md. [dates]
  Managed up to 500 customer loan and real estate accounts. Generated new business leads, cross-sold financial services, and refinanced loans through cold-calling, telemarketing, and field sales.

EDUCATION

Bachelor's Degree, Marketing,[1] Temple University, Philadelphia, Pa. [date]

COMPUTER SKILLS [3]

Proficient in popular applications, including Microsoft Windows, Excel, Word, Access, PowerPoint, Outlook, and Works; Lotus Notes; WordPerfect; Adobe Acrobat, Illustrator; Internet applications. Expertise with specialized data management, mail merge and analytical software.

Retailing. <u>Retail sales worker</u>. Reverse chronological. Retail worker seeks assistant manager position. Requirements: 1-2 years of retail experience,[1] positive sales attitude and proven sales leadership,[2] strong verbal and written communication skills,[3] strong customer service skills,[4] and basic computer skills.[5]

CYNTHIA MARIE ROMANI

Alexandria, VA   Cell: 555-444-0909   Email: cmromani@gmail.com

OBJECTIVE: Assistant Manager, Retail Beauty Company

PROFILE: Motivated **retail sales professional** with three years[1] of outstanding customer service experience.[4] Demonstrated sales leader,[2] with ability to consistently surpass goals and build client base. Positive attitude,[2] able to go above and beyond for customer satisfaction. Skilled in problem resolution, time and asset management and team leadership. Strong administrative and visual merchandising skills, with keen attention to detail. Excellent verbal and written communication skills.[3] Prior management experience in food service.

RETAIL EXPERIENCE

Key Holder, Sales Representative
Perfect Skin Co., Arlington, Va.   [dates][1]

➤ <u>Customer Service:</u>[4] Build customer base through friendly, attentive service. Educate customers in skin care and make-up products and techniques. Perform facials and color makeovers. Drive revenue by communicating and demonstrating benefits of products and special offers to new and returning customers. Maintain customer files and follow up on sales to create brand loyalty and increase customer retention. Answer questions and resolve customer complaints and problems.

➤ <u>Merchandising/Loss Prevention:</u> Plan and organize displays to correspond with current promotions and best-selling products. Maintain store appearance and stock shelves; identify and respond to security risks and thefts.

➤ <u>Sales Administration:</u> As Key Holder, open/close store; prepare daily deposits and sales reports. Process customer payments, balance cash drawers and maintain sales records. Interact with other stores as needed. Motivate staff to meet goals.[2]

Key Accomplishments:
➤ Promoted three times in 18 months, from part time to full time, then to Key Holder.
➤ Exceeded personal daily, weekly and monthly sales goals. Ranked top seller for [year].

OTHER EXPERIENCE

Administrative Assistant, National Fleet Leasing, Co., Fairfax, Va.   [dates]

Teacher, KinderCare Learning Center, Kingstowne, Va.   [dates]
➤ *Key Accomplishment:* Employee of the Quarter [date]

EDUCATION: Howard University, Washington, D.C., General Education   [dates]

COMPUTER SKILLS: MS Word, Excel, Outlook, PowerPoint; Internet; proprietary databases; hardware, software and peripheral troubleshooting. [5]

Food Service. Server. Functional. Experienced restaurant worker seeks higher-paying job. Requirements: 2 years of experience in reputable dining establishment,[1] ability to communicate using a positive and clear speaking voice, listen to and understand requests, and respond appropriately,[2] ability to perform essential physical job functions,[3] ability to work under pressure,[4] and be a team player.[5]

RENEE MARGARET JONES

Mesa, AZ

Cellular: 999-777-3434 • Email: rmjones@gmail.com

RESTAURANT SERVER

PROFILE: Over 5 years of customer service experience in restaurant and retail settings. Highly motivated, able to multi-task and prioritize workload under pressure, as well as increase pace as workload demands.[4] Excellent interpersonal skills, with ability to build rapport and develop regular clientele. Team player,[5] noted for volunteering to work additional shifts, in other departments. Keen attention to detail.

KEY SKILLS

- **Customer Service/Sales:** Skilled in essential physical job functions[3] — anticipating needs and empathizing with diverse customers. Speak clearly, quickly identify and resolve problems, listen and respond to requests, and follow up to assure complete satisfaction.[2] Outstanding upselling ability, without over-selling.

- **Server:** Accurately and quickly take and place all food orders. Answer all questions about cooking methods, menu items, specials and prices. Prepare and/or deliver food, beverage, and dessert orders. Check food for appearance, temperature and portion size, and deliver food orders in a timely fashion. *Recognized as top server. Routinely manage 6-table station on busy Friday and Saturday night shifts.*[3] *Consistently achieve sales goals.*

- **Team Lead/Trainer:** Experienced in leading teams, delegating work, enforcing policies, and ensuring assigned tasks are completed. Motivate co-workers.

- **Accounting/Inventory:** Accountable for cash and credit transactions. Also, skilled in receiving deliveries and verifying 400-piece orders; noted discrepancies, damages, and missing items.

- **Computer Proficiencies:** Various POS software programs, including QuickBooks POS Pro and Keystroke POS System.

PROFESSIONAL EMPLOYMENT

Server [1]   [dates]
Olive Garden, Mesa, Az.
Server [1]   [dates]
Ruby Tuesday, Phoenix, Az.
Student Marshall   [dates]
Arizona State University, Tempe, Az.
- *Received Outstanding Service Award, [date]*

EDUCATION
Undergraduate Coursework, Health Science Policy; Arizona State University, Tempe, Az.,
93 credits.   [dates]

Healthcare. Office manager. Hybrid. Recent healthcare management graduate with medical office experience seeking Medical Office Business Manager position. Requirements: 5 years' experience as medical practice administrator,[1] 3 years' supervisory experience,[2] experience with marketing and referral development,[3] experience in billing and accounts receivable[4] and demonstrated accomplishments and career growth in the healthcare field.[5]

MARY L. TREY

Anaheim, CA * 111-998-5555 * maryltrey@yahoo.com

CAREER FOCUS

Healthcare Management
Administration • Operations & Processes • HR • Generalist • Sales • Education Coordinator

PROFILE & SKILLS VALUED BY YOUR COMPANY

- Five years' direct experience in Healthcare Administrative Management.[1] Professional working knowledge of procedures applicable to hospital and physician settings. Completed healthcare internship while earning Bachelor of Science degree in Healthcare Management.

- Multi-task/detail oriented: provide functional guidance on multifaceted projects. Prioritize and distribute workloads, carefully balancing skill sets. Manage calendars and schedules, meeting fast-paced deadlines. Oversee staff.

- Accomplished professional with refined interpersonal and communications skills. Ensure smooth flow of communications between management, patients/clients, and team members, speaking frequently with patients and medical or insurance professionals. Maintain strict confidentiality of sensitive information following HIPAA regulations.

• Resilient & Energetic	• Relationship Builder	• MS Word, Excel, PowerPoint
• Leader	• Medical Terminology	• Information Management
• Manager	• Medical Insurance	• Medical Billing/Coding
• Diplomatic & Tactful	• Risk Management	• Medical Legal Requirements

EXPERIENCE

Office Manager, Plumbing Inc., Irvine, Calif. [dates]
- Manage administrative and financial tasks for company of 15. Complete AP/AR, weekly payroll, banking, and invoices. Construct quarterly business taxes.[4]
- Conduct research and compile information to generate bids (for construction contracts).
- Provide excellent customer service and answer multi-line telephone system.

Key Accomplishments:
- Analyzed and streamlined business processes, reducing paper records and input time. Reduced labor expenditures by 10%.[5]
- Researched providers and reviewed bids for equipment lease and service; secured better price/product for copier and telecommunications. Achieved cost savings of $12,000 per year.[5]

Medical Office Coordinator, Doctors & Associates, Brea, Calif. [dates]
- Hired as Medical Office Coordinator and within eights months, was informed center would close. Shifted into high gear to oversee difficult task of managing operating medical clinic, while

simultaneously closing the clinic. Successfully met closure deadline with all patient files copied and sent to selected doctors.

- Worked closely with patients to find new doctors, ensuring they had proper medications during transition period.
- Copied charts for new medical practitioners, sent closure notices to all patients, and mailed medical records to each patient or made arrangements for storage.
- Operated Medical Information Management software (patient registration, charge entries, and appointment scheduling). Scheduled appointments, checked patients in and out of clinic, prepared encounter forms, prepared daily log sheet, posted charges daily, entered and updated insurance information, entered ICD and CPT codes, and made daily bank deposits.

Medical Secretary, Klebanow Family Care; **Maintenance Supervisor,** Property Management Company: Kelly Personnel Services, Yorba Linda, Calif.   [dates]
- Scheduled appointments, checked patients in and out of clinic, prepared encounter forms, prepared daily log sheet, posted charges daily, entered and updated insurance information, entered ICD and CPT codes, and made daily bank deposits.
- Greeted patients with professionalism and courtesy to set appointments or resolve complaints/conflicts.
- Managed administrative requirements as temp employee in various offices.

Office Manager, Intensive Care Ambulance Service, Fullerton, Calif.   [dates]
- Managed office requirements including bookkeeping and AP/AR, payroll for 10 employees, and marketing. Balanced four separate bank accounts. Produced financial/statistical reports and worked closely with the CPA. Directed two assistants.**2**
- Supervised and dispatched eight EMTs and paramedics.
- Scheduled appointments with nursing homes and hospitals for patient transport.
- Wrote correspondence and marketing materials to gain new business with nursing homes, dialysis clinics, and hospitals.**3**
- Worked with vendor companies to purchase ambulance supplies including stretchers, wheel chairs, IV bags, bandages, uniforms, and medications issued during transport of patients.

EDUCATION

Bachelor of Science Degree, Health Care Management [5]
California State University, Fullerton, Calif.   [dates]

Relevant Health Care Management Courses:
- Health Policy
- Anatomy & Physiology
- Management Problems
- U.S. Health Care System
- Public Speaking
- HR & Labor Relations
- Facilities Fiscal Aspects
- Marketing
- Risk Management/Health Care
- Legal Aspects of Health Care
- Health Care Services Analysis
- Equipment & Materials Mgmt.

Healthcare Administrative Internship: [dates]

Shadowed **Healthcare Administrator** (an RN) of assisted living facility with 50 residents. Cross-trained in all departments: **HR and Office Manager's offices** (staff scheduling and administration; interviewed job candidates), **Admissions** (interviewed hospital applicants and processed applications for admission), **Health Inspection** (shadowed health inspector), and **Marketing** (visited local hospitals and medical offices).

Business. Business Analyst. Reverse Chronological. Technical Writer seeks Business Analyst position. Requirements: college degree,[1] minimum five years of relevant work experience,[2] experience/understanding of business process reengineering and business modeling concepts,[3] awareness of the business and information technology functions,[4] and strong analytical and technical writing skills.[5]

MICHELLE ANN GERSHON

Cell: 555-333-6767 • Email: m-a-gershon@hotmail.com • St. Louis, MO

BUSINESS ANALYST

Over 10 years' experience in managing and integrating information technology (IT) applications[2] for financial service and healthcare providers. Expertise: business and end-user requirements, project management, communicating business needs to IT staff, and quality assurance (QA) testing. Strong technical written communications skills, including ability to convey complex IT and industry-specific information clearly.[5] Deadline-driven. Pay attention to detail. Excel in team and individual work settings.

RELEVANT PROFESSIONAL EXPERIENCE

Technical Writer
Medical Billing Co., Chesterfield, Mo.   [dates]

Technical writing for non-profit medical billing and collection company, serving 50 major hospitals in the Midwest. Hired to author Health Insurance Portability and Accountability Act (HIPAA) compliance and IT information security policies.

- Policy Development: Wrote corporate and IT security policies to satisfy HIPAA regulations. Created corporate standard for policy and procedure documentation. Wrote and edited IT software documentation, policies, and procedures.[4]
- Project Management: Facilitated company's conversion from paper to automated data tracking and recordkeeping. Led project team to develop online Documentation Center. Researched commercial off-the-shelf and open-source software.
- Disaster Recovery: Worked with contractor to develop and implement disaster recovery plan and established business continuity plan. Managed disaster recovery testing; taught system to users.

Key Accomplishment
Successfully passed 2 external audits with no items of concern. (Company had previously been cited/fined for lack of information security policies with regard to HIPAA regulations.)

Project Coordinator (Contract position)
First Credit Co.,Clayton, Mo.   [dates]

Hired to coordinate several high-profile IT projects for this global financial services provider. Reported directly to a VP of the Consumer Internet Group. Supported project management staff (5 project managers with up to 30 people per team) to complete 15 IT projects, including Disney custom Internet site, Disney Rewards Card, Disney reporting, and Verified by Visa.

- Project Coordination: Developed and maintained project documentation including Project Plans, Action Items/Issues Logs, Critical Tasks lists, and Meeting Minutes.
- Resource Management/Liaison: Balanced changing priorities and business expectations to meet strict deadlines. Served as point of contact and liaison for all project staff.

Key Accomplishment
Significant contributor to Disney Rewards Card project—completed on time and under budget.

Business Analyst
College Finance Co., St. Louis, Mo.   [dates]
Performed business process analyses for this national postsecondary education loan services company.

- Business/Process Analysis: Reviewed and analyzed business modeling operations; flowcharted all company processes and functionality.[3] Developed and recommended business process improvements, identifying end-user and business requirements. Designed and prepared reports.

Key Accomplishment
Critical contributor to implementation of Phone Pay system, a PC application which automated loan payment process, saving over 100 manhours per month. Worked extensively with developers and QA testing; trained end-users.

Business Analyst/Technical Writer
Applied Card Systems, St. Louis, Mo.   [dates]
Initially hired as Technical Writer; promoted to Business Analyst for this growing financial services company.

- Project Management: Managed projects according to System Development Lifecycle, ranging from application processing and collection system enhancements to new products, using MS Project. Identified end-user requirements and developed business requirements documents.
- Software Implementation: Developed documentation (user and technical manuals) for software applications and procedural documentation for all IT units.

Key Accomplishment
Provided liaison for IT-related projects with multiple business units serving 1,000 internal users.

EDUCATION, TRAINING, & CERTIFICATIONS
B.A.,[1] English, University of Missouri, Columbia, Mo.   [date]
    Webmaster Certificate, Penn State University   [date]
    Spherion eSQM Training Course (Internet Software Quality Management Methodology) [date]

COMPUTER PROFICIENCIES
MS Office: Word, Excel, PowerPoint, Access; SharePoint, Visio, MS FrontPage, MS Project; Adobe Acrobat, FrameMaker, Photoshop; TYPO3; HTML; Javascript; Test Director 6.0; Winrunner 6.02

Chapter 15

A Sampling of OnTarget Resumes by Experience Level and Age

··

*H*ave reason to think that you have too much experience — or not enough — to rack up the job offers you want? Or that you're too young — or too old? Or that even when you're barely out of your mid-40s (a kid, really), you're stuck in low gear? The sample resumes in this chapter show techniques aimed at downplaying negative perceptions about your experience or your age.

A text box atop each sample resume contains a mission statement — that is, what the job seeker aims to accomplish, which usually is a better job. The mission statement also includes the requirements for a specific position — or a summary of the typically requested requirements for an occupation or career field.

Within the mission statement, each of the job's requirements has a number next to it. The same number also appears in the body of the resume next to the job seeker's matching qualification for that requirement.

The cross-matched numbers between a job's requirements and the candidate's qualifications shown here are just for illustration, *not for your actual resumes.*

These samples are intended to laser your attention to requirement-and-qualification matching, the single most important factor in causing your candidacy to get noticed in an online swarm of resumes.

New Graduate. <u>Business Administration degree</u>. Hybrid. Candidate seeks Junior Financial Analyst position. Requirements: BS Business or Finance,[1] 1-3 years' relevant experience,[2] strong Excel skills,[3] independent work style,[4] highly motivated,[5] strong problem-solving skills,[6] excellent communication skills[7] and team player.[8]

JOSHUA GANSL

Charleston, SC 29401   Tel: 555.111.1712   joshgansl@yahoo.com

OBJECTIVE: Junior Financial Analyst

SKILLS & QUALIFICATIONS

- Strong financial, quantitative/qualitative analytical, and problem-solving skills.[6]
- International and domestic summer work experience. Gained essential knowledge evaluating properties, structuring financing, conducting pro-forma cash flow analysis, and executing leases for residential and commercial real estate sales and acquisitions.
- Poised, self-confident. Proven public speaking, interpersonal and multicultural communications skills.[7]
- Highly motivated with strong work ethic.[5] Well-developed team player abilities.[8] Able to prioritize tasks, work independently,[4] and meet deadlines.
- Competitive and ambitious. Welcome new challenges.
- Computer Skills: Advanced proficiencies in Microsoft Windows, Word, Excel,[3] and PowerPoint.

EDUCATION

B.S.,[1] Business Administration, Clemson University, Clemson, S.C., GPA 4.0   [date]

- **Relevant Courses:** Corporate Finance, Accounting, Financial Statement Analysis, Micro/Macro Economics, Business Statistics, and Management Information Systems
- **Team Project:** In-depth business case analysis of sporting goods industry. Conducted top-down financial statement analysis to determine predictors of future stock prices.

WORK EXPERIENCE

Tillman Securities, PLC, London, England [2]   [dates]

Worked directly with CFO on commercial real estate acquisitions and financing. Reviewed properties and conducted future cash flow analysis. Prepared and presented regulatory and financial documentation to financial institutions.
- Involved in executing purchase of over $100 million in commercial real estate properties.
- Part of team that refinanced several multimillion dollar real estate properties.

JOSHUA GANSL *Page 2*

Seaside Realty Partners, Inc., Los Angeles, Calif. [dates]

Summer [year]**:** Participated in successful acquisition of 18 commercial properties leased to U.S. Drugstore Corporation in upstate New York. Created Excel spreadsheets, performed due diligence, analyzed and prepared leasing agreements, conducted pro-forma cash flow analysis, and conducted on-site inspections with acquisition team.

- Presented summary financial data to outside investors and the company's executives to be used for acquisition decision-making.

Summer [year]**:** Shadowed Vice Chairman. Gained valuable experience evaluating real estate properties, and predicting future cash flow and property income. Developed passion and talent for identifying, structuring, and executing sound commercial real estate investments.

Gansl and Greenberg, LLP, Los Angeles, Calif. [dates]

- Delivered administrative and operational support for high-volume law firm. Ensured all documents were accurately filed. Provided customer service and supported legal staff.

Camp International, Jerusalem, Israel [dates]

Camp counselor at an international summer camp for 200 campers from all over the Americas and Europe; including England, France, and Belgium.
- Led broad range of team activities and supervised tours throughout Israel.
- Promoted open communications and camaraderie among all campers. Reinforced importance of respecting cultural differences.
- Developed talent for fostering communication despite language barriers.

SPECIAL INTERESTS & ACTIVITIES

Community Service
- Chai Lifeline Volunteer, an organization that supports cancer patients and their families. Maintained ongoing relationships with seriously ill youngsters. Participated in "Big Brother" program for two years.

Team Sports
- Captain of college basketball team, 2 years.

International Travel
- Extensive travel to over 10 European countries, as well as trips to the Middle East. Enjoy experiencing and learning about other cultures, history, and customs.

Foreign Languages
- Write and speak Hebrew.
- Conversational Yiddish — an international dialect of German.

Reading
- Avid reader. Especially enjoy financial publications.

Mid-Career Trades. HVAC expert. Functional. Experienced heating/cooling specialist seeks HVAC Manager, Technical Training & Service position. Requirements: Min. 15 years of experience in theory and practice of HVAC – installation, service, repairs, heat pumps, air conditioners, gas/oil furnaces, boilers, and standard controls,[1] strong communication and leadership skills,[2] must be performance-driven, motivated,[3] and computer savvy.[4]

GREG BOREK

903 Longmeadow Lane • Raleigh, NC 27602
Cell: 999-333-2323 • Email: greg_borek@comcast.net

HVAC/Refrigeration Systems Expert

OBJECTIVE: HVAC Manager, Technical Training and Service

AREAS OF EXPERTISE

- **HVAC/R Expert**, with over 20 years' experience. Highly skilled in every phase of heating and air conditioning, chillers, heat pumps, furnaces, and boilers for residential, commercial, plumbing and refrigeration lines: **design, installation, troubleshooting, service, and repair**.[1] Experienced with Metasys and Johnson 350 controller. Proficient in Control systems design and installation–Analog and DDC.

- Experienced **project manager and team leader**,[2] with jobs averaging $500,000, up to 500 tons. Adept at estimating job schedules, choosing quality, cost-effective materials and designing and installing control systems, as well as supervising apprentices, journeymen and subcontractors on the job.

- Mentor, coach, and train junior staff. Develop and implement work standards and provide guidance on technical processes, safety, and operations.

- Performance-driven and motivated;[3] consistently complete job ahead of schedule and under budget. Regularly receive written and verbal recognition and bonuses.

- Strong customer service, interpersonal and communications skills.[2]

- Skilled at any and all **electrical** or **electronic diagnosis** and **repair**.

- Knowledgeable A/C systems **programmer**; PC proficient and familiar with HVACPRO software.[4]

CERTIFICATIONS

North Carolina Licensed Journeyman, #6666; EPA Certified, Universal & Automotive, #999999999

SAMPLE PROJECTS

Designed and installed controls systems for:
WNCN 17 NBC • Fool Lion food stores
Borders book stores • Wake Forest University

Installed & set up Metasys system for:
Durham Regional Hospital • CVS drugstores
State government building, Raleigh

WORK HISTORY

Johnson Controls, *Controls Technician*	[dates]
Aire Right Mechanical, *Commercial A/C*	[dates]
Servicemark Mechanical Services, *Residential A/C and Refrigeration; Appliance Repair*	[dates]

EDUCATION/SPECIALIZED TRAINING

Metasys ASC engineering, Johnson Controls, [date]
DDC control, M & M Controls, [date]
Trane Microcontrol Voyager, Trane, [date]
Pneumatic Controls I & II, [date]
Honeywell: Fireye, M & M Controls, [date]

Carrier Parker System, Carrier, [date]
Wake Tech. Comm. College, 36 credits [dates]
Diploma, Roosevelt High, Raleigh, SC [date]

Young Adult. <u>Intern</u>. Reverse Chronological. Recent MPA graduate seeks Program Officer/Researcher position with nonprofit or public policy organization. Requirements: Bachelor's degree (preferably Master's),[1] strong research, writing, and legislative skills,[2] experience working on policy and advocacy campaigns,[3] solid Microsoft Office skills,[4] and strong attention to detail and ability to multi-task.[5]

ROCHELLE HENDERSON

Brooklyn, NY
Cell: 888-444-9090
E-mail: r_henderson@ny-u.edu

EXPERIENCE

[dates]   **UNITED NATIONS DEVELOPMENT PROGRAMME**   New York, N.Y.
Programme Assistant Intern, Equator Initiative   [dates]
Mid-term Evaluation Intern, United Nations Capital Development Fund   [dates]

- Researched and wrote [2] reports and position papers on capacity building in local communities.
- Authored and edited [2] articles for *Between the Lines* newsletter.
- Evaluated and analyzed documents to extract recommendations for improving design and cost effectiveness of microfinance donor training workshops.

[dates]   **NEW YORK UNIVERSITY SCHOOL OF MEDICINE**   New York, N.Y.
Research Associate, [2] **Center for Immigrant Health**

- Conducted highly detailed [5] research in English and Spanish on quality of medical services for immigrant populations for advocacy campaign,[3]
- Designed and implemented quality assurance mechanisms to improve accuracy of study's data.[5]
- Supervised and trained staff of 9 research interns.

[dates]   **PEACE CORPS**   Tarija, Bolivia
Gender and Development Representative   [dates]
Natural Resources Management Extensionist   [dates]

- Directed all logistical components, drafted budget, and raised funds for 4-day national gender and development conference for 35 high school students and 5 community representatives.
- Selected to use participatory modules to train 28 volunteers for gender mainstream projects.
- Managed locally focused natural resources projects for over 80 indigenous women.
- Planned, prioritized, and managed multiple tasks and assignments in fast-paced environment.[5]

[dates]   **WORLD WILDLIFE FUND**   Washington, D.C.
Government Relations Intern [2]

- Wrote and edited documents on environmental legislation and international development concerns to educate staff on policy issues. Represented lobbyist at World Bank and Capitol Hill meetings.

[dates]   **THE WHITE HOUSE**   Washington, D.C.
President's Council on Sustainable Development Intern [2]

- Prepared overviews of environmentally sustainable strategies presented to international delegations.
- Edited *Towards a Sustainable America* report presented to President William Clinton.

EDUCATION   **Master of Public Administration,**[1] New York University, New York, N.Y., [date]
     Specialization: International Public and Nonprofit Management and Policy
   Bachelor of Arts,[1] Environmental Science and Policy, Hood College, Frederick, Md., [date]
     Concentration: Environmental Policy; Minors: Sociology and International Economics

COMPUTERS   Microsoft Office [4] (Word, Excel, Outlook, PowerPoint, Access, Visio) and SPSS

LANGUAGES   Fluent in Spanish. Intermediate proficiency in Portuguese and Quechua.

Mid-Career Professional. <u>Teacher</u>. Reverse chronological. Experienced drama teacher seeks community college drama director position or chair of drama department. Requirements: 5-10 years' teaching theater in educational setting,[1] master's degree in theater arts.[2]

TERESA LYNN MORROW

Catonsville, MD
Residence: 444-555-1234 • Cellular: 444-555-5678
Email: dramacate@aol.com

Talented **Drama Instructor** with 10 years[1] plus of hands-on theatre and teaching experience. Outstanding ability to build programs and interest, both at school and community levels, as well as to develop rapport, relationships, and resources. Innovative and creative, willing to try new ideas; strongly committed to fostering the next generation of playwrights, actors, and production staff. Master's degree in theater arts (this year).[2]

TEACHING EXPERIENCE

Drama Teacher/Director of Drama [dates]
Lincoln High School, Columbia, Md.

Revitalized struggling drama department of this former tech-magnet Howard County high school. (Program went through 10 teachers in year prior to hire.) Built interest in drama program as well as offerings and opportunities. Currently teach 5 drama classes and direct Drama Club.

✓ <u>Productions:</u> Direct 3 large stage productions and 2 smaller classroom productions per year. Coordinate student technicians, directors, production staff, and actors. As appropriate, select plays, direct casting, coordinate auditorium calendar and events, and supervise design and construction of scenery and costumes. Manage production budget and direct marketing of productions. Continually challenged to present quality, award-winning productions on small budget.

Provide advice, support, and direction to students, encouraging high level of student involvement.

Productions include *Get Bill Shakespeare Off the Stage, George M!, A Night with Edgar, Starmites, Sugar, The Princess Bride, The Wizard of Oz, Finian's Rainbow, After Juliet, Seven Brides for Seven Brothers, Anything Goes,* and *The Importance of Being Earnest.*

✓ <u>Teaching:</u> Prepare and present materials on drama and communications for culturally diverse student base. Classes include: Introduction to Drama, Advanced Drama, Stagecraft, Musical Theatre, and Speech Communications. Incorporate variety of teaching strategies, including Essential Elements of Instruction, cooperative learning, and portfolio writing.

✓ <u>Curriculum Development:</u> Designed "Theater as Resource" Instructional Projects for middle school English classes, to introduce/integrate theatre and increase interest in drama prior to entering high school. Participate on Curriculum Development team; as a contributor, drafted guidelines, goals, and recommendations, as well as outlines and lesson plans.

✓ <u>Community Festivals/Field & Class Trips:</u> Coordinate student participation/attendance of variety of theatre presentations and workshops, locally, nationally, and internationally, including the Shakespeare Festival, the Folger Theatre Festival, Howard County Drama Festival, Magic Music Days (Epcot Center), and the Stratford Theatre Festival (Canada).

Achievements:

✓ Received 9 statewide awards for "best in" categories (Long Reach High School students).

✓ Organized trip to prestigious Stratford Theatre Festival in Canada, Summer [date]. Orchestrated invitations for 20 students and 4 adults—partially government-supported program is usually only open to Canadian students/teachers. Festival included workshops, backstage tours, and plays.

✓ Created Stagecraft class, teaching students to plan and create sets.

Substitute Teacher   [dates]
North Hill High School, Hampstead, Md.

Taught Mythology and 11th grade English. Voted Teacher of the Month for [date]. Also, recruited as substitute Theatre Director for [date]. Supervised/performed selection, casting, costuming, set design and construction; produced *Anne of Green Gables*.

VOLUNTEER & OTHER EXPERIENCE

Coordinator, Howard County (Maryland) Drama Festival   [dates]

Organized and coordinated one-day festival with 250 student attendees and support/teaching staff of 20. Scheduled seminars, entertainment, and workshops, including room planning and lunch. Served as co-coordinator for [date] festival.

Instructor, The Teaching Shakespeare School (Stratford, Canada)   [dates]

Specially invited to participate in program open to Canadian teachers. Additionally, paired with Stratford actor to team-teach *The Tempest* and *As You Like It* to 20 Long Reach students. Served as Teachers' Festival Liaison (3 years) for Stratford Festival teacher's conference, [date].

Graduate Assistant, New York University Study Abroad Program   [dates]

Made daily preparations for on and off campus classes at Trinity College (Dublin, Ireland). Coordinated receptions for students, visiting dignitaries, and professors; provided administrative support to Program Director.

Producer/Technical Director, The Howard County (Maryland) Players   [dates]

Coordinated musical theatre performances for program that pairs high school students and adults.

EDUCATION

Master's Degree, in progress, Educational Theatre, Community Concentration, New York
      University, New York, N.Y., 24 credits; expected completion: GPA: 3.75   [dates]

Bachelor of Arts, English and Theatre, York College of Pennsylvania, York, Penn.,   [dates]
      received Helen Gotwald Drama Award

Secondary Certification, English Theatre, York College of Penn., York, Penn.,   [dates]

Continuing Education, The Academy at the Stratford Festival, Stratford, Canada.   [dates]
      Classes completed: Shakespeare: Text and Performance, Voice and Movement, Set Building
      and Scene Painting, and Design in the Theatre

Young Professional. <u>Graphic Artist/Visual Information Specialist</u>. Reverse chronological. Graphic Artist seeks corporate communications graphics position. Requirements: Bachelor's degree,[1] 3 years' experience in graphics design and photography,[2] experience in production management and utilizing video, 35MM and audio equipment,[3] knowledge of advertising and marketing communications,[4] excellent communications skills,[5] and willing to travel 50% of the time.[6]

SCOTT E. PASQUALE

340 Decatur Lane
Cell: 111.444.4444   Baton Rouge, LA 70801   E-mail: spasquale@gmail.com

GRAPHIC ARTIST/VISUAL INFORMATION SPECIALIST

Skilled graphic artist, photographer, and video producer with three years' professional experience.[2] Creative and resourceful in coordinating and producing training videos, photography for print and Web and graphic design. Proficient in production management, as well as use of video, graphics software, 35 MM, digital and audio equipment and systems[3] to produce advertising and marketing materials, Web content, and training programs.[4] Strong communications skills;[5] able to travel.[6]

Professional **Experience**	**Computer and Information Specialist** [dates] *Training Professionals, Inc.; Baton Rouge, La.* • Maintain Web site utilizing HTML, scanning and forms management • Develop graphics, photographic images, and content for print and electronic media • Maintain customer service, evaluate customer feedback, and determine appropriate action • Produce videos and edit into training films • Photograph training sessions for Web site production
	Commercial Photography Intern and Independent Contractor [dates] *Online Real Estate Listing Service; New Orleans, La.* *Judith Salmona, Freelance Photographer; Kenner, La.* • Accomplish portrait, real estate, and documentary photographic assignments • Produce professional quality custom color prints and graphic images • Scan negatives and slides; manipulate and correct images • Maintain and service printing and graphics equipment • Organize and catalog negatives and proof sheets
	Technical Supervisor: *Performance Anxiety* **Installation** [dates] *Smith College; Northampton, Mass.* • Produced interactive video exhibition combining real-time computer image processing with variety of short videos • Used Image software and Infusion Systems' I-Cube X hardware
Education	**B.A.,**[1] Visual and Performing Arts, Louisiana State University, Baton Rouge, La. [date] *Relevant Coursework:* Introduction to Computers, Programming in C, HTML, Dreamweaver, Illustrator, Quark, Macromedia Flash, B&W Photography, Color Photography, Advanced Photography, Electronic Image Processing, Final Cut Pro, Alternative Processes, Visual Concepts, Ideas in the Arts, Introduction to Recording Techniques, History of Photography, Contemporary Art in Process, History of Film, American Life in Films
Skills	*Computer:* Macintosh and PC – Word, Excel, PowerPoint, Photoshop, Illustrator, Acrobat, QuarkXpress, Flash, digital imaging, scanning, Corel Draw, non-linear video production and editing, C Programming, HTML Web page development, database management *Photography:* digital video production, 35mm photography, B&W and color processing, printing and toning, studio portraiture, and dry mounting

Baby Boomer. Director of Marketing and Communications. Reverse chronological. Marketing expert seeks Director of Marketing position for international nonprofit. Requirements: Bachelor's degree (Master's preferred)[1] and a minimum of 10 years' experience in marketing, brand management, and corporate communications,[2] experience conducting market research and utilizing market research to guide planning and decision making,[3] knowledge of the not-for-profit fundraising environment,[4] excellent communications, presentation and negotiation skills,[5] and willing to travel 20% of the time.[6]

CONSTANCE M. CONNOLLY

Cell: 555.444.5656 Sioux Falls, SD E-mail: c_connolly@hotmail.com

Director of Marketing

Creative, dynamic Marketing professional with 14+ years of experience.[2] Demonstrated success developing and implementing strategic and tactical global marketing plans to improve product positioning, brand management, corporate communications, and competitive market share.[2] Results-oriented team leader with proven expertise managing marketing programs from concept through project completion. MBA in Marketing. Key strengths include:

✓ Superior communications, presentation, negotiation, and management skills[5]

✓ Experience formulating and implementing comprehensive multi-media campaigns.

✓ Expertise developing global and product-specific marketing plans, strategies, and budgets for nonprofit and for-profit organizations [4]

✓ Strong analytical capabilities. Extensive market research expertise, including demographic and market trend analyses; competitive assessments; and consumer segmentation and needs studies to guide planning and decision making.[3]

✓ E-Commerce & Web creation, development, and management experience.

✓ Proficiency in new product development, launch, and evaluation.

✓ Published writer and accomplished presenter, able to travel for meetings, trainings, and conferences.[6]

✓ American Marketing Association, American Society for Association Executives.

PROFESSIONAL EXPERIENCE

Director, Marketing and Communications
MUSCULAR DYSTROPHY ASSOCIATION, Sioux Falls, S.D. [dates]

Develop and implement marketing and communications strategies to support major, organization wide refocusing of MDA's operations, role and relevancy, community impact and image. Reached funding goal. Charged with conceptualizing and designing central messaging strategies to reposition MDA as leading health and human service organization.

CONSTANCE M. CONNOLY   555.444.5656   **Page 2**

✓ Aggressively promote notable accomplishments, and develop communications tools to improve internal branding, public relations, and sales.

✓ Develop and execute annual marketing program integrating television, radio, direct mail, print, electronic media, and special events.

✓ Conduct in-depth market research to evaluate public/customer perception and satisfaction, guide organizational investments in set-vices and impact areas, and support special projects to drive improvements.

Key Contributions & Achievements

✓ Developed technical blueprint that provided foundation for software development for new Volunteer Matching Program that will facilitate marketing and matching of volunteer opportunities.

✓ Conceived and spearheaded development of first Speakers Bureau to improve visibility of key constituencies (volunteers, health and human service representatives) in community. Speakers Bureau set for launch in [date].

Director of Marketing, Research, and Product Development
SCHOLARLY ASSOCIATION, INC., Washington, D.C.   [dates]

Supported global marketing needs of four distinct product lines: special interest groups, membership, conferences, and publications. Worked directly with Executive Director, internal management team, Board of Directors, and 62 committees to translate collective vision into strategic marketing plan.

✓ Built key consumer relationships, designed and implemented solutions-based sales strategies, and positioned company as market leader in scholarly publishing market.

✓ Developed and managed integrated, multimedia marketing program. Implemented new product development, launch, and evaluation. Developed strategies for increased product sales, brand awareness, and communications.

Key Contributions & Achievements

✓ Co-developed and implemented pricing model that created financially-sound basis to increase professional journal subscription revenues by $1 million on sustained basis.

✓ Conceptualized innovative direct mail marketing program that boosted new consumer base by 40% in one year.

✓ Spearheaded organization's first-ever global consumer satisfaction and performance improvement study, enabling management to formulate decisions based on consumers' expressed needs and desires.

✓ Strategic player in company's entrance into arenas of e-commerce and Web communications. Co-initiated effort to restructure Web site to increase navigability, aesthetics, brand, and commerce opportunities.

✓ Reevaluated vendor network and negotiated more competitive terms, resulting in savings of over 30%.

✓ Named 'Marketer of the Year' by Council of Educational Organizations   [date]

Director of Marketing and Public Relations
ARCHDIOCESE OF SIOUX FALLS, Division of Catholic Schools, Sioux Falls, S.D.   [Dates]

Launched one of the first programs in nation to market Catholic schools to counter 20-year trend of declining enrollment. Collaborated with Superintendent and Marketing Advisory Committee to generate marketing vision. Conceptualized message and developed strategies for multimedia advertising. Primary liaison with advertising agency and media. Managed advertising designs, scripts, and placement of spots. Maintained press relations and briefed educational reporters. Hired as Marketing and P.R. Assistant: promoted after 3 years.

Key Contributions & Achievments

- ✓ Launched successful multi-media campaign that increased Catholic school enrollments by 13% and generated construction of three new schools. By [date], there were more applicants than placements for county schools.

- ✓ Co-negotiated exclusivity contract with local TV station and advertising agency to produce commercials for Archdiocese on pro-bono basis, reducing campaign costs by 50%.

- ✓ Wrote, presented, and received grant to fund position and program for three-year period.

- ✓ Authored demographic study to guide Archdiocesan leadership in new school construction.

- ✓ Designed training program that incorporated facets of the marketing position: marketing, public relations, and development work. Trained school boards and committees at 101 schools to maximize local impact.

EDUCATION

Master of Business Administration, [1] [date], University of South Dakota, Vermillion, S.D.

Bachelor of Business Administration/Marketing Major, [date], Dakota Wesleyan University, Mitchell, S.D.

PUBLICATIONS & PRESENTATIONS

"Strategic Planning for State and Local Associations" – Guest speaker at National Association of Home Builders, Destin, Ha., [date]

"Application of Market Research to New Product Design: Case Studies" – Guest speaker at Council of Engineering and Scientific Society Executives, Houston, Texas, [dates]

Connolly, C. [date], **"Using Market Research to Make Strategic Decisions"** Association Management

Connolly, C. [date], **"Applying Marketing Success Principles to International Organizations,"** New Organizations World.

Connolly, C. [date], **"Nonprofits When Effectivly Marketed Can Save Lives,"** Nonprofits Review.

Young Professional. <u>Sales and Marketing Manager</u>. Hybrid. Seeks Marketing Coordinator position in larger company in advertising field. Requirements: 3-5 years of marketing experience – printing industry experience a plus,[1] degree in business, marketing, advertising or related discipline,[2] highly motivated,[3] detail and goal-oriented,[4] and high proficiency with MS Word, Excel, PowerPoint – Quark and Photoshop a plus.[5]

YOEL MORECK

Las Vegas, NV
Cell: 555-333-3939
Email: yoel_morick@gmail.com
Twitter: @YMoreck

MARKETING COORDINATOR with 5 years of marketing experience.[1]

- Sales, marketing, and advertising in printing/publishing,[1] real estate, and landscaping.
- Highly motivated,[3] with demonstrated ability to develop and maintain new sales territories and accounts, create new revenue streams, and increase profits.
- Strong ability to develop customer rapport and build loyal relationships.
- Excellent attention to detail and ability to meet and surpass sales goals.[4]

SALES & MARKETING EXPERIENCE

Sales and Marketing Manager/Field Supervisor
Local Lawn Services, Las Vegas, Nev.   [dates]

Recruited to spearhead sales and marketing efforts for this growing landscaping company.

<u>Marketing:</u> Develop marketing and advertising programs and materials, including direct mail and internet. Conduct market and customer research and develop new revenue streams to build business. Advise on market penetration and business development strategies.

<u>Sales:</u> Manage customer relationships from initial contact through consultation/estimate and service delivery. Develop sales leads, estimate projects, and write service contracts. Determine customer needs and recommend best options. Resolve customer problems and follow up to ensure customer satisfaction and loyalty.

<u>Management:</u> Analyze business operations and processes and identify improvements. Review profit and loss statements; recommend ways to reduce costs and maximize profits. Develop and implement policies. Direct laborers onsite; track time and attendance.

Key Accomplishments:

- Achieved year-on-year growth, increasing revenue by 31% in first year to $550,000; and an additional 18% the following year, for total revenue of $650,000. Established 70+ new accounts.
- Authored 14-page Employee Handbook; developed formal standards and policies for labor staff.
- Created new business line, hardscaping. Also created Web site for retail mulch sales.

Account Executive
Star Publishing, Las Vegas, Nev.   [dates]

Sold advertising to local and national clients for primarily business-to-business publications, including area chamber of commerce directories. Total circulation was approximately 100,000.

Maintained established accounts and developed new leads and clients. Consulted directly with clients' executive staffs to secure ad sales. Kept track of and met multiple, concurrent publication deadlines. Worked with creative design staff to develop advertising concepts and content. Managed full sales-cycle, ensuring client satisfaction.

Key Accomplishments:

- Consistently met/exceeded sales goals; sold $100,000 of advertising in 6 months.
- Established territory for newly won contract — Susquehanna Chamber of Commerce Quality of Life Guide, a full-color directory. Landed 35 new accounts, worth $35,000.

President

Your Lawn and Garden, LLC, Henderson, Nev.   [dates]

Founder/operator of landscaping business. Oversaw all aspects of company start-up and operation, including sales and marketing, business development, accounting, and management.

Researched market and identified specific demographics of targeted client base. Developed marketing strategy; created and distributed advertising materials. Managed customer relationships; met with potential clients, negotiated contract, and closed sale. Directed staff of 1-3, coordinating projects and ensuring completion.

Sales Manager

Sailor's Restaurant and Seaside Guide, San Francisco, Calif.   [dates]

Sold advertising for 2 regional editions of full-color, glossy boating magazine, circulation of 110,000.

Created sales territory for new regional edition of this yearly publication, distributed at local marinas. Generated leads through direct contact and cold calls. Clients included hotels, restaurants, yacht brokers, and retail shops. Negotiated contracts, established payment schedules, and designed ads. Managed billing and publication distribution. Once established, maintained and expanded client base.

OTHER WORK EXPERIENCE

Flight Attendant

Delta Airlines, Las Vegas, Nev.   [dates]

Provided customer service, resolved passenger and employee problems, and responded to emergency situations. As Chief Purser, supervised crews of 2-10; provided liaison with captain. Received numerous commendations and customer appreciation letters.

Editor: [dates]

Created and published 20-page bimonthly staff newsletter. Selected and compiled content and artwork; edited, formatted, designed, proofread, and laid out publication.

EDUCATION

B.S.,[2] Marketing, in progress, University of Nevada, Las Vegas, Nev.; 96 credits. Expected graduation: [date]

A.A.,[2] Business, City College of San Francisco, San Francisco, Calif.,   [date]

COMPUTER SKILLS:[5] MS Word, Excel, Outlook, Publisher, PowerPoint; Photoshop; ACT! database

Baby Boomer. <u>Publisher turned Author.</u> Hybrid. Retired from a successful publishing career and self-published his own book. Author Publisher seeks speaking engagements via radio, TV, and conferences about life experiences and career successes. Requirements: strong, professional speaking skills and appearance,[1] a message to give,[2] energetic,[3] people-person [4] and drive to share experiences. [5]

FRANK S. JUDAKIS

555 Warren Pl. • Providence, RI 99999

Phone 666-777-4040 • Twitter: @FSJudakis • E-mail: fjudakis@comcast.net

MOTIVATIONAL SPEAKER

Seasoned, popular speaker,[1] energetic,[3] inspirational, witty, and direct. Passion to share life experiences and expertise[5] and enrich lives of others. Enjoy reaching out to diverse groups[4] to communicate message.[2] Topics include publishing, journalism publicity, marketing, entrepreneurship, and contemporary business professionalism.

HIGHLIGHTS OF EXPERIENCE

BEST-SELLING AUTHOR, *To Love Mercy,* published by MidAtlantic Highlands, Huntington, W.V. A non-fiction book of memoirs and close-to-true-life fiction by residents of Mid-Atlantic States. Completed two successful book tours, interviews on more than 20 radio shows, and second printing in just three months. Featured in the Chicago Sunday Sun-Times.

PUBLISHER/CONSULTANT, COMMUNICATIONS GROUP, Chevy Chase, Md.
Provide publishing, marketing, editorial and strategic consulting to publishers and other clients. Published over 60,000 FEDERAL PERSONNEL GUIDES until [date]; readership averaged 70,000 per print and on-line guide. Previously published nationally influential newsletters including Health Policy Week, Managed Care Report, Prospective Payment Guide, Law Firm Profit Report and others.

PARTNER, AMERICAN COMMUNICATIONS GROUP, Bethesda, Md.
One of three partners in firm that published six newsletters and one database service serving gasoline marketers, credit unions, small banks, day care providers and business mailers.

ASSISTANT EDITOR, THE WASHINGTON POST, Washington, D.C.
Edited Watergate copy for L.A. Times/Washington Post News Service client newspapers.

REPORTER AND EDITOR, THE ASSOCIATED PRESS, Chicago, Ill.
Covered numerous famous disorders, riots, and demonstrattions.

OTHER ACCOMPLISHMENTS/EXPERIENCE

Gold (first prize), best newsletter promotion, by The Newsletter Clearinghouse, [date]

Adjunct Professor, American University School of Communications, Washington D.C., [dates]
Adjunct Professor, George Washington University, Washington D.C., [dates]
Chair, Small Publishers Working Group, Newsletter Publishers Association, [year]

Young Professional. Associate Editor. Reverse chronological. Journalist seeks features/projects designer position. Requirements: 3 years of weekly newsroom design experience,[1] solid news judgment,[2] communication skills,[3] attention to detail,[4] and knowledge of InDesign.[5]

JANCIE ULREY
Boston, MA • Mobile: 617-777-6767 • Email: jan_ulrey@gmail.com

JOURNALIST/LAYOUT & DESIGN SPECIALIST

OBJECTIVE: Features/Projects Designer

PROFILE: Nearly six years' experience in weekly newspaper settings, serving as writer, editor and page designer.[1] Passionate about newsgathering and creating eye-catching, reader-friendly content. Solid news judgment and design skills,[2] coupled with imagination and creativity, able to produce aesthetically pleasing pages. Organized, detail-oriented [4] and deadline-driven. Strong time management and communications skills;[3] excel in team and individual work settings. Proficient in AP Style. **Computer Skills:** Word, Outlook, Excel, PowerPoint, Access; Quark Express; InDesign;[5] Photoshop; HTML

~ **A.A.S.,** Communications, Bunker Hill Community College, Boston, Mass., [date] ~

RELEVANT EXPERIENCE

Associate Editor   [dates]
Bay Windows   Boston, Mass.

Design, layout and write for weekly newspaper, averaging 64-136 pages, with circulation of 16,000.

- Design/Layout: Plan and execute advertising and editorial page design, including front and back pages, news and features sections, headlines, column titles, and cutlines. Review weekly ad sales and determine page count and color slots. Formulate layout design and presentation using InDesign, including style and size of type, photographs, and graphics. Take layout direction from editor and work with advertising and design staff to correct problems. Use Photoshop to make color corrections on photos and crop and rotate images; track photo archives.

- Writing/Editing: Research, develop and write news and feature stories. Contribute to editorial planning, develop story ideas and arrange and conduct interviews. Review copy and correct errors in content, grammar and punctuation, following appropriate formatting and AP style guidelines. Write/rewrite cutlines and headlines. Correct final copy and prepare files for Web upload.

Key Accomplishments:
- Successfully completed layout/production on largest paper (136 pages) in publication's history for 30th anniversary issue.
- Supported new editor, staff writer and editorial assistant during major staff transition.
- Wrote over 40 feature and news stories while handling design/production responsibilities.

Staff Writer   [dates]
The Sunday Voice   Cambridge, Mass.

Key player on four-person staff of this small weekly community newspaper.

- Writing/Content Selection: Contributed to and/or managed news coverage, determining emphasis, length, and format. Wrote hard/soft news, including school news and obituaries. Gathered information through research, interviews, experience, and attendance of events.

- Production/Administration: Planned and executed layout of school news section and obituaries, as well as determined page count and scanned photos. Edited and proofread editorial content. Assumed managing editor's duties as needed, leading news meetings, assigning stories, and gathering news content. Also, screened phone calls and purchased supplies.

Mid-Career Professional. <u>Vice President</u>. Reverse chronological. Banking executive seeks regional finance manager position. Requirements: Bachelor's degree in finance or accounting, MBA or CPA preferred,[1] 5-7 years experience in accounting, finance, and auditing,[2] proficient in SAS, SQL, Access, Excel, and PowerPoint,[3] results oriented,[4] and strong written and verbal communication skills.[5]

DAVID M. SHERLE

9080 Hopscotch Circle • Denver, CO 80012
Residence: 555-777-9090 • Cell: 303-333-4545
Email: sherle_dm@comcast.net

FINANCIAL SERVICES EXECUTIVE

Special Assets/Credit Administration/Risk Management

Over 7 years' broad banking experience, including accounting, finance, and auditing.[2] Technical expertise in special assets, loan workout, and credit administration. In-depth knowledge of foreclosure and multiple bankruptcy procedures. Excellent ability to communicate and build consensus with diverse groups having dissimilar interests. Results oriented,[4] with strong negotiation, organization, and written/verbal communication skills.[5] Proficient in MS Word, Excel, Outlook, PowerPoint, Access; SQL; SAS.[3]

Leadership & Organizational Expertise

- Business & Market Development
- Strategic Planning & Development
- Team Building & Performance Improvement
- Inter- & Intra-Banking Relationships

Financial Expertise

- Corporate & Individual Credit Analysis
- Cost Benefit Analysis
- Asset Recovery
- Risk Management

PROFESSIONAL EXPERIENCE

Vice President
Community Bank, N.A., Denver. Colo.   [dates]

- Senior Workout Officer/Credit Administration Division. Monitor due diligence and integrity of distressed commercial loan, commercial real estate, and charged-off loan portfolios in excess of $15M.
- Loan Workout. Reduce non-performing assets via restructure, renegotiation, or vacate strategy. Meet with client to discuss loan status and ascertain best options to improve and/or recover loan and related expenses. Conduct cost-benefit analysis, consider credit/cash flow constraints and bankruptcy/legal remediation prior to formulation of Action Plan.
- Implement Action Plan. Work with bank's legal counsel from default initiation through account reconciliation and/or exit.
- Establish bid-in guidelines, coordinate, and finalize public auctions of real estate.
- Manage Other Real Estate Owned.
- Standing Member, Problem Loan Committee.

DAVID M. SHERLE, page 2
555-777-9090

- Perform Quality Review, examining select loans for regulatory and internal policy compliance. Prepare reports for senior management.

Key Accomplishments:
- Reduced delinquencies from 8.85% to 2.05% of aggregate loans outstanding ($150M), net charge-off recovery of $1.95M or 36% of assigned footing ($5.48M).
- Liquidation of all Other Real Estate Owned properties.

Assistant Vice President, Special Assets Department
Southern Trust Co., Denver, Colo.   [dates]

- Managing Officer of Commercial Loan/Mortgage Workout Department. Generated monthly Action Plans for assets classified/criticized by Office of the Comptroller of the Currency.
- Underwriting Officer of SBA loan portfolio and agency leasing program.

Key Accomplishments:
- Garnered "Favorable" department rating for [dates] O.C.C. examinations.
- Reduced delinquency from 8.78% to 1.05% of aggregate loan/mortgage base ($97.5M).
- Downsized Other Real Estate Owned by 95% ($2.98M).

Assistant Vice President, Special Assets Department
Bank of the West, Tacoma, Wash.   [dates]

- Vice President of a bank subsidiary, specifically created for the sale of Other Real Estate Owned commercial properties and industrial machinery/equipment; aggregate portfolio tiered at $17.5M, with collections approximating $3.5M.
- Workout Officer for Credit/Support Services Division. Collected or restructured non-performing outstandings under commercial loan, real estate and equipment leasing portfolios. Maximized monetary recovery through credit/collateral risk analysis and distressed-asset liquidation under auction and direct sale. Managed loan portfolio in excess of $18M.
- Special Assets Officer.

Vice President, Commercial/Consumer Loan Department   [dates]
Ado State Bank, Alamosa, Colo.

- Senior Credit Officer, overseeing dual-loan portfolio in excess of $42.5M. Supervised two managers and five support staff. Implemented operational procedures and regulatory controls as required by Federal statutes.

Early Professional Career
Business Development Officer, Central Bank   [dates]
Loan Review Officer, Corporate Loan Group, Mercantile Bank   [dates]
Regional Loan Officer, Community Banking Division, Union Trust Company of Colorado [dates]

EDUCATION
MBA,[1] University of Colorado at Denver, Denver, Colo. 3.80 GPA   [date]
BA, Accounting, Adams State College, Alamosa, Colo., 3.75 GPA   [date]

New Graduate. <u>Veterinary Technician</u>. Reverse chronological. Worked in field while student; now seeks better job in larger vet hospital. Requirements: Medically assist veterinarians,[1] bachelor's degree,[2] instrumentation,[3] office software.[4]

DONNA LUNA

4214 Kensington Rd. • Dallas, TX 99999
Cell: 111-869-4716 • E-mail: DLuna@hotmail.com

PROFILE: Recent BS Biology plus 8 years' experience in veterinary and medical fields. Skilled in latest technology. Work cheerfully on team or independently. PC proficient. Dependable, conscientious veterinary paraprofessional ready for senior level veterinary hospital staff position.

LABORATORY SKILLS

- ✓ Dexterous use of laboratory equipment and instrumentation, including isolating environmental samples, performing assays, and identifying samples. Prepare, analyze, and test laboratory specimens. Stain slides to microscopic test for specific disease pathogens and unknowns.

- ✓ Assist with veterinary surgical and autopsy procedures. Perform micro animal surgeries and anesthetizations.

- ✓ Collect blood, and other samples from animals. Perform red/white blood cell counts.

- ✓ Keep comprehensive lab notes and researched, prepared, and presented detailed reports and papers. Lead and organized group project work.

WORK EXPERIENCE

Veterinary Technician   [dates]
Westview Animal Hospital, Dallas, Tx.

<u>Veterinary Support</u>:[1] Assist veterinarians to diagnose and treat variety of animal diseases and conditions including surgeries. Take and test blood, urine, and fecal samples, testing for disease, viruses, and parasites. Skilled with instrumentation, including radiograph and ultrasound.[3] Use Avimark, MS Word, & QuickBooks software.[4]

<u>Reception</u>: Receive and direct calls and visitors, answering customer inquiries and resolving problems. Assure customer satisfaction, exercising empathy and tact. Take and relay detailed messages regarding animal patients. Collect and process payments. Set appointments and send reminder notices. Update and maintain electronic and paper filing systems. Direct and provide guidance to Animal Care Assistants.

Receptionist   [dates]
Dr. Roger Lax, Plano, Tx.
<u>Administration</u>: Receptionist for busy private practice. Answered phones and received patients. Created and updated medical files. Gained competence with medical terminology.

EDUCATION

Bachelor of Science,[2] Biology; Towson University, Towson, Md.   [dates]

Relevant Coursework: Biostatistics, Biology: Ecology, Evolution, & Behavior, Botany, Chemistry, Comparative Animal Physiology, Dangerous Diseases, Fish Biology, Genetics, Medical Microbiology, Organic Chemistry, Physics, Zoology.

Mid-Career Professional. Project Manager. Reverse chronological. PM seeks Managerial HRIS (Human Resource Information Systems) position. Requirements: Bachelor's degree in computer science, management information systems, or equivalent, MS/MBA a plus,[1] five+ years increasing responsibility in HR Technology and/or HR discipline leading medium to large scale projects,[2] three+ years experience in project management,[3] knowledge of current HRIS technology,[4] good analytical, interpersonal, leadership and managerial skills,[5] and strong oral and written communication skills.[6]

JANICE E. DEMER

Anaheim, CA   Day/night: 999-555-5555   E-mail: Janiceedemer@aol.com

MANAGER
HUMAN RESOURCE INFORMATION SYSTEMS

- Project Management
- Implementation Consultant
- Quality Customer Service
- Corporate Start-ups
- Procedural Development
- Corporate & Government Contracts

- Skilled Negotiator
- Strategic Planner
- Sales Process/Full Life Cycle
- Market/Competitor Research
- Product Solutions
- Payroll

Over 5 years' solid career history in HRIS operations including start-ups, reviewing and determining software solutions for payroll and HR issues, training, and large scale project management.[2] Keen eye for analyzing problems and determining viable solutions. Demonstrated experience in effectively managing implementation cycles. Expertly control high-level client problem resolution. Develop and establish 'customer service first' environments, attaining significant levels of customer retention. Proven ability to build and lead teams, establish rapport and manage personnel.[5] Excellent written, presentation, and negotiation skills.[6]

TECHNICAL PROFICIENCY [4]

Web Based Recruiting Tools	HRIS	LANs/WANs	Visio	Word
Internet & Research	Web-based HR/PR	Pivotal	Networks	Excel
Database Management	Tools	MS Project	Access	Outlook
Client Server Technology	SQL Reporting			PowerPoint

PROFESSIONAL EXPERIENCE

Treemont Employer Services, Irvine, Calif.   [dates]
Treemont is a payroll and HR solutions outsourcing company.

Project Manager [3]   [dates]
- Implement and manage responsibilities of multiple, integrated projects. Ensure consistent success of service initiatives across customer segments and business units.
- Collaborate with senior and functional managers to plan business and technology initiatives and budgets. Use formal and informal networks to accomplish objectives.
- Manage cost, schedules and performance of large, highly complex projects. Fully accountable for complex/diverse projects with high degree of business risk.

Janice Demer, Page 2

Key Projects:
- Managed multi-product Web-based implementation worth $250K. Successfully moved a 4,000 employee global client from Windows-based PR/HR software to a Web-based HR/Payroll package. Supervised project team of 17, completing project on time and under budget.
- Carefully managed sensitive outstanding balance issue with hostile client. Directed team of five to troubleshoot complex issues, retain the account, and collect balance in full, equaling $400K.

System Consultant   [dates]
- Generated leads and secured new HRIS clients. Created and delivered proposals and demonstrations to key management personnel (user, technical user, buyer and decision-makers), meeting customer specific requirements. Maintained $8.2 million quota annually. Proposed product solutions and applications working with IT directors for system requirements and functionality. Wrote RFPs.
- Effectively tailored responses and proposals using strategic models to best position firm in marketplace. Managed large and complex client accounts, averaging 500 to 5,000 personnel.
- Reviewed current technology trends. As product expert, educated field staff on cutting edge advances in payroll & HR, recruiting, employee self-service and benefit outsourcing.

Account Executive   [dates]
- Selected at regional level for special project team studying customer retention to proactively manage and develop profitable, long-term customers.
- Met with clients to ensure complete customer satisfaction. Reviewed and recommended solutions to HRIS problems and suggested specific software. Managed conflict resolution.
- Developed account strategies to establish trends and identify opportunities to capitalize on retaining and growing customer base. Coordinated customer training. Negotiated long-term agreements.

Consultant/Implementations   [dates]
- Analyzed customers' payroll needs and provided recommendations for streamlining payroll processes. Negotiated contracts up to $5M.
- Trained customers on Source 500 software. Provided quality on-going customer support, ensuring successful implementation of payroll, human resources, and tax filing accounts.

Mountain High Health Services, Villa Park, Calif.
                                                                             [dates]
Mountain High held a government contract for the military insurance program—housing multiple large databases with hundreds of thousands of files and records.

Operations Supervisor
- Developed and implemented start-up plans/operations/audits to employ and operate call center with 700 employees. Implemented new database software and controlled large databases.
- Hired and trained 60 direct-report employees, set-up department, and staffed call center with 500 additional personnel. Determined all staffing requirements, providing timely hiring and training.

EDUCATION

    M.A.,[1] Information Access and Management, University of California, Irvine, GPA: 4.0   [date]
    B.A., Human Resources Management, California State University Fullerton, GPA: 3.85   [date]

             Project Management Institute, Irvine, Calif., Member

Chapter 16

A Sampling of OnTarget Resumes for Special Circumstances

● ●

*J*ust because you're changing careers or stepping out of your military uniform, or explaining resume gaps, or running away from home back into the workforce, or are ready to belt the next person who calls you "overqualified," don't think you're necessarily at a disadvantage. You can create a riveting resume. The samples in this chapter give you some ideas about how to do just that by deftly handling your special circumstances.

A text box atop each sample resume contains a mission statement — that is, what the job seeker aims to accomplish, which usually is a better job. The mission statement also includes the requirements for a specific position — or a summary of the typically requested requirements for an occupation or career field.

Within the mission statement, each of the job's requirements has a number next to it. The same number also appears in the body of the resume next to the job seeker's matching qualification for that requirement.

The cross-matched numbers between a job's requirements and the candidate's qualifications shown here are just for illustration, *not for your actual resumes.*

These samples are intended to laser your attention to requirement-and-qualification matching, the single most important factor in causing your candidacy to get noticed in an online swarm of resumes.

Career Change. <u>Flight Attendant</u>. Reverse chronological. Experienced flight attendant seeks new career in sales/account management outside travel field. Requirements: Bachelor's degree,[1] 5+ years' Customer Service Support or Sales Experience,[2] proficiency in Word, Excel, and Outlook,[3] excellent communication, organization, time management, and presentation skills,[4] and willingness to be part of a high-performing team![5]

Pamela Wright

Seattle, WA

Day/Evening: (777) 333-2525   p_wright@yahoo.com

OBJECTIVE: Customer Service Account Manager

QUALIFICATIONS SUMMARY:

Results-driven Customer Service professional with over 5 years of customer service support experience.[2] Self-confidence, integrity, and commitment to customer service excellence. Creative, pragmatic and proactive problem-solver. Organized and attentive to detail, with demonstrated time management skills. Strong research, mediation, and negotiation skills gained from work place experience. Dynamic oral, writing, interpersonal, and presentation skills.[4] Energetic team member.[5] PC proficient.

PROFESSIONAL EXPERIENCE

Lead Flight Attendant   [dates]
Northwest Airlines, Inc., Seattle, Wash.

Supervise Staff, Customer Liaison:
- Answer customer inquiries and resolve problems, working with diverse clientele. Anticipate and assess needs; assist passengers with baggage and boarding. Build customer rapport; use diplomacy and tact to avoid confrontational situations and defuse hostile customers.
- Oversee work performance of up to four flight attendants during flights. Consult with cockpit and cabin crew for trip briefings. Use communication log to update staff and management.

Plan and organize in-flight services flow and ensure safety and comfort of passengers. Collect payment for retail products. Account for meals, beverages, and other supplies.

Leadership of Flight Attendants.
- Elected to lead 525 flight attendants. Coordinated six employee support committees.
- Developed and managed database systems to track and distribute information.
- Developed leadership training and budget requirements.

Maintain knowledge of government regulations.
- Interpret and communicate complex regulations, policies, and procedures in language the public can understand.
- Continually analyze work processes and recommend ways to improve operations and services.

Notable Achievements:
- Awarded three Certificates of Excellence for providing exceptional service to customers.
- Developed new procedure to improve flexibility for handling emergencies.

EDUCATION/COMPUTER SKILLS

Bachelor of Arts,[1] Communication   [date]
The George Washington University, School of Media and Public Affairs, Washington, D.C.

Windows; Word, Outlook, PowerPoint, Excel.[3]

Returning Homemaker. <u>Nurse</u>. Functional. Homemaker seeks R.N. position. Requirements: Current Registered Nurse license,[1] graduate of approved School of Nursing,[2] current physical assessment skills,[3] comprehensive knowledge of nursing principles,[4] current CPR certification,[5] strong attention to detail,[6] and patient/family interaction skills.[7]

Pearl Izumi, R.N.

Dallas, TX
Cell: 222-888-4040 • Email: pearlizumi@hotmail.com

SUMMARY: Licensed Registered Nurse[1] with comprehensive knowledge of nursing principles.[4] Three years of field/classroom experience. Dependable and highly organized, with excellent attention to detail[6] and follow through. Personable, able to develop positive rapport and empathize with patient and family.[7] Strong communication skills—speaking, listening, and writing. Experienced in managing crisis situations and resolving problems. Enjoy working as a team member or individually. Experienced instructor.

KEY SKILLS/QUALIFICATIONS

➤ Direct patient care; patient charting and client care documentation; robust physical condition[3]
➤ Assessing patient condition, planning appropriate treatment and administering patient care and discharge plans
➤ Educating patients and family for home care[7]
➤ Maintaining sterile fields and applying dressings; catheter, IV, and suctioning training; cleaning instruments and surgical equipment
➤ CPR certified, valid through [date][5]

EARLIER EXPERIENCE

Trainer   [dates: more than a decade ago]
Best Solutions Group, Irving, Texas
➤ Developed training program and presented software curriculum for healthcare companies.
➤ Analyzed client needs and created appropriate training materials. Wrote curriculum and materials for companies in four states. Designed/presented "The Trainer's Trainer" program for Canadian counterparts.

EDUCATION

A.A.,[2] Nursing, El Centro College, Dallas, Texas; GPA 4.0   [date]
Clinical: Parkland Memorial Hospital, Irving Coppell Surgical Hospital, Dallas Southwest Medical Center, Renaissance Hospital

General coursework, Boston College, Boston, Mass., 60 credits   [dates: more than a decade ago]

Military to Civilian. <u>Operations Manager</u>. Hybrid. Army officer seeks to transition into Supply Chain Management for Government Contractors. Requirements: 10+ years supply chain management experience,[1] 10+ years supervisory experience,[2] degree in Logistics, Industrial Engineering, or related discipline,[3] strong relationship-building skills,[4] and excellent communication and presentation skills; high integrity.[5]

JERRY W. THOMAS

CR 475 Box 12 * APO AE 09000
011-49 (0) 555-5555555 (c) * jerryw.thomas@yahoo.com

CAREER FOCUS
SUPPLY CHAIN MANAGEMENT

TRANSPORTATION • OPERATIONS • INSTRUCTOR • FORCE PROTECTION

PROFESSIONAL AND PERSONAL VALUE OFFERED

- Current Secret Clearance
- Twenty years' professional experience as an Operations Manager with specific expertise in large-scale transportation and supply management operations.[1]
- Superior technical and interpersonal communications, building strong relationships and alliances.[4] Excellent written, verbal and presentation skills.[5] Thoroughly enjoy challenges and creative problem resolution. Maintain high integrity.[5]
- Draft and implement policies and procedures. Manage logistical and administrative requirements for hundreds of personnel supporting thousands of customers in multiple countries—knowledge of treaties and regulations governing arms control and property book control.
- Quickly assess operations and initiate improvements in staffing, organization and procedures. Manage multiple, simultaneous and complex projects and programs.
- Assemble, motivate, train, and inspire talented working teams/staffs. Consistently produce quality.

PROFESSIONAL EMPLOYMENT AND SELECTED EXAMPLES OF QUALIFICATIONS IN ACTION

MANAGER, RANGE CONTROL & SAFETY [dates]
U.S. Army, Deployed to Kosovo

- Manage administration, resource planning, safety coordination, and operations for a range serving complex 30 separate organizations in Europe. Create schedules and communicate with customers for scheduling requirements. Write reports and submit documentation.
- Serve as a consultant and advisor to Director on safety, operations, and specific issues.
- Formulate safety guidelines and policies and provide operational guidance. Assure that customers adhere to safety policies and procedures.
- Acted as consultant to area managers to prepare quotes, negotiate contracts, monitor shipments, and coordinate deliveries within Europe and Eastern Asia.

OPERATIONS MANAGER   [dates]
ACCOUNT MANAGER   [dates]
Brown and Root Contractor, Germany

- Supervised warehouse operations including receiving merchandise and delivery. Supervised 38 personnel[2] including five administrative staff, seven subcontractors, 23 warehouse personnel, and three contract security personnel responsible for warehousing and storage of $33M perishable and non-perishable products. Supervised, evaluated work performance, and rated employees.

- Coordinated incoming shipments with shipping contractors (military and civilian), managed the workload, monitored manpower requirements, processed special orders and critical deliveries.

- Managed customer service, ensuring customer satisfaction. Developed an SOP to track shipments.

- Supply Center Program – Europe Account Manager: Managed new and existing requisition and supply accounts. Supervised and coordinated resources with local vendors for purchases up to $15M.

U.S. Army (Senior Noncommissioned Officer)   [dates]
SENIOR ADMINISTRATOR   [dates]
First Infantry Division, Germany

- Managed and supervised logistical operation procedures. Oversight direction for administration and coordination of training support, safety control, and supply requirements during deployment and contingency training in a split-country operation.

- Directed logistical operations for 42 sub-divisional units including field deployments, division gunneries, and maneuver densities. Managed $900K worth of equipment.

- Assisted the Food Service Supervisor in interpreting and implementing Army's Food Service program and provided multifunctional logistical support for operations in garrison and field. Supervised staff of 89, provided class I support to 1,200 soldiers, accounted for $7M in equipment, and managed annual budget of $90,000.

- Selected to provide logistical training support and foreign military training in Hungary. Coordinated logistical requirements for 4,200 personnel and trained individual delegations on logistical support from setting up a command to managing a supply channel.

OPERATIONS SUPERVISOR, Korea   [dates]

- Coordinated and directed maneuvers, supply operations, inventories, hand-receipts, special procurements and other logistical requirements for 20 sub-divisional organizations including inspections and evaluations.

- Implemented emergency, disaster, and combat feeding plans (computed supply usage factors). Developed SOPs for safety, security, and fire prevention programs.

Education, Training & Awards

> **B.S.,[3]** Business/Integrated Supply Chain & Operations Management,   [dates]
> University of Phoenix, Phoenix, Az
>
> > International Merchant, Purchase Authorization Card training, [date] • Requisition and Local Procurement Management Training, [date] • Senior Advisor and Management Course, [date] (3 weeks) • Automated Management Information System, [date] • Advanced Leadership and Management Course, 6 weeks, [date]

Overqualified. <u>Manager</u>. Reverse chronological. Equal Employment Program Administrator seeks lighter responsibility as EEO consultant or investigator.(Candidate has a master's degree but doesn't mention it because the job ad doesn't call for an advanced degree. She would mention the fact in an interview. And the candidate would include her master's if the job ad stipulated a preference for an advanced or professional degree.) Requirements: Minimum of three years' Human Resources, EEO Claims, Employment Law and/or related experience,[1] Bachelor's degree in Business Administration, Human Resources or related field.[2] Solid investigative and writing skills,[3] organizational, time-management, and interpersonal skills.[4]

PAMELA THIERRY

Kansas City, MO   E-mail: pam_thierry@aol.com   Cell: 111-444-0909

OBJECTIVE

EEO Consultant. Energetic and dedicated, though no longer enjoy frantic managerial pace. Seeking challenging non-managerial position.

PROFESSIONAL SUMMARY

- Exceptional conflict resolution, investigation and mediation skills [3]
- Proven ability to organize work, prioritize tasks and produce high quality work products in a timely manner [4]
- Expert knowledge of EEO laws and procedures.
- Demonstrated interpersonal,[4] written and oral communications skills [3]
- Results oriented and effective team leader
- Dedicated, with strong work ethic
- Word, Excel, Outlook, Access, PowerPoint, Internet research skills

PROFESSIONAL EXPERIENCE

CENTERS FOR MEDICARE & MEDICAID SERVICES   [dates] [1]
Kansas City, Mo.

Supervisory Equal Employment Opportunity Specialist
- Team Leader for the Office of Equal Opportunity and Civil Rights' EEO complaints processing team. Consult with customers to acquire information, collect and analyze evidence, and prepare investigative reports. Negotiate conciliations and interact with complainants, agency staff, and legal staff.
- Direct and monitor Alternative Dispute Resolution (ADR) Program for EEO complaints.
- Direct and monitor EEO Contract Investigations Program.
- Prepare and deliver presentations and training for agency EEO counselors, Federal ADR professionals, and agency managers and employees.

PAMELA THIERRY Cell: 111-444-0909

Key Accomplishment:
- Brought agency into 100% compliance with all EEO regulatory time frames. Reconciled EEO complaint inventory. Eliminated backlog of complaints. Improved quality of written work products. Established office as a model for complaint processing.

U.S. EQUAL EMPLOYMENT OPPORTUNITY COMMISSION [dates]
St. Louis, Mo.

Held a series of increasingly responsible positions in **Equal Employment Opportunity** and **Alternative Dispute Resolution**.
Alternative Dispute Resolution Coordinator (Acting), [dates]; Mediator/Facilitator, [dates]; Intake Supervisor, [dates]; Investigator/ADR Coordinator, [dates]; Systemic Investigator, [dates]; Investigator, [dates]

- Managed and evaluated EEOC, St. Louis District Field Office's mediation program.
- Used variety of ADR processes to resolve employment discrimination complaints involving private companies and state, local, and Federal agencies.
- Investigated class allegations of employment discrimination.
- Investigated individual charges of discrimination involving private companies and state and local government agencies.
- Managed and responded to Congressional inquiries, White House correspondence, interagency referrals, and public inquiries.

Key Accomplishments
- Effectively managed inventory of 100 cases, while consistently receiving positive feedback from clients regarding timeliness, responsiveness, and outcome of mediation sessions. Expanded Field Office use of ADR.
- Recognized for high level of success in resolving complex cases.
- Contributor to development of nationwide Mediation Training Program for staff and contract mediators.
- High percentage of investigations resulting in findings of discrimination and conciliation agreements.

ADDITIONAL PROFESSIONAL EXPERIENCE

U.S. Department of Justice, Community Relations Service; Internship
U.S. Office of Personnel Management; Investigator
National Institute on Aging, Gerontology Research Center; Library and Research Assistant

EDUCATION

Bachelor's Degree,[2] Business Administration, Truman State University, Kirksville, Mo.

PROFESSIONAL AFFILIATIONS

Co-Chair, Federal Executive Board, Alternative Dispute Resolution Council
Volunteer Mediator, Federal Executive Board, Mediation Services Program
Volunteer Mediator, Department of Justice, Office of Civil Rights, Disability Rights Section

Grouping Temp Jobs. <u>Legal Assistant</u>. Reverse chronological. Legal Assistant seeks Paralegal position, based on recent certification and 7 years' experience in legal field. Requirements: Paralegal certificate,[1] at least 5 years' experience in legal setting,[2] experience in preparing contracts and agreements,[3] excellent communications skills,[4] advanced computer skills,[5] minimum typing speed 75 wpm,[6] project management skills,[7] professional demeanor.[8]

BRINDA BASU

333 Bladensburg Avenue • Dallas, TX 12345
Residence: (444) 777-1212 • Cell: (444) 999-1919
Email: brinda_basu@gmail.com

OBJECTIVE: Paralegal

Over 7 years' experience as legal assistant and legal secretary,[2] with additional administrative experience. Expertise in legal research, drafting pleadings and motions, scheduling depositions and coordinating hearings, case file management and analysis, record keeping and data tracking, client interviewing and recommending actions. Law experience includes Personal Injury, Medical Malpractice, Family Law, Estate Planning, Workers' Comp and Corporate Law.

Core competencies include efficiency, organization, working well under pressure and deadlines and attention to detail. Professional demeanor,[8] with excellent interpersonal and communications skills.[4] Typing speed: 75 wpm.[6]

COMPUTER PROFICIENCIES [5]

Expert in MS Office: Word, Excel, Outlook, Access; WordPerfect; Quicken; Internet; familiar with Lexis-Nexis and various legal billing and litigation management software

EMPLOYMENT HISTORY

Paralegal Intern   [dates]
Public Defender's Office, Dallas, Texas

• Reported directly to and provided support for Public Defender in busy city district. Researched cases and transcribed tapes. Summarized police reports and compiled trial notebook. Maintained and updated legal case files. Wrote speedy trial motion.

Legal Assistant
Harlow Staffing Services, Dallas, Texas   [dates]

Assigned to Dallas/Fort Worth law firms, including: James & Marks; Dean M. Holly; Linda K. Ryan; Gonzalez & Gonzalez; Dixie and Moor

- Office Management: Coordinated office functions for small law firms, including client file management, billing and accounts payable and receivable. Supervised administrative and word processing staff.

- Research/Writing: Conducted thorough research of federal and state statutes, using Internet and law libraries. Identified and summarized relevant points in primary and secondary authorities of law. Applied court opinions, statutes and court rules in writing recommendations for course of action on complex personal injury and property damage claims. Prepared contracts, agreements and other legal documents.[3]

- Litigation Support/Case Management: Served as project manager for casework and litigation support.[7] Summarized depositions, medical records, employment records and other relevant documents. Organized documents for trial. Drafted various pleadings and documents for medical malpractice, personal injury and family law actions. Coordinated expedited hearings and met all filing deadlines. Scheduled and assisted with depositions.

- Personal Injury, Tort Law/Medical Knowledge: Experienced in tort law, case analysis procedures, discovery and client/witness interviewing. Knowledge of medical terminology.

Legal Assistant
The Ramirez Law Firm, Dallas, Texas   [dates]

- Executive assistant to Senior Partner and associate. Wrote and followed up on longshoremen and workers' compensation claims. Interviewed claimants for relevant information and summarized cases. Scheduled depositions and ensured all parties received notices. Provided liaison with opposing counsel to determine and/or confirm course of action. Contacted insurance companies to follow up on claims and communications.

Legal Secretary
Law Offices of Danes and Smith, Dallas, Texas   [dates]

- Assisted in timely and complex preparation of cases from discovery to trial phase. Prepared case files, including case summaries, supporting forms and documentation. Processed wide range of business contracts. Researched cases, decisions, laws and statutes.
- Managed scheduling functions. Received and reviewed all incoming correspondence. Prepared outgoing correspondence, including client, court and opposing counsel communications. Screened and directed calls and visitors.

EDUCATION/TRAINING

Paralegal Certificate,[1] Southeastern Career Institute, Dallas, Texas, GPA: 4.0/4.0   [date]

Mediation & Conflict Resolution Certificate, Texas Women's University   [date]

A.A. Degree, Liberal Arts, Camden County College, Camden, N.J.   [date]

Military Spouse. <u>Military Family Member</u>. Reverse chronological. Instructor and Training Coordinator seeks Trainer position. Requirements: Bachelor's degree,[1] minimum of 5 years of experience in adult education, curriculum design and development,[2] experience coordinating and administering training programs,[3] knowledge of curriculum evaluations including qualitative and quantitative analysis,[4] excellent communications and program marketing skills,[5] and willing to travel.[6]

MELODY ANN RICHARDS

456 Pine St. • Falls Church, VA 99999
Cell: 666-333-3333
Email: melody.richards@comcast.net

TRAINER

Training and Curriculum Specialist, Instructor, Coordinator

✓ Experienced instructor with 5+ years' experience in training and curriculum design [2]
✓ Public speaking, teaching professional adults clearly, comfortably and memorably [5]
✓ Excellent content developer utilizing interactive exercises and multi-media images in PowerPoint presentations
✓ Skilled in curriculum design and lesson planning
✓ Critical analysis, including qualitative and quantitative review of course evaluations for continuous improvement [4]
✓ Excellent listening and consulting skills meeting management and personal training objectives; willing to travel [6]

PROFESSIONAL EXPERIENCE

Employment Readiness Assistant   [dates]
Army Community Service, Ft. Myer Military Community, Va.

<u>Career Instruction.</u> Instruct military personnel and family members in job search strategies, interview skills and resume writing techniques.

<u>Employment Counseling.</u> Train military community in employment strategies both individually and in classroom settings. Coordinate appointments and group trainings.[3] Assist clients with job search, resume writing and interviewing skills. Market qualified applicants to local employers in private industry, county, state and federal government.

<u>Job Fair and Special Event Coordination.</u> Organize and facilitate job fairs, career expos and luncheons. As team member, manage events for up to 200 family members seeking employment.

Accomplishments:
✓ Successfully developed relationships with more than 20 local small and mid-sized businesses for consideration of spouse employment.[5]
✓ Established cooperation with federal agency human resources recruiters to establish placement opportunities with Federal Career Internship programs.
✓ Developed successful interactive curriculum, which has resulted in excellent class attendance and evaluations.

Senior Core Instructor   [dates]
Universal Movement, Virginia Beach, Va.

Program Design. Developed syllabus and implemented marketing strategies for numerous yoga classes and workshops. Coordinated program offerings and class schedules.[3] As Core Instructor, managed program oversight, assessment and evaluation.

Coaching and Instruction. Regularly met with students to review required hours and complete grid for registry application.

Accomplishment:
✓ Co-designed initial teacher training program in accordance with industry guidelines.

Program Developer/Instructor   [dates]
Adult Learning Center, Virginia Beach, Va.

Course Development and Marketing.[5] Expanded yoga program from one class to eight classes per week in addition to monthly weekend workshops.

Curriculum Design and Evaluation. Wrote class descriptions and syllabus. Developed marketing materials, class evaluations, and lending library for students.

Accomplishment:
✓ Increased classroom enrollment by 110% over one year.

EDUCATION

B.S.,[1] Business Administration, University of Nebraska, Lincoln, Neb.   [date]

AFFILIATIONS AND LICENSES

Career Masters Institute   [dates]

Association of Job Search Trainers   [dates]

Licensed Yoga Instructor   [dates]

Licensed Yoga "Train the Trainer" Instructor and Curriculum Design   [date]

TRAINING COURSES

Training and Presentation Coaching, Worldwide Media, New York City   [dates]

Training in PowerPoint Design and Program Marketing, 16 classroom hours   [date]

Extensive Yoga Training and Development, US and International courses   [date]

COMPUTER SKILLS

Microsoft Office: Word, Excel, Outlook, PowerPoint, Access; Adobe Photoshop (basic skills).

Too Many Layoffs. Information Technology. Hybrid. Information technology network expert seeks Network Analyst position. (Through no fault of his own, candidate has been laid-off three times in about four years. To prevent employer's assuming he was terminated for cause or is a job hopper, candidate makes exception to the resume rule of giving no reasons for leaving a job.) Requirements: Bachelor's degree in Computer Science or equivalent training and several years of related full-time experience, [1] experience operating and configuring security and networking on enterprise systems, [2] excellent customer service skills, [3] knowledge of networks routing and switching equipment, authentication systems, network diagnosis tools, [4] and experience with Windows and Unix. [5]

JASON P. KING

Cell: 555-444-1010   Email: jpking@gmail.com   Pittsburgh, PA

Network analyst and security administrator more than three years of LAN administrative experience.[1] Recognized for expert troubleshooting, using network analyzers and test equipment to quickly solve network hardware problems. Able to research past problem resolutions and develop new solutions. Adept in planning, coordinating, and controlling automated systems.

AREAS OF EXPERTISE

- <u>Local Area Networks:</u> Experienced in installation/configuration of new software modules, user training, diagnostic and problem resolution, testing and providing operational support and maintaining/monitoring automated systems.

- <u>System Design:</u> Adept at analyzing, designing and implementing computer software to manage central systems.

- <u>Customer Service & Communications:</u> Good at understanding and resolving client problems.[3] Outstanding documentation, written and verbal communication skills. Comfortable in high-pressure, 24/7 on-call environment. Team member and mentor.

IT KNOWLEDGE AND SKILLS

Software: [4,5] Novell NetWare 3.1/4.0, Win95/98/XP/Vista, IIS, Linux (RedHat), Checkpoint Firewall1/VPN1, Visio, Cisco PIX, Unix Citrix

Hardware: [4] PC maintenance/installation, servers, desktops and laptops, Cisco Routers/Catalyst Switches, Cabletron Ethernet/Fast Ethernet, Ascend/Lucent ISDN

Networking: Peer-to-Peer, Client/Server, TCP/IP, DHCP, WINS, DNS, Routing, Network Cabling, FDDI, Gateways, Firewalls, Ethernet, VPN

CERTIFICATIONS [1]

MCSE, MCP+Internet,	[date]
MCP: NT Workstation, Server, Enterprise, TCP/IP, IIS3.0,	[date]
A+ certified,	[date]

JASON P. KING   Cell: 555-444-1010   Email: jpking@gmail.com

PROFESSIONAL EXPERIENCE

Network Administrator   [dates]
Allegheny Computer Systems, Inc., Pittsburgh, Penn.
(Company being sold.)

- Administer, direct and integrate networks in multiple platforms.

- Develop, assess, maintain and configure LAN/WAN network hardware, software
  telecommunications and systems solutions.[2] Troubleshoot network security, servers, LAN/WAN
  hardware, software and integration. Perform vulnerability assessment testing.

- Manage corporate network and servers. Configure routers, switches, servers and firewalls.

Key Accomplishment:
Managed selection, installation, configuration and testing of monitoring software, ensuring 99.99%
uptime. Spent half of allotted $50,000 budget.

Firewall Administrator/Contractor   [dates]
GBH Consulting, Ingram, Penn.
(Company closed.)

- Built firewall security policy from the ground up; created security policy for customers based on
  need and services provided. Monitored and maintained customer firewalls, building and
  troubleshooting VPNs and secure dial-in connections

- Troubleshot customer issues.

- Technical point-of-contact for sales staff; trained personnel in networking and firewall security.

Cisco Engineer/Contractor   [dates]
TechSys Solutions, Mt. Oliver, Penn.
(Company lost major contract, resulting in significant staff layoffs.)

- Monitored and maintained 135+ diverse and complex Web hosting client network environments.
  (24/7, 99.99% uptime.)

- Reviewed router and switch configuration, checked for anomalies, anticipated/averted problems.

- Monitored and managed multiple data lines through six global data centers.

Systems Integration Manager   [dates]
Three Rivers Computers, Pittsburgh, Penn.

- Managed, trained and supervised production staff of 11 technicians.

- Configured, integrated and serviced PCs; installed and configured software applications for
  workstations, servers and laptops. Troubleshot hardware and software.

EDUCATION

     BS Degree, Computer Science*, College of Allegheny County   [date to present]

     *48 of 62 required credits completed

Employment Gap. Program Manager. Hybrid. Former project officer seeks to return to professional project work after 5-year unemployment gap and recent teaching experience. Focused on employment with government contractors. (Education showing updated skills positioned before outdated 10-year old technical relevant experience. Unemployment gap explanation buried at end of resume.) Requirements: significant senior experience as Project Manager,[1] demonstrated success in coordinating with government contracting personnel,[2] negotiating and managing expectations with senior government executives,[3] managing task order operations on time and on budget,[4] hiring and managing staff,[5] and program administration.[6]

JACKSON FELS

Atlanta, GA   777-999-1212   E-mail: jacksonfels@aol.com

Summary of Qualifications

Integrity-driven, versatile **Project Manager** 17 years of increasingly responsible experience in the government sector; 6 years of project management experience.[1] Cross-functional expertise supporting core business functions, including Technical Research, Contract Development/Procurements, Customer Relations, Project Planning/Coordination, Budget Analysis, and Technology Utilization. Strong analytical, organizational, and administrative skills. Positive, adaptable, and motivated.

Areas of Expertise

- **Organization:** Logical and highly-organized. Excel in prioritizing and completing tasks and meeting budget goals and deadlines without compromising quality or productivity.[4] Extensive project management, budget management, scheduling, and procurement experience.
- **Expert Technical Skills:** Ability to define systems requirements, coordinate hardware/software purchases, and adapt commercial-off-the-shelf software (COTS). Programming background.
- **Oral/Written Communications:** Experience interfacing with people of diverse backgrounds, including coordinating tasks with government and contracting personnel.[2] Skilled in writing and editing.
- **Client/Customer Service:** Excellent negotiation and customer interface skills. Direct liaison to senior management,[3] external clients, vendors, and consultants.

Selected Education & Certifications

Master of Education, University of Georgia, Athens, Ga.,   [date]
A+ and Network+ Certifications   [date]
B.S., Computer Science, Georgia Institute of Technology, Atlanta, Ga., Honors graduate   [date]
B.A., Organizational Communications/Journalism, Minor: Government,   [date]

Relevant Professional Experience

Technical Intelligence Project Officer   [dates]
Defense Intelligence Agency (DIA)
Directed information technology program[6] to upgrade information security and improve intelligence data management and dissemination. Developed requirements, budgets, and schedules. Coordinated all project phases from development through implementation. Liaison to internal and external clients, vendors, contract officers, consultants, military and national intelligence organizations.

- **Contracts/Logistics:** Oversaw procurements of large computer systems. Wrote Request for Proposals and Statements of Work. Defined and documented technical requirements. Reviewed funding.
- **Personnel/EEO Support:** Resolved personnel matters. Held successful conflict resolution meetings with military and civilian staff. Selected by supervisor to serve on Personnel Hiring Panels. Oversaw interview and hiring of professional and administrative personnel.[5] Trained and managed staff of 10.
- Researched and analyzed Counter Intelligence Research Branch operations to determine computer systems requirements to support intelligence data collection, analysis, retrieval, and dissemination.
- Interviewed senior intelligence staff to gather source data. Planned and executed in-depth study of DIA intelligence work stations. Managed deadlines and briefed branch chiefs on project progress, status, and timelines.

Selected Accomplishments:
- Successfully executed all team projects on schedule and within budget.
- Planned and implemented organizational studies to evaluate workflow, system requirements, and collection needs. Summarized and presented detailed analyses to DoD officials.
- Successfully planned and accomplished the total hardware and software automation of the Human Intelligence and Counter Intelligence Offices.

Computer Systems Project Officer   [dates]
Computer Programmer [dates]
Department of Defense (DoD), U.S. Army

Computer Systems Project Officer [dates]: Oversaw the contractual, logistical and financial processes for large-scale office automation projects. Planned and executed analysis of the INSCOM center's operations. Provided technical advice and support to cross-functional teams. Independently planned and conducted in-depth research and analysis of ADP system design, interrelationships, operating mode, software, and equipment configuration. Promoted from Computer Programmer.

Other Experience & Additional Information

Substitute Teacher   [date to Present]
Atlanta City Public Schools, Atlanta, Ga.

Roving substitute for Title 10 schools in Atlanta, Ga. Teach reading, implement lesson plans, and manage classrooms for first to fifth grade students with learning and physical disabilities and behavioral problems.

Full-Time Student   [dates]

While still caring for now school-aged child, completed Master's degree in Education. Also, volunteered as reading instructor and coach.

Caretaker   [dates]

Resigned full-time position to adopt and care for toddler and care for dying elder relative, allowing spouse to retain full-time position. Also, resolved stress-related illness.

Military to Civilian. <u>Sourcing Manager</u>. Hybrid. Newly retired Army Contracting Officer seeks senior private-sector job with federal government contractor (Note: Unlike most private-sector businesses, military terminology/jargon is understood and valued by civilian government contractors). Requirements: minimum 10 years' procurement,[1] college degree (advanced degree preferred),[2] ability to coordinate overall material management effort,[3] strong leadership and decision-making skills,[4] and excellent computer skills.[5]

MICHAEL HSIEH

6565 S. Northway Dr.   Cell: 999-444-9090
Jackson, MS 92000   Email: michael_hsieh@army.mil

MATERIAL MANAGEMENT SENIOR MANAGER

Sourcing Manager with over 12 years' experience managing full contract life cycle for multi-million dollar procurements in military/federal area.[1] Combine in-depth knowledge of federal acquisition regulations and performance-based acquisition solutions with Six Sigma project management expertise. Expert on logistics and supply chain management, acquisition planning, material management, pre/post-award contract documentation, and contractor compliance monitoring.[3] Innovative problem solver with keen business acumen, demonstrated skill in making sound decisions, motivating leadership skills,[4] and demonstrated win-win philosophy. Excellent computer skills.[5] Clearance: DOD Secret.

CERTIFICATIONS

DAWIA Level II Certification (Contracting) [date]
Contracting Officer Warrant: $5 million

EXPERTISE

- **Acquisitions:** Manage full procurement life cycle, from acquisitions planning through solicitation, selection, award, and contract management.

- **Logistics:** Plan, coordinate, and evaluate logistical actions in support of agency mission.

- **Program Analysis:** Conduct program and cost analysis in the preparation of Business Case alternatives to achieve short- and long-term strategic goals.

- **Consulting:** Provide expert planning, analysis, and advice on program alternatives, strategies, and costs.

ACCOMPLISHMENT HIGHLIGHTS

- Awarded over 170 contracts valued in excess $160M during six-month deployment. Major awards include a $25M bus transportation requirement and $78M agreement between the United States and the Hashemite Kingdom of Jordan to train Armed Forces.

- Completed site survey and $32M contract awards to complete a major building in 18 days.

- As Contractor Administrator with Contingency Contracting Administration team overseas, realized $1.5M in cost savings for construction of camp to house refugees.

MICHAEL HSIEH, Page 2   Residence: 999-444-9090

PROFESSIONAL EXPERIENCE

United States Army   [dates]

Emergency Essential Contingency Contracting Officer   [dates]

As a warranted ($5M) Contracting Officer for the Project and Contracting Office (PCO), directed full contract life cycle for wide range of complex acquisitions with high visibility in Iraqi Reconstruction Effort. Acquisitions have supported construction projects throughout the country, primarily focused on renovation of critical police stations and commodities for Armed Forces. Administered and awarded Delivery Orders against $20M requirements contract for clothing and textile commodities in support of the nation's uniformed services. Developed Solicitation Plan for $200M vehicle maintenance contract. Applied Six Sigma principles to develop continuity files and contracting templates to streamline acquisition process.

Supply Chain Management Analyst, Fleet Industrial Supply Center   [dates]

Provided program management support for Supply Chain processes in Southeast Asia. Identified inefficiencies and redundancies achieving annual cost savings of over $830K [date]. Orchestrated bottom up review of Personal Property program. Reconciliation of 3,356 line items and $11M worth of Minor Property resulted in "Outstanding" rating.

Chief Logistics and Contracting Officer   [dates]

Managed all logistical support for 250-solider detachment deployed to Camp Zama, Japan. Supervised 25 officer and enlisted soldiers managing wide range of services including budget, contracting, payroll, retail sales, mail, and hazardous materials. Reduced base-wide inventory costs by 10% ($150K) by application of automated inventory control systems. Prepared $900K budget request for an Unfunded Requirement resulting in 100% funding for critical programs.

Deputy Logistics Director, Regional Contracting Center   [dates]

Managed Logistics Support Center operations, including oversight for all contract administration, warehousing, stock, transportation, mail, fuel supply management, and support for troops operating in Southeast Asia and Australia. Developed a Business Case resulting in approval of $1.1M for Web-enabled Enterprise Resource Management solution, projected to save $1.5B.

Contingency Contract Specialist, Defense Contract Management Agency   [dates]

Managed all DCMA post-award functions including evaluating contractor performance, interpreting contract laws and provisions, negotiating contract modifications, determining price and cost analysis, and ensuring timely delivery. Coordinated with United Nations Health Care Relief, Halliburton, and U.S. Navy and Air Force LOGCAP program managers to execute multi-million Cost-Plus Award Fee contracts. Realized $1.5M in cost savings by reducing procurement lead times.

EDUCATION

Master of Business Administration,[2] University of Baltimore, Baltimore, Md. [date]

Bachelor of Science,[2] General Science/Math, Jackson State University, Jackson, Miss., [date]

Too Many Jobs. Administrative Security Specialist in federal agency. Functional. Seeking Administrative Security Manager position in civilian government contracting firm. (Because candidate risks being perceived as job hopper, she uses two techniques: Group jobs by theme, and make exception to rule of not giving reasons for leaving jobs.) Requirements: Experience with facility, personnel, information, operations, personnel and physical security,[1] 3 years security experience,[2] strong interpersonal, speaking and writing skills,[3] must pass background investigation.[4]

MOLLY DANNER
Web Portfolio: www.MollyDanner.com

Cell 555-555-9999   molly.danner@comcast.com

OBJECTIVE: Administrative Security Manager

PROFILE: Security specialist with three years of security experience;[2] former contract administrator and budget analyst. Expertise includes gathering information and preparing security reports, conducting security training, and establishing and enforcing security procedures. Strong interpersonal, speaking and writing skills.[3] Fast learner, adaptable. Hold SCI Security Clearance.[4]

SECURITY SKILLS ON JOB

- Ensure compliance with departmental security policies, procedures and instructions to safeguard classified information, facilities, equipment and human resources.
- Advise senior staff on security awareness, classification, travel, courier and communications policies. Develop and update Security Operating Procedures and Training Manuals/Materials.
- Implement security violation detection, prevention and reporting programs.
- Areas of security expertise: information, physical, personnel, operations and facility.[1]

SECURITY/LAW ENFORCEMENT EXPERIENCE

SPACE & MISSILE DEFENSE COMMAND, COLORADO SPRINGS, COLO.   [dates]
Administrative Security Manager

Referred by OP communications (training vendor) as best person for this security-sensitive position. Operate and administer computer equipment and Directorate of Combat Development's (DCD) Sensitive Compartmented Information (SCI) Program and collateral facilities. Administer SCI program and ensure that SCI data is properly accounted for, controlled, transported, sorted, packaged, safeguarded and destroyed. Ensure continuous systems integrity and secure communications within SCI facility.

- Conduct inspections, investigations, inquiries and assistance visits and provide reports. Make recommendations for corrective actions. Develop security plans and procedures to safeguard classified information.
- Establish and maintain emergency action plans (EAP) and Standard Operating Procedures (SOPs).
- Oversee physical security program for operations in two facilities. Ensure compliance with national and agency security directives and policies. Monitor Fixed Facility Checklist and access controls.
- Manage SCIF intrusion detection system, including, CCTV system, alarms and central panel operations. Establish alarm response procedures, perform live testing and document findings.
- Responsible for personnel security program. Prepare Visit Requests for over 65 staff members and officers for field trips and temporary duty assignments. Ensure staff has appropriate level of access.

OP COMMUNICATIONS, COLORADO SPRINGS, COLO.   [dates]
Manager and Registrar

Coordinated Security Operations Officer Qualification Course Training for 350 students. Performed administrative duties for instructors and administrators.

CITY OF COLORADO SPRINGS, COLORADO SPRINGS, COLO.   [dates]
Metropolitan Police Officer

Resigned to care for critically ill family member, who passed away after two months.
Completed 8-month police study program and 3-month advanced field training courses.

- Certified in 9mm handgun, shotgun, police equipment, cameras, automated police information retrieval systems, crime scene evidence collecting equipment and use of chemical aerosol irritants.

CONTRACTING & ADMINISTRATIVE EXPERIENCE

ALLEN CONSTRUCTION, INC., COLORADO SPRINGS, COLO.   [dates]
Contractor Administrator

Recruited to more challenging position.
Provided support to project managers on Federal contracts, ranging in value from $300,000 to $8M.

STATE OF WYOMING, CHEYENNE, WYO.   [dates]
Contract Administrator and Budget Analyst

This was a 9-month contract position
Performed accounting and contract review for $50M Wyoming State Prison Construction Project. Important liaison to senior attorney general, with direct interface on arising construction issues and discrepancies. Supervised one employee located in another location and served as purchasing agent.

- Prepared legal notices and correspondence for each phase of construction contracts, including review, closeout and final retainage release. Composed correspondence and reports.
- Compiled construction progress and financial reports, including accounts receivable and payable.

EDUCATION, TRAINING, CERTIFICATIONS & COMPUTER SKILLS

Undergraduate Coursework, Business Administration, Wyman College, Cody, Wyo., 42 credits, [dates]

Professional Training & Certifications

- Joint Personnel Adjudication System Training for Security Professionals, in progress
- Certified Information System Security Officer (ISSO),   [date]

Proficient in Microsoft Word, Outlook, Publisher, Excel, Access, PowerPoint, Quattro Pro, QuickBooks, Dac Easy Payroll & Accounting, Internet. Familiar with AutoCAD 12.

Chapter 17

A Sampling of Extreme Resume Makeovers

· ·

*E*ach of five before-and-after sets of resumes in this chapter makes a specific point: Bare-bones quick notes don't make the sale; attention wanders with too much (unusable) information; persuasive information grabs attention; credibility grows when focus meets accomplishments; and white space encourages readability.

A text box atop each resume in this chapter contains a mission statement — that is, what the job seeker aims to accomplish, which usually is a better job. The mission statement also includes the requirements for a specific position — or a summary of the typically requested requirements for an occupation or career field.

Within the mission statement, each of the job's requirements has a number next to it. The same number also appears in the body of the resume next to the job seeker's matching qualification for that requirement.

The cross-matched numbers between a job's requirements and the candidate's qualifications shown here are just for illustration, *not for your actual resumes.*

The samples are intended to laser your attention to requirement-and-qualification matching, the single most important factor in causing your candidacy to get noticed in an online swarm of resumes.

BEFORE

Military to Federal. Wounded veteran wants entry-level job at Veterans Hospital. He includes key information like "purple heart" and "10 points veterans' preference." But otherwise, he writes the equivalent of a telephone message with no accomplishments or reasons why he's a better qualified candidate than another wounded veteran.

DAVID YOUNG

Walter Reed Army Medical Center   *Permanent Address:* P.O. Box 3901
Malogne House Omaha, NE 68105-3901   Omaha, NE 99999
6900 Georgia Ave., N.W.
Washington, D.C. 20307
Cell: 402-777-3030   Email: davidyoung@yahoo.com

I received a purple heart and I will be a 10 point vet pref.

EMPLOYMENT

[dates]   INTERN, VETERAN'S AFFAIRS
                 Congressman Gene Taylor, 4th Congressional District of MS

                 I assisted his staff in office work during Hurricane Katrina and had my own project
                 which I worked on. There was a soldier's home in Gulfport that had to be evacuated.
                 Over 300 vets had to be brought up here to the D.C. soldier's home. My job was to make
                 sure they were being taken care of. I got them in touch with their families and friends and
                 made sure everyone was accounted for. I worked with different organizations to set up
                 clothes drives and phone card drives.

[dates]   MILITARY POLICE OFFICER
                 Nebraska Army National Guard

                 I received police officer training, both garrison and combat MP. As soon as I graduated,
                 our brigade was deployed to Iraq as combat MP's. While deployed, I completed all the
                 MP duties: convoy escorts, personal security, mounted patrol, holding and transporting
                 prisoners, searches, etc.

[dates]   EQUIPMENT OPERATOR AND SUPERVISOR
                 Pepper Turbines, Inc.

                 I operated heavy machinery, vehicles, and forklifts.

EDUCATION

                 Approx. 60 college credit hours in the fields of criminal justice and social work

                 High School Diploma

AFTER

Military to Federal. Active Duty Reserves. Reverse chronological. Wounded veteran seeks Program Support Clerk job at VA Hospital, GS-5 position, $37,000. Federal resumes must include SSN, prior hours and earnings, citizenship, military service & federal job announcement number. Requirements: knowledge of VA policies, procedures, objectives and regulations pertaining to patient care,[1] ability to tactfully and courteously deal with a variety of people from diverse backgrounds and with varied levels of understanding,[2] working knowledge of PC software packages,[3] ability to work independently and under pressure,[4] and ability to organize, plan and prioritize work.[5]

DAVID YOUNG

Cell: 402-777-3030

Email: davidyoung@yahoo.com

Current Address:
Walter Reed Army Medical Center
Malogne House
6900 Georgia Ave., N.W.
Washington, D.C. 20307

Permanent Address:
P.O. Box 3901
Omaha, NE 99999-3901

Social Security Number: 123-45-6789
Military Service: Nebraska National Guard [dates]

Citizenship: United States of America
Veteran's Preference: 10 points

OBJECTIVE: Program Support Clerk, GS-0303-5, Announcement Number: ATL-06-06-031TA

JOB SKILLS

- Experience communicating with soldiers and veterans from various backgrounds, both in active duty and hospitalized for serious injuries sustained in Operation Enduring Freedom. Able to build rapport and use tact, courtesy and professionalism in interpersonal relations.[2]
- Knowledgeable of physical therapy and medical terminologies.
- Skilled in office administration procedures, including answering calls, preparing correspondence and documents and filing. Type 40 wpm.
- Able to work under pressure effectively, both independently and in team settings.[4]

PROFESSIONAL EXPERIENCE

Intern, Veteran's Services   [dates]
Congressman Gene Taylor, 4th Congressional District of Mississippi
Rayburn House Office Building, Washington, DC
Salary: n/a; 15 hours/week
Supervisor: Rep. Gene Taylor, 202-444-9090. May be contacted.

- Administrative Assistant: Performed administrative duties such as word processing, managing files and records, designing forms, and other office procedures. Prepared correspondence and producing reports on veteran's benefits activities and research.
- Constituent Services: Provided customer and personal services to veterans concerning benefits and programs. Answered written and phone inquiries, providing information on policies, procedures, objectives and regulations pertaining to patient care and services.[1]
- Veterans' Benefits Research: Researched TRICARE health insurance issues for national guardsmen and reservists while not on active duty. Advocated for veterans' benefits and provided

DAVID YOUNG	Cell: 402-777-3030
Announcement Number: ATL-06-06-031TA	SSN: 123-45-6789

information to Department of Veterans Affairs representatives. Wrote summaries of veterans' problems and situations concerning processes and treatment services.

Key Accomplishment:

- Hurricane Katrina/Veterans Home Coordinator: Coordinated relocation of 300+ veterans from Armed Forces Retirement Home in Gulfport, Miss. to U.S. Solders' and Airmen's Home located in Washington D.C. during aftermath of Hurricane Katrina. Established phone card and clothing drives to ensure that each veteran had sufficient clothing. ***Awarded Humanitarian Service Medal and Nebraska Emergency Service Medal.***

Military Police Officer [dates]
Nebraska Army National Guard
155th Separate Armored Brigade
2222 Hwy 51 South, Lincoln, NE 99999
Salary: $21,500/year; 40 hours/week
Supervisor: Capt. James Sutter, 402-444-9090. May be contacted.

- Security: Performed law enforcement duties for U.S. forces and commands, preserving military control and providing perimeter, escort and physical security. Investigated, processed and prepared incident reports. Debriefed and interviewed witnesses and sources for pertinent information concerning investigations and incidents; wrote reports and summaries.
- Operational Support: Provided ordnance and logistical support to operational forces. Coordinated compound and work projects.

Equipment Operator and Supervisor [dates]
Pepper Turbines, Inc.
5555 Wilkens Boulevard, Omaha, NE 99999
Salary: $25,500/year; 40 hours/week
Supervisor: Mike Jones, 402-555-3434. May be contacted.

- Supervisor: Managed equipment operators in safety and operations for this government contractor manufacturing firm. Organized, prioritized and planned workload; assigned tasks.[5]
- Equipment Operator: Operated vehicles, forklifts and heavy machinery.

EDUCATION

Undergraduate Coursework, Criminal Justice and Social Work, Metropolitan Community College, Omaha, NE 99999, 56 credits [dates]

Diploma, Pine Grove High School, Omaha, NE 99999, [date]

AWARDS

Army Commendation Medal, Iraq Campaign Medal, Global War on Terrorism, Expeditionary Medal, Purple Heart, Humanitarian Service Medal, Mississippi Emergency Service Medal, National Defense Service Medal, Army Service Ribbon, Armed Forces Reserve Medal

COMPUTER SKILLS [3]

MS Office: Word, Outlook, Excel, PowerPoint, Access; Internet

- 2 -

BEFORE

Sales to Administration. Salesperson who wants to return to administration writes a generic resume with a cliché objective that focuses on what she wants, not what she brings to the employer. Nor does she strategically position her administrative experience but begins with sales, although she no longer wants to work in sales. The makeover resume that follows addresses both of these problems.

LEAH C. JENKINS
CELL(212)768-4545•LEAH_JENKINS@YAHOO.COM
999 AMESBURY PLACE•NEW YORK,NY 11111

OBJECTIVE

To obtain a challenging full-time position in a dynamic atmosphere where my hard work and customer service capabilities can be efficiently utilized. Should be career oriented and allow for an opportunity for growth within the company.

EXPERIENCE

[dates]   Ikea   Long Island, NY

Sales Worker

- Assist customers with purchases, such as planning wardrobe systems and bathrooms. Recommend options and answer customer and co-worker inquiries. Place customer orders using automated system; search database for item availability.

[dates]   Medix School   Towson, MD

Admiissions Receptionist

- Supported Director and Director of Admissions. Typed letters, scheduled meetings, and maintained student files. Managed receptionist duties.

[dates]   Outback Steakhouse   Baltimore, MD

Restaurant Administrator

- Coordinated all special and charity events, such as first Baltimore Marathon, Charity Golf Classic, etc.
- Employee of the year for [date], employee of the month [dates].
- Implemented training system for all servers, bartenders, hosts, and bussers.
- Handled all payroll, accounts payables/receivables, employee issues, corporate reports (monthly P&L, daily sales reports, etc.) and all money handling responsibilities.

[dates]   Hycalog Drilling Co.   Houston, TX

Office Manager

- Created annual operating plan using PowerPoint.
- Established and maintained new office for regional manager.
- Reviewed engineer's expense reports, handled all travel arrangements, administered petty cash box, and acted as English/Spanish translator.

[dates]   Law Offices of Leonard Bunch, P.C.   Houston, TX

Receptionist/Secretary

- Prepared legal documents such as last wills and testaments, trusts, corporation & association papers, IRS forms and claims.
- Greeted clients, answered 5-line phone system, and scheduled all appointments for attorneys. Completed general filing and office duties.

EDUCATION

[dates]   Cooper Union School of Art   New York, NY
Pursuing Continuing Studies Certificate in Photography.

[dates]   Lamar State University   Beaumont, TX
45 credits toward B.A. in Business Administration and Spanish.

[dates]   Juan Agustin Maza University   Mendoza, Argentina
90 credit hours toward B.S. in Industrial Engineering.

SKILLS

Dilingual Spanish/English, Computer proficient, Extensive experience in customer service; International work experience; High attention to detail and ability to multitask

AFTER

Sales to Administration. Sales Worker. Targeted. Salesperson seeks to return to administrative field. Requirements: Minimum of 3-5 years' administrative experience,[1] some college coursework,[2] expert skills in Word, Excel and PowerPoint,[3] bilingual English/Spanish, written and verbal,[4] and can-do attitude.[5]

LEAH C. JENKINS
999 Amesbury Place • New York, NY 11111
Cell: (212) 768-4545 • Email: leah_jenkins@yahoo.com

EXPERTISE: Administrative Management

Motivated and accomplished office manager and administrative professional with over 5 years' experience.[1] Attentive to detail, able to take initiative, prioritize multiple tasks and manage workload. Resourceful with can-do attitude;[5] team player. Bilingual: Spanish/English (fluent).[4]

SKILL SUMMARY

- **Administration:** Managing office workflow, purchasing, developing policies and procedures to improve operations, maintaining filing and database systems, meeting/event planning,

- **Accounting:** Managing and monitoring financial transactions, accounts, invoices and payroll.

- **Communications:** Preparing business documents, letters and memos, serving as receptionist, POC and first contact.

- **Expert Computer Skills:**[3] MS Word, Excel, PowerPoint, Outlook; Internet; Photoshop; CAD; Peachtree; Quicken; proprietary databases and software programs

ADMINISTRATIVE EXPERIENCE

Admissions Receptionist
Medix School, Towson, Md.   [dates]

- Reception: Served as first contact for callers and visitors; determined nature of contact and directed/forwarded to correct department. Provided information, answered inquiries, took messages and scheduled appointments.

- Administration: Provided direct support to Director and Director of Admissions. Scheduled and coordinated meetings, arranging for refreshments, reserving meeting space, inviting attendees and preparing materials. Coordinated service for and procured new/upgraded equipment, technology, service plans and office supplies. Developed and implemented administrative policies and procedures, maintained student records and files and managed incoming and outgoing correspondence. Prepared and typed letters, minutes, memos and other documentation. Assured correct use of grammar, punctuation, language, format and spelling.

- Admissions Support: Tracked and managed student information via database. Scheduled appointments with Admissions Counselor. Served as proctor for student testing; prepared and sent admissions letters to applicants and students.

Key Accomplishments:
- Discovered accounting error, saving $4,700 in purchasing overcharges.
- Created new form letter templates and developed database system to manage mailings.
- Upgraded postage and phone systems, securing more cost-effective service and better equipment.

Office Manager
Hycalog Drilling Co., Mendoza, Argentina   [dates]

- Office Management: Tapped to establish new regional office. Coordinated initial furnishing and set up; managed continual administrative operations. Supported regional manager and engineering staff. Served as Point of Contact, resolving customer and staff issues. Managed all

Leah C. Jenkins — 2 — Cell (212) 768-4545

correspondence, travel arrangements and purchasing. Prepared letters and reports, including P&L and annual operating plan for senior management. Maintained files. English/Spanish translator.

- Accounting: Managed all A/R and A/P. Reviewed, processed, coded and paid invoices and expense reports. Sent invoices and collection letters, audited accounts and managed petty cash.

Receptionist/Secretary
Law Offices of Leonard Bunch, P.C., Houston, Texas   [dates]

- Managed office workflow and reception. Greeted, screened and directed visitors and callers. Scheduled appointments and managed attorney calendars. Sorted and forwarded incoming mail; prepared outgoing correspondence. Typed, formatted and prepared letters, memos and legal documents. Maintained and updated filing system.

OTHER WORK EXPERIENCE

Sales Worker
Ikea, Long Island, N.Y.   [date to Present]

- Sales/Customer Service: Assist customers with room planning and purchases. Ascertain needs, recommend options and answer customer and worker inquiries. Place customer orders using automated system; search database for item availability.

- Administrative/Inventory: Take daily inventory and input requisitions into database. Maintain communications with coworkers, including written updates on tasks, projects and goals. Write weekly product updates for staff. Conduct yearly and need-based inventories.

- Design/Merchandising: Plan and design space and furniture layout and systems, using automated programs and paper sketches. Design customer and internal room settings.

Key Accomplishments:
- Received excellent performance evaluations: "Exceeds job expectations."   [dates]
- Received 5 Ambassador Awards, for excellent customer service.

Restaurant Administrator
Outback Steakhouse, Baltimore, Md.   [dates]

- Accounting: Managed payroll, A/R, A/P and cash deposits. Tracked and submitted payroll for staff of 75; reviewed payroll report, identified errors and made corrections. Received and tracked invoices, entered and coded accounting data and paid vendors. Prepared daily, monthly and yearly corporate reports, including P&L. Maintained and stored files and records.

- Administrative: Scheduled part-time administrative staff; trained employees and replacement. Purchased office supplies and coordinated equipment maintenance. Coordinated all special and charity events. Contacted corporate and business donors, scheduled time and location, prepared invitations and gift bags for participants and coordinated events with kitchen and waitstaff.

Key Accomplishments:
- Promoted twice in less than 2 years. Hired as server, promoted to bartender and then to RA.
- Employee of the Year, [date]; Employee of the Month, [date].
- Implemented new training system for all new servers, bartenders, hosts, and bussers

EDUCATION

Undergraduate Studies,[2] Business Administration/Spanish, Lamar State University, Beaumont, Texas, 45 credits completed,   [dates]

BEFORE

> **Data to Education.** Data analyst transitioning to Instructional/Curriculum Design based on new education. Resume with laundry list of skills and duties is overwhelming and hard to follow. Also, lists only last two jobs – about 3 years' experience; she's been working for about 10 years. Small font makes it hard to read.

Evelyn Baker

55 Keswick Ct.
Honolulu, HI 99999   **ebaker@gmail.com**   Home Phone: (808) 444-1212
Cell Phone: (808) 333-6060

Objective: To obtain a position as a Curriculum Design Specialist in an organization that would allow me to develop my skills, while contributing to organizational goals.

Professional Profile: An ambitious, organized individual experienced at working in a fast paced environment demanding strong, organizational, technical and interpersonal skills. Prioritize tasks and meet deadlines.

Technical Skills

- **Languages**: C/C++, Visual Basic 2005, Java, HTML
- **Operating Systems**: UNIX, DOS, Windows 95 – 2003, XP
- **Applications**: Microsoft Office (Excel, Access, Word, PowerPoint, Outlook), PeopleSoft, GroupWise
- **Database**: Oracle8i Database Administrator Track Training for SQL and PL/SQL, Enterprise DBA Part 1A: Architecture and Administration, Enterprise DBA Part1B: Backup and Recovery, Enterprise DBA Part 2: Performance and Tuning, Enterprise DBA Part3: Network Administration
- **Instructional Design and Development**: Apply theories, philosophies, and current research driving learning, teaching, and Instructional Design. Create basic Internet-based instructional content, and basic multimedia-based instructional content. Manipulate current database technologies, desktop publishing technologies, spreadsheet technologies, and digital graphic editing technologies.
- **Information Technology Infrastructure**: Hands-on experience of Information systems architectures including software systems, hardware, operating systems, databases, object-oriented technology, networking, and enterprise-wide systems.
- **Internet and Network Security:** Footprinting, scanning, and enumeration tools, testing Windows security (95-2000), testing UNIX/Linux security, testing network devices and firewalls, scanning for remote control and testing backdoors and Trojans, testing Internet users.
- **Technical Writing:** Develop and edit technical communication such as user manuals, installation instructions, Marketing Collateral: Grant Proposals. Researches, analyzes, and edit system information and perform technical writing. Interpret and simplify information technology concepts for defined audiences.
- **MIS Capstone Project**: Developed an Information System for an organization. Made modifications in design techniques and strategies to accommodate several different contingencies.

Professional Experience

The Queen's Medical Center, Honolulu, HI   [dates]
Adult Intensive Care Unit – APACHE 11 Data Analyst/Coordinator
- Collate data of all admissions into the Adult ICU on a daily basis using the APACHE 11 System.
- Collate data of all admissions into the Adult ICU and prepare quarterly reports with that data.
- Prepares Summary Sheets for each ICU patient noting all appropriate statistics.
- Coordinate the daily activities of the Adult ICU.
- Performs data management and data analysis for research.
- Gathers data requirements, design reports, analyze the results and implement and test Reports.
- Maintains data collected for research purposes (including acquisition, editing and reporting); providing statistical consulting primarily in collaborative studies involving the Adult Intensive Care Unit.
- Follow up with various ancillary departments to obtain statistics necessary to be presented in the quarterly report.

Evelyn Baker

Home Phone: (808) 444-1212   ebaker@gmail.com   Cell Phone: (808) 333-6060

- Design and implement new Reports and modify existing Reports.
- Maintain user security within the Reporting application and make changes/updates as necessary.
- Support and maintain Reporting and Data Analysis Tools.
- Work with business users to understand business requirements and develop appropriate solutions.
- Direct day-to-day office operations, providing fundamental support to Director, Assistant Director and three Intensivists in the Adult Intensive Care Unit.
- Manage accounts payable, receivable, and billing charges.
- Oversee administrative budget. Prepare expense reports and credit card/bank reconciliations.
- Train Medical Residents in use of office computer resources.

Volunteer Experience

Bridgestone Classic, Honolulu, HI   [dates]
PGA Tournament Intern

- Assist Event Coordinator and work in conjunction with the tournament site Operations staff on certain aspects of the event.
- Conference planning.
- Serves as point of contact with clients and committees.
- Provides onsite supervision for conferences and meetings.
- Prepares contracts for corporate review and signature.
- Compile, sort, code and enter clients' invoices into computer.
- Account reconciliation experience.
- Maintain communication with clients' regarding payments.
- Responds to clients inquires regarding conference billings and procedures.
- Management of event database (volunteers, sales, VIPs, club members).
- In conjunction with Bridgestone, create and maintain Tournament Web site.
- Post event; generate letters from Tournament Director to all contestants and sponsors thanking them for participating in the tournament.
- Distribute and process volunteer applications.
- Coordinate with tournament, Bridgestone, and P.E.J. Productions regarding volunteers.
- Coordinate registration packets/credentials, yardage books and uniforms.

Education

- **Master of Science: Instructional Technology,** Instructional Design and Development
  Certificate in Information Security and Assurance
  Hawaii Pacific University, Honolulu, HI; [date]
- **Bachelor of Science: Management Information Systems**
  University of Hawaii at Manoa, [date]
- **Oracle 8i Database Administrator Training**
  University of Maryland Baltimore County, [date]
- **Associate of Applied Science: Computer Information Systems**
  Leeward Community College, Pearl City, Hawaii, [date]

Professional Affiliations

- Member of Beta Alpha Pi (Accounting and Information Systems Organization), Hawaii Pacific University
- Member - Computer Club, Leeward Community College

Honors

- Honors List, Meritorious Scholar

References and salary requirements available upon request.

AFTER

Data to Education. Career Change. Reverse chronological. Data analyst with new degree in instructional technology seeks position in instructional systems design and development. Requirements: Master's degree in instructional systems design or closely related field,[1] experience in multimedia authoring of instructional systems,[2] demonstrated ability to work in teams,[3] project management experience,[4] and experience with Web development technologies.[5]

EVELYN BAKER

55 Keswick Ct. • Honolulu, HI 99999
Cellular: 808-333-6060
Email: ebaker@gmail.com

PROFILE: Over 7 years of experience in administration, instruction and information technology. Broad range of skill sets in Instructional Design, IT and office management. Organized, with demonstrated ability to manage workload and meet deadlines. Strong written and oral communications skills.

KEY COMPETENCIES

- **Instructional/Curriculum Design and Development:** Maintain knowledge of theories, philosophies and current research driving learning, teaching and Instructional Design. Create Internet-based and multimedia-based instructional content.[2] Use and apply database, desktop publishing, spreadsheet and digital graphic editing technologies.

- **Information Technology Expertise:** Hands-on experience in Information Systems architectures including software, hardware, operating systems, databases, object-oriented technology, networking and enterprise-wide systems. Special project management:[4] Developed MIS Capstone Information System for organization. Conducted needs assessment, developed, implemented and tested system. Made modifications in design techniques and strategies to accommodate contingencies.

- **Technical Writing:** Experience in developing and editing technical communications such as user manuals, installation instructions and grant proposals. Able to research, analyze and edit system information, as well as interpret and simplify IT concepts for defined audiences.

EDUCATION

M.S.,[1] Instructional Technology, Instructional Design and Development, Hawaii Pacific University, Honolulu, Hawaii; Certificate in Information Security and Assurance   [date]
  Relevant Coursework: Applied Psychology of Learning, Research and Information Technology, Computer Based Instruction, Information Technology and Infrastructure

B.S., Management Information Systems, University of Hawaii at Manoa, GPA: 3.75   [date]

PROFESSIONAL EXPERIENCE

Data Analyst/Coordinator
Adult Intensive Care Unit (ICU), The Queen's Medical Center, Honolulu, Hawaii   [dates]

- **Data Management:** Collect, enter, update and manage Adult ICU data, ensuring data accuracy and integrity. Track for management analysis, resource allocation, financial management. Prepare statistical reports with interpretive summary narratives. Work with other departments to obtain or verify data. Maintain user security.
- **Office Administration:** Manage daily office operations, providing support to director, assistant director and 3 intensivists in Adult ICU. Administer budget, managing all accounts payable and receivable functions. Train new and current staff on processes and technology systems.

Intern

Bridgestone Classic, (PGA Tournament), Honolulu, Hawaii   [dates]

- **Event Management Support:** Assisted Event Coordinator and as team member,[3] worked with tournament site operations staff. Provided onsite supervision for conferences and meetings. Prepared contracts and performed accounts receivable activities and reconciliation; sorted, coded and entered invoices.

- **Data Management/Communications:** Served as point of contact for clients and committees. Updated and maintained event database. Created and maintained tournament website. Drafted and sent thank you letters to contestants and sponsors.

Teacher

Manoa Elementary School, Honolulu, Hawaii   [dates]

- **Computer Instruction/Curriculum Development:** Taught computer fundamentals to students in grades K-5th. Prepared daily lesson plans. Collaborated with other teachers on technology integration curriculum.

Lab Assistant

Leeward Community College, Peal City, Hawaii   [dates]

- **Computer Specialist:** Provided user support for 6,000 college students in computer lab. Managed 72 multimedia workstations.

COMPUTER COMPETENCIES

Languages: C/C++, Visual Basic 2005, Java
Operating Systems: Windows 95-2003, XP
Applications: MS Office (Excel, Access, Word, PowerPoint, Outlook), PeopleSoft, UNIX, DOS, GroupWise, HTML, Dreamweaver, CSS, XML, PhP, Macromedia Flash, Macromedia Captivate [5]
Databases: Oracle8i Database Administrator Track Training for SQL and PL/SQL, Enterprise DBA Part 1A; Architecture and Administration, Enterprise DBA Part1B: Backup and Recovery, Enterprise DBA Part 2: Performance and Tuning, Enterprise DBA Part3: Network Administration

PROFESSIONAL AFFILIATIONS

Beta Alpha Pi (Accounting/Information Systems Organization)   [dates]
Hawaii Pacific University, Honolulu, HI

Computer Club, Leeward Community College, Pearl City, HI   [dates]

BEFORE

Culinary Career. Sous Chef seeking Chef position. Lacks focus, direction, organization, visual appeal.

MATTHEW BELASKI
Hartford, CT
Cell: 860-999-1212
Email: matthew_b@comcast.net

EDUCATION

[dates]	Computer Programming Degree, Anne Arundel Community College, in progress
[dates]	A.A., Degree, Restaurant Cooking Skills, Baltimore International College
[dates]	B.S., Business Administration, Shepherd University

EMPLOYMENT

[dates] Sous Chef, Government House
- Logistical kitchen planner for food and beverage events for the Governor of Connecticut.
- Plan, purchase and execute specific menus. Coordinate meeting and convention service requests. Inventory, inspect and rotate fresh, frozen and grocery stocks.
- Coordinate and communicate relevant information with the Governor's office, State Police and other state agencies.
- Provide and deliver personal needs of the first family.
- Protect privacy of the first family, as well as, proprietary information pertaining to Government House. Provide information to the media as needed.
- Direct usage of Department of Corrections trustees.
- Develop, implement and insure sanitation programs.
- Maintain and reconcile departmental petty cash funds.
- Successful implementation of private sector ideas and technologies to a public sector environment.

[dates] Banquet Chef, Hartford Marriott
- Designed and executed high-end food operations for exclusive catered events.
- Led production team by communication of specific customer directed protocols regarding national and international clients.
- Implemented quality assurance and cost control measures.
- Made purchasing, cost and quality recommendations to upper management.
- Was recognized by management for innovative ideas that improved operational effectiveness.

[dates] Food and Beverage Director; Executive Chef, Aramark
Food and Beverage Director: Executive Dining Room at Sprint Network Services.
- Supervised staff of 8 employees, both front and back of the house.
- Designed and directed production of breakfast and lunch menus for service 5 days a week.
- Increased new catering sales, while maintaining repeat customer clients.
- Developed and led employee training sessions for customer service, food production and sanitation.
- Updated computer technology to modernize purchasing and just in time inventory systems.
- Developed marketing and advertising campaigns to grow business. Installed thorough accounting and customer service tracking systems.
- Introduced and maintained hazardous area critical control points program to promote safe food handling.
- My duties also included management of all vending operations.

AFTER

> **Culinary Career.** <u>Sous Chef</u>. Reverse Chronological. Sous Chef seeks Chef position. This customized resume addresses requirements with matching qualifications, and directs reader's eyes to "sell don't tell" achievements. Requirements: bachelor's degree or related culinary degree,[1] 8+ years of industry and culinary management experience,[2] ability to manage staff in a diverse environment with focus on client and customer services,[3] experience controlling food and labor cost,[4] menu development,[5] and skill in development of culinary team.[6]

MATTHEW BELASKI

Cell: 860-999-1212 • Email: matthew_b@comcast.net • Hartford, CT

CHEF

Over 10 years of kitchen management experience[2] in state government and corporate settings. Demonstrated expertise in project management, team building, budget management and improving operations. Able to assess needs, processes and performance and recommend and implement improvements. Strong skills in customer service, as well as interpersonal, written and verbal communications. Excellent ability to establish priorities, multi-task and meet strict deadlines. Proven proficiency in developing innovative solutions to problems and achieving results. PC competent.

PROFESSIONAL EMPLOYMENT

Government House, State of Connecticut   [dates]
SOUS CHEF, HARTFORD, CT

- <u>Operations Management:</u> Direct daily operations of full-service kitchen, planning, coordinating and preparing formal and informal meals and events for up to 3,000 people, both planned in advance and last minute, with range of guests from international dignitaries to constituents. Continually analyze operations and recommend and implement range of process improvement initiatives. Develop, implement, apply and interpret policies, regulations and directives.

- Project Management: Conduct needs assessment surveys and determine needs based on event specifications and labor demands. Plan event menus with consideration to protocol, preferences, caliber of event, attendees and lead time.[5] Create project timeline; assign tasks and monitor progress. Manage multiple task lists to complete projects with adjacent deadlines. Resolve problems and issues, including crisis situations. Conduct post-event assessments.

- <u>Supply Management:</u> Take inventory and plan orders to regulate flow of product and ensure stock levels meet event and daily needs. Research best products and vendors to comply with state purchasing regulations. Rotate stock, monitor usage and storage to ensure efficiency, sanitation and security and reduce waste. Negotiate, administer and oversee vendor and service contracts.

- <u>Budgeting/Funds Management:</u> Develop pricing and cost accounting procedures. Analyze and forecast product and labor costs estimates. Resolve budget issues and develop food and labor cost-cutting solutions to ensure budget adherence.[4] Brief management and recommend cost control improvements and budget adjustments.

- <u>Personnel Management:</u>[6] Direct diverse kitchen and wait staff,[3] promoting teamwork and communication. Provide continual training and coaching to improve employee performance, job knowledge and career advancement; serve as point of contact for benefit information. Write position descriptions and assist in hiring process. Resolve employee issues and provide employee input and feedback to management.

- Logistics Management: Integrate logistics of event planning, including manpower and personnel, supply, training, storage and facilities. Research and plan manpower, equipment and fiscal resources.

- Customer Service: [3] Serve as personal and administrative assistant to First Family. Anticipate and respond to needs, maintaining flexible and service-oriented attitude. Purchase personal and business related goods. Protect privacy and security of First Family at all times.

- Communications/Information Management: Build rapport with internal staff and external departments to improve operations and flow of information. Develop and utilize spreadsheets, databases and documents to improve operational readiness, manage projects and research information. Maintain records on events, including menus, demographics and after-action reports.

Key Accomplishments:

- Plan, coordinate and execute breakfast, lunch, dinner for First Family and other events, including seated dinners and open houses for up to 4,000, with usually 3-5 events per week, up to 2 per day.

- Instituted process changes to alter staff mind-set from reactive to proactive. Created plan to work one meal ahead, enabling accommodation of last minute requests and events.

- Received letter of appreciation from the White House for organizing luncheon attended by President with less than 24-hour notice.

- Implemented industrial production system, automated systems and information management for production, scheduling and cost control.

- Actively built team mindset and morale, achieving improved attendance and performance. Stressed employees' role in organizational success and interdepartmental cooperation.

Downtown Marriot   [dates]
BANQUET CHEF, HARTFORD, CT

- Designed and executed high-end food operations for exclusive catered events. Led production team, communicating customer-directed protocols for national and international clients. Implemented quality assurance and cost control measures. Recognized by management for innovative ideas that improved operational effectiveness.

Aramark   [dates]
FOOD AND BEVERAGE DIRECTOR; CHEF, HARTFORD, CT

- Food and Beverage Director, Executive Dining Room: Sprint Network Services. Designed and directed production of breakfast and lunch menus for service 5 days a week, for 100 employees. Supervised staff of 8. Increased new catering sales and established new client services. Developed and led employee customer service, food production and sanitation training sessions. Updated computer technology to modernize purchasing and just in time inventory systems. Implemented hazardous area critical control points program to promote safe food handling.

- Chef, *Hartford Pride*: Oversaw menu design, coordination and execution for lunch, dinner and catered events on 450-passenger vessel. Led galley team of 20 employees and 2 supervisors. Employed commercial and banquet-style food production methods to achieve time and product management. Directed purchasing, inventory control and training involved with menu execution. Achieved increased efficiencies in purchasing, inventory and scheduling using computer technology. Developed, trained and employees in sanitation and food safety.

EDUCATION

B.S.,[1] Business Administration, Shepherd University, Shepherdstown, W.V.   [date]

A.A.,[1] Restaurant Cooking Skills, Baltimore International College, Baltimore, Md.   [date]

BEFORE

Law Enforcement/Security. Protection Professional. Reverse chronological. Overcrowded, challenging to read. Mid-career government security professional seeks senior position with large corporate firm or government contractor. Requirements: related MA/MS/MBA plus 15 years experience, [1] knowledge of security program planning, funding, and information management systems, [2] ability to coordinate and evaluate staff and programs, [3] adjust plans and schedules to meet requirements, [4] and must be eligible for Secret Security Clearance. [5]

MARION J. JACOBI, CPP
P.O. Box 1111 • San Diego, CA 99999
email: **m_jacobi@juno.com**

Day: (111) 444-6565   Evening: (111) 333-1212

Senior Executive • Law Enforcement & Security Operations

Results-driven **Certified Protection Professional (CPP)** with more than 20 years of progressively responsible national security and federal investigative experience, [1] in the public sector preceded by a career in municipal law enforcement and emergency medical services. A hands-on senior executive with extensive experience planning and managing investigative operations and personnel in a 24/7 environment. Exceptional qualifications in strategic planning, program development and management, budget development and administration, team building, staff development, and human resources management. Advanced knowledge of public administration law, police operations, and national security issues. Strong public speaker. Top Secret Security Clearance. [5] PC proficient.

Areas of Expertise:

- Criminal/Administrative Investigations
- Internal Affairs Investigations
- Physical Security / Antiterrorism Programs
- Investigative Case Management
- Personnel Security/ Background Investigations
- Training & Performance Measurement
- Non-traditional & Traditional Investigations

- Strategic / Budget Planning & Execution
- Law Enforcement Operations & EMS Leadership
- Program Administration / Project Management
- Organizational Management
- Risk, Fraud Management / Regulatory Compliance
- Human Resources Management, Union/Salaried
- Tactical Field Operations / Electronic Surveillance

PROFESSIONAL EXPERIENCE

DEPARTMENT OF HOMELAND SECURITY (DHS)   [dates]
U.S. Immigration and Customs Enforcement (ICE) / Immigration & Naturalization Service (INS)
-- Promoted through increasingly responsible national security supervisory and law enforcement positions.

Section Chief / Supervisory Special Agent, San Diego, Calif. (dates)

Selected to lead DHS/ICE's Law Enforcement Support Center (LESC), a national, non-traditional operations center supporting local, state, and federal law enforcement investigations 24/7, 365 days/year. LESC uses government and commercial criminal history databases to provide current immigration and identity information.

Lead five key departments: Investigations Branch, Computer Services Division, Operations, Program Analysis Unit, and the Administrative Section. Oversee 250+ union and salaried employees. [3] Concurrently serve as Facility Security Manager and NCIC Criminal Justice Information Services Officer. Scope of responsibility:

- Managing development and implementation of internal and external operations protocols affecting investigations, communications, and administration; long and short-range budget planning and execution. [2]
- Provide liaison to FBI, National Crime Information Center (NCIC), Advisory Policy Board, National Law Enforcement Telecommunications System (NLETS) Board of Directors and other investigative agencies. Provide operational, procedural, and compliance oversight.
- Senior advisor to multi-agency state and federal executive working groups on national and international enforcement and security initiatives involving critical infrastructure industries, employment, law enforcement communication, and information sharing.

Current Leadership Projects & National Security Initiatives:

- Consultant for the new Federal Air Marshal NCIC program. Advised on and contributed to creation of policy recommendations for new handheld wireless device initiative.

- Leading and managing Task Force for $200,000 project to transfer the national U.S. Customs and Border Protection (CBP) tip-line (1-800-BE-ALERT) to ICE, merge the two systems, create a new internal telephone system, and new national policies and procedures affecting information processing.
- Consultant to Transportation Security Administration for developing background check procedures.

Major Accomplishments:

- Orchestrated reorganization of NCIC national program, resulting in its centralization at LESC. Totally redesigned policies, procedures, and institutional practices, agency-wide.[4]
- Directed start-up of LESC to provide enhanced investigative support to federal, state, and local security agencies investigating criminal foreign nationals (in the post 9/11 environment). Developed and implemented highly effective new search and response protocols that improved response time and records accuracy.
- Established DHS toll free tip-line (1-866-DHS-2ICE) for public use to facilitate reporting of suspicious activities affecting national security and public safety.
- Streamlined methods for investigative records management, established strategic partnerships with FBI management and staff. Effectively led major organizational changes and staff growth of 280 employees.
- Authored and implemented Emergency Occupant/Site Disaster Recovery Plan and contract security guard post orders, driving improvements in facility security.

Organized Crime Drug Enforcement Task Force Coordinator, INS (dates)
Senior Special Agent, Atlanta, Ga.

Directed the West Central Organized Crime Drug Enforcement Task Force (OCDETF), a region encompassing 12 states and four INS District Offices. Decision-making responsibility for all immigration task force matters, including the role of the regional task force, investigative case planning and management, and INS resource allocations. Advisor to INS district and regional components investigating criminal activities. Federal task force team leader. Evaluated personnel performance, mediated interagency disputes, and led regulatory training.

- One of only two national coordinators selected to define, implement, and manage an international human trafficking investigation. Served as INS liaison to the Criminal Division in the Department of Justice.
- Frequently selected for long-term assignments at the Central Region Investigations Branch in Dallas. Formulated national guidelines on undercover operations and consensual monitoring.

Senior Special Agent, INS, Detroit, Mich. (dates)

- **Violent Gang Task Force (VGTF) Program**: Developed and orchestrated complex narcotics distribution investigations employing standard investigative techniques, undercover operations, and electronic surveillance. Led two long-term investigations as an undercover operative.
- Successfully dismantled active human trafficking/identity document vending organizations. Made calm, sound judgments based on experience and initiated appropriate enforcement actions.

Journeyman Border Patrol Agent, San Diego, Calif. (dates)
Captain / Paramedic Operations Supervisor, Louisville, Ky. (dates)
Police Officer, City of Plantation Police Department, Plantation, Ky. (dates)

EDUCATION, LAW ENFORCEMENT CERTIFICATIONS, & TRAINING

M.A., Security Management,[1] Webster University Graduate School, St. Louis, Mo.

B.S., Liberal Studies, University of the State of New York, Albany, N.Y.

Certified Protection Professional (CPP), [date], American Society for Industrial Security (ASIS)

Certified Police Officer, Kentucky Department of Criminal Justice, Police Academy, Richmond, Ky.

MEMBERSHIP ORGANIZATIONS

American Society for Industrial Security (ASIS) / Federal Law Enforcement Officers Association (FLEOA)

AFTER

Law Enforcement/Security. Protection Professional. Reverse chronological. White space makes reading easier. The previous and identical 2-page resume presented here as a 3-page resume. Mid-career government security professional seeks senior position with large corporate firm or government contractor. Requirements: related MA/MS/MBA plus 15 years' experience,[1] knowledge of security program planning, funding, and information management systems,[2] ability to coordinate and evaluate staff and programs,[3] adjust plans and schedules to meet requirements,[4] and must be eligible for Secret Security Clearance.[5]

MARION J. JACOBI, CPP

P.O. Box 1111 • San Diego, CA 99999

Day: (111) 444-6565   email: **m_jacobi@juno.com**   Evening: (111) 333-1212

Senior Executive • Law Enforcement & Security Operations

Results-driven **Certified Protection Professional (CPP)** with more than 15 years of progressively responsible national security and federal investigative experience,[1] preceded by a career in municipal law enforcement and emergency medical services. A hands-on executive with extensive experience planning and managing investigative operations and personnel in a 24/7 environment. Exceptional qualifications in strategic planning, program development and management, budget development and administration, team building, staff development, and human resources management. Advanced knowledge of public administration law, police operations, and national security issues. Strong public speaker. Top Secret Security Clearance.[5] PC proficient.

Areas of Expertise:

- Criminal/Administrative Investigations
- Internal Affairs Investigations
- Physical Security/Antiterrorism Programs
- Investigative Case Management
- Personnel Security/Background Investigations
- Training & Performance Measurement
- Non-traditional & Traditional Investigations

- Strategic/Budget Planning & Execution
- Law Enforcement Operations & EMS Leadership
- Program Administration/Project Management
- Organizational Management
- Risk, Fraud Management/Regulatory Compliance
- Human Resources Management, Union/Salaried
- Tactical Field Operations/Electronic Surveillance

PROFESSIONAL EXPERIENCE

DEPARTMENT OF HOMELAND SECURITY (DHS)

U.S. Immigration and Customs Enforcement (ICE)/Immigration & Naturalization Service (INS)   [dates]
Section Chief/Supervisory Special Agent, San Diego, Calif.   [dates]

MARION J. JACOBI *Page* 2 Evening: (111) 333-1212

Selected to lead DHS/ICE's Law Enforcement Support Center (LESC), a national, non-traditional operations center supporting local, state, and federal law enforcement investigations 24/7, 365 days/year. LESC uses government and commercial criminal history databases to provide current immigration and identity information.

Lead five key departments: Investigations Branch, Computer Services Division, Operations, Program Analysis Unit, and the Administrative Section. Oversee 250+ union and salaried employees.[3] Concurrently serve as Facility Security Manager and NCIC Criminal Justice Information Services Officer. Scope of responsibility:

- Managing development and implementation of internal and external operation protocols affecting investigations, communications, and administration; long- and short-range budget planning and execution.[2]

- Liaison to FBI, National Crime Information Center, Advisory Policy Board; National Law Enforcement Telecommunications System Board of Directors.

Current Leadership Projects & National Security Initiatives:

- Consultant, Federal Air Marshal NCIC program. Advisor: new handheld wireless device initiative.

- Leading and managing Task Force for $200,000 project to transfer the national U.S. Customs and Border Protection (CBP) tip-line (1-800-BE-ALERT) to ICE, merge the two systems, create a new internal telephone system, and new national policies and procedures affecting information processing.

- Consultant to Transportation Security Administration for developing background check procedures.

Major Accomplishments:

- Orchestrated reorganization of NCIC national program, resulting in its centralization at LESC. Totally redesigned policies, procedures, and institutional practices, agency-wide.[4]

- Directed start-up of LESC to provide enhanced investigative support to federal, state, and local security agencies investigating criminal foreign nationals (in the post 9/11 environment). Developed and implemented highly effective new search and response protocols that improved response time and records accuracy.

- Established DHS toll free tip-line (1-866-DHS-2ICE) for public use to facilitate reporting of suspicious activities affecting national security and public safety.

- Streamlined methods for investigative records management, established strategic partnerships with FBI management and staff. Effectively led major organizational changes and staff growth of 280 employees.

- Authored and implemented Emergency Occupant/Site Disaster Recovery Plan and contract security guard post orders, driving improvements in facility security.

Organized Crime Drug Enforcement Task Force Coordinator, INS   [dates]

Senior Special Agent, Atlanta, Ga.

Directed the West Central Organized Crime Drug Enforcement Task Force (OCDETF), a region encompassing 12 states and four INS District Offices. Decision-making responsibility for all immigration task force matters.

- One of only two national coordinators selected to define, implement, and manage an international human trafficking investigation. INS liaison to Department of Justice.

- Frequently selected for long-term assignments at the Central Region Investigations Branch in Dallas. Formulated national guidelines on undercover operations and consensual monitoring.

Senior Special Agent, INS, Detroit, Mich.   [dates]
- **Violent Gang Task Force (VGTF) Program**: Developed and orchestrated complex narcotics distribution investigations employing standard investigative techniques, undercover operations, and electronic surveillance. Led two long-term investigations as an undercover operative.

- Successfully dismantled active human trafficking/identity document vending organizations. Made sound judgments based on experience; initiated appropriate enforcement actions.

Journeyman Border Patrol Agent, San Diego, Calif.   [dates]

Captain/Paramedic Operations Supervisor, Louisville, Ky.   [dates]

Police Officer, City of Plantation Police Department, Plantation, Ky.   [dates]

EDUCATION, LAW ENFORCEMENT CERTIFICATIONS, & TRAINING

M.A., Security Management,[1] Webster University Graduate School, St. Louis, Mo.   [date]

Certified Protection Professional (CPP), American Society for Industrial Security (ASIS)   [date]

Certified Police Officer, Kentucky Department of Criminal Justice, Police Academy, Richmond, Ky.   [date]

MEMBERSHIP ORGANIZATIONS

American Society for Industrial Security, Federal Law Enforcement Officers Association

Part V
The Part of Tens

The 5th Wave
By Rich Tennant

"This is your resume? A bit long-winded don't you think?"

In this part . . .

*H*ere you find quick tips and checklists to help you put a gleaming shine on the document that sells you. I show you ways to back up your claims. I give you guidance for finding a resume professional, and I close this part by taking you through all the notes your resume needs to hit in one short chapter.

Chapter 18

Ten (×3) Ways to Prove Your Claims

In This Chapter

▶ Number statements to prove your accomplishments

▶ Percentage statements to document your claims

▶ Dollar-amount statements to back your results

So you have excellent communications skills, or you meet people well, or you can make a computer work magic. At least, that's what you assert. How can I (an employer) believe you?

I'm more likely to believe your claims of skills and accomplishments when you back them up with specifics. A good start on backing up your statements is *measuring* them with numbers, percentages, and dollar amounts.

Compare the following statements in Column A with the statements in Column B. Which is the strongest, most attention-grabbing, most convincing?

Column A	*Column B*
Easy Ways to Be More Popular	50 Easy Ways to Be More Popular
Towels on Sale	Towels 40% Off
Designed internal company insurance plan to replace outside plan at great savings.	Designed $30 million self-insured health plan, saving estimated $5 million per year over previous external plan

I think you'll agree that the Column B statements win hands down! The take-home message is *measure, measure, measure.* Look at the following statements in the three categories of numbers, percentages, and dollar amounts. Fill in the blanks as a reminder to measure your accomplishments and results.

with Numbers

__ (#) years of extensive experience in _____ and _____.

2. Won _____ (#) awards for _____.

3. Trained/Supervised _____ (#) full-time and _____ (#) part-time employees.

4. Recommended by _____ (a number of notable people) as a _____ (something good that they said about you) for excellent _____ (an accomplishment or skill).

5. Supervised a staff of _____ (#).

6. Recruited _____ (#) staff members in _____ (period of time), increasing overall production.

7. Sold _____ (# of products) in _____ (period of time), ranking _____ (1st, 2nd, 3rd) in sales in a company of _____ (#) employees.

8. Exceeded goals in __ (#) years/months/days, establishing my employer as _____ (1st, 2nd, 3rd, or whatever number) in industry.

9. Missed only _____ (#) days of work out of _____ (#) total.

10. Assisted _____ (#) (executives, supervisors, technical directors, others).

Say It with Percentages

1. Excellent_____ (your top proficiency) skills, which resulted in _____ (%) increase/decrease in _____ (sales, revenues, profits, clients, expenses, costs, charges).

2. Recognized as a leader in company, using strong skills to effect a/an ____ (%) increase in team/co-worker production.

3. Streamlined _____ (industry procedure), decreasing hours spent on task by ____ (%).

4. Used extensive _____ (several skills) to increase customer/ member base by ____ (%).

5. Financed ____ (%) of tuition/education/own business.

6. Graduated within the top ____ (%) of class.

7. Responsible for an estimated ____ (%) of employer's success in _____ (functional area/market).

8. Resolved customer relations issues, increasing customer satisfaction by ____ (%).

9. Eliminated _____ (an industry problem), increasing productivity by ____ (%).

10. Upgraded _____ (an industry tool), resulting in ____ (%) increase in effectiveness.

Say It with Dollar Amounts

1. Supervised entire _____ (a department) staff, decreasing middle-management costs by ____ ($).

2. Purchased computer upgrade for office, saving the company ____ ($) in paid hours.

3. Eliminated the need for _____ (one or several positions in company), decreasing payroll by _____ ($).

4. Averaged _____ ($) in sales per month.

5. Collected _____ ($) in memberships and donations.

6. Supervised the opening/construction of new location, completing task at _____ ($) under projected budget.

7. Designed entire _____ program, which earned _____ ($) in company revenues.

8. Implemented new _____ system, saving _____ ($) daily/weekly/monthly/annually.

9. Reduced cost of _____ (substantial service) by developing and implementing a new _____ system at the bargain price of _____ ($).

10. Restructured _____ (organization/system/product) to result in a savings of _____ ($)

Chapter 19

Ten Ways to Improve Your Resume

Think your resume could sparkle with a few tweaks? Feeling like you've busted your chops and still are on the outside looking in? Close but no cigar? Here are ten easy fixes to power up your resume to OnTarget status.

Match Your Resume to the Job

To dart past job software filters, a resume must closely meet the requirements in the job description. If you know what company recruiters are looking for, make sure you put it in the top quarter of your resume. If instead you're posting your resume in databanks, research the career field for typical requirements and include those that apply to you.

Use Bulleted Style for Easy Reading

Using one- or two-liners opens up your resume with white space, making it more appealing to read. Professional advertising copywriters know that big blocks of text suffocate readers. Let your words breathe!

Discover Art of Lost Articles

Although using articles — *a, an,* and *the* — in your resume isn't *wrong,* try deleting them for a crisper and snappier end result. Recruiters and employers expect to read resumes in compact phrases, not fully developed sentences. The first person *I* is another word that your resume doesn't need. Look at the following examples:

With Articles	**Without Articles**
I report to the plant manager of the largest manufacturer of silicone-based waxes and polishes.	Report to plant manager of largest manufacturer of silicone-based waxes and polishes.
I worked as the only administrative person on a large construction site.	Worked as only administrative person on large construction site.

Sell, Don't Tell

Forget sticking to the old naming-your-previous-responsibilities routine. Merely listing "Responsible for XYZ" doesn't assure the recruiter that you met your responsibility or that the result of your efforts was worth the money someone paid you.

By contrast, read over your resume and make sure you have answered that pesky "So what?" question, which is lying in ambush for each bit of information you mention. Try to imagine what's running through a recruiter's mind when you relate that you were responsible for XYZ: *So what? Who cares? What's in it for me?* Anticipate those questions and answer them before a recruiter has a chance to toss your resume. (Chapter 10 discusses this advice in more detail.)

Show Off Your Assets

Recruiters are wild about snaring the cream of the crop. If you're in the top 5 percent of any significant group (graduation, sales, attendance record, performance ratings), make sure that fact appears prominently on your resume.

Make Sure Your Words Play Well Together

Old wisdom: Use a lot of action verbs to perk up reading interest in resumes (see Chapter 10). *Later wisdom:* Cash in some of the action verbs for nouns, the keywords that ward off anonymity in sleeping resume databases. *New wisdom:* Use both nouns and verbs.

Just don't mix noun and verb phrases in the same resume section. The following example explains.

> ***Highlights:***
>
> • Founded start-up, achieving positive cash flow and real profits in the first year. (verb)
>
> • President of point-of-sale products. (noun)
>
> • Proven ability for representation of high technology products. (noun)
>
> • Consistently achieved highest profit in 45-year-old company history. (verb)

Change the noun statements to be consistent with the verb statements:

> • Served as president of point-of-sale products.
>
> • Proved ability to represent high-technology products.

Writing instructors call this agreeable notion *parallel construction*.

Reach Out with Strength

Highlight the qualifications and past job activities that speak to the kind of job you want and the skills you want to use. If, for instance, you want to transition from military training to civilian training, remain riveted to your training skills without diluting your message by mentioning your ability to use several simple computer programs.

Don't muddle your resume's message with minor skills or skills you no longer want to use; stay on message.

Trash a Wimpy Objective

Imagine an actor striding onto a stage, stopping, and then standing there like a log addressing the audience: "I came to find out what you can do for me."

Not exactly a curtain raiser — any more than beginning your resume with simply awful objective statements like: "Seeking a chance for advancement," or "where my skills will be utilized."

Retire trite messages like this one: "To obtain a responsible job with challenging and rewarding duties." Does someone out there really want an irresponsible position? One that's dull and unrewarding?

Be an editor! Draw a line through wussy wording that leaves everyone wondering whether you're a washout. Your statement can be simple, yet effective: "Management position in finance where more than ten years' experience will strengthen the bottom line."

Check the Horse's Mouth

Pick up the phone and call the HR department where you want to work and are about to submit your resume. Ask: "Before I send you my resume online, I want to get the facts. Do you accept MS Word attachments, store them as formatted documents, and route them to line managers as images?"

If the answer is *yes,* wrap fish in that ugly ASCII plain text resume and throw it away, reveling in the fact that you get to send the attractive version of your resume. If the answer is *no,* well, good try in this era of transition. After all, ugly is still better than unreadable.

Erase the "Leave-Outs"

Eliminate clutter by removing useless information that doesn't support reasons you're a qualified candidate. Here's a short list of the worst offenders:

- "References available on request." Listing the actual references on your resume is even worse.
- Your Social Security number or driver's license number.
- The date your resume was prepared.
- Your company's telephone number.
- Your high school or grammar school if you're a college graduate.
- Dates you spent involved in college extracurricular activities.
- Dates you were involved with professional or civic organizations unless using them to fill in gaps or add heft to your claims.
- Names of (human) past employers; put these on your reference sheet with contact information.

Chapter 20

Ten Tips for Choosing Professional Resume Help

*I*n addition to reading this book, how do you best come up with a resume that ushers you into prime interviewing territory? Should you hire a professional resume writer or go it alone?

There's plenty to be said in favor of hiring a professional writer, who not only is expert in classic marketing principals but is tuned into the brave new world of job search — from swirling social media to racing-ahead technology.

Professionally crafted resumes not only boost your confidence but actually make money for you by shortening your job search — for example, when you are searching for a $50,000-a-year job, each week of unemployment costs you about $950 in lost pay. The downside is that professional resume creation costs money that you may have budgeted for other current needs. Good arguments exist on both sides of whether you should pay a pro or tackle the writing challenge solo.

Here's my take: I have witnessed dramatically good, life-changing results produced by the efforts of talented professional resume writers. If you want to employ a professional to write your resume and can make the investment, why not?

Organize your own material to present to the professional writer just as you organize your taxes to hand over to an accountant. Organizing your information primes your mind for job interviews.

In an age of personalization — personal financial advisers, personal trainers, personal career coaches — why not a personal resume pro? Prime candidates for resume services are first-time resume writers, people in a competitive professional or managerial job market, people with a checkerboard history, and people who haven't thought about resumes in years. Follow these tips to avoid hacks and select a resume pro wisely.

Choose a Resume Writing Service, Not a Clerical Service

Many clerical services do a competent job of word-processing your resume for a fair price of $100 or so. A clerical service is a useful option if that's all you need.

But most people need much more, and clerical services are a different business from *professional resume writing services.* Clerical services sell processes like keyboarding and printing. Resume firms sell specialized knowledge in fluently articulating what you want to do and the evidence that backs up your claim that you can do it.

A resume pro knows a great deal about the business of marketing you to employers, has the latest trends and buzzwords on tap, and coaches you through potholes in your history.

Ask Around for a Great Resume Pro

After you decide to use a resume professional, your next step is finding a winner. Winners are talented writers who also possess strong analytic skills.

The best way to find a winner is to get a referral, either from a satisfied client or from someone in the business — a local career center consultant, recruiter, or outplacement consultant. Review prospective writers' Web pages to see samples of their work.

If you're being laid off, inquire within your corporate human resource department. These people often know who's doing the best work.

The fact that a resume firm has been in business for a long time and has done thousands of resumes is no guarantee of competence — but it's a sign that some clients must like what they deliver and have spread the word. The acceptance of major credit cards is another indicator of stability.

Request a Free Initial Consultation

Request a free, brief, get-acquainted meeting in person or on the phone. Speak not to the boss or a sales representative, but to the writer. The same firm can have good and poor writers. Ask the writer what general strategy the writer will use to deal with your specific problems. If you don't hear a responsible answer, keep looking.

A responsible answer does not imply discussion of the specifics of how your resume will be handled. Much like people shop retail stores to look at the merchandise and then order from a discount catalog, people shop professional resume services to pick writers' brains and then write their own resumes. Resume pros caught on to this move and developed laryngitis.

Moreover, going into detail about how the resume pro intends to handle your resume is irresponsible before the professional knows more about you. Find out instead about the writer's general approach and viewpoint on the strategies discussed in this book.

Watch Out for Overuse of Forms

Most resume pros ask you to fill out a lengthy, detailed form — much like the one new patients fill out in a doctor's office. The form is a good start, but it's far from enough. Eliminate firms that don't offer dialogue with the writer. The resume pro should interview you to discover your unique experience and strengths. You and the resume pro are colleagues, sharing a task.

The problem with form dependency is you may merely get back your own language prettied up in a glitzy format. That's not what you want a resume pro to do for you.

Look for a Fair Price

Prices vary by locale and depend upon a number of factors, but expect to pay between $250 and $1,000 for most resumes. Single-page junior resumes may cost less. Executive resumes often range between $750 and $2,000.

You pay the most in these situations:

- ✔ **Heavy time investment:** The professional must spend many hours to document your value, as when you're changing careers.

- ✔ **Killer job market:** Hoards of people want the job you want, and the professional has the expertise to make you stand out from the crowd.

✓ **Challenging problem:** When you have a background of job-hopping, employment gaps, and other kinds of issues discussed in Chapter 13, the professional has to have the expertise to present your qualifications in a favorable light.

✓ **Customizing resumes:** If you're using a two-page resume, for example, you can probably pay for a core resume and customize only the first page for each different job, retaining the second page across your search. You pay extra for a few customizations of your core resume to see how it's done.

✓ **Document packages:** Many job seekers now understand that cover letters, cover notes, online profiles, accomplishment sheets, follow-up letters and other career marketing documents described in my book, *Cover Letters For Dummies,* 3rd Edition (Wiley), are the nuts and bolts of 21st century job search and turn to professional resume writers for assistance.

Check Out Samples

Ask the resume pro to show you sample resumes. Choose an expert who is comfortable with state-of-the-art technology (See Chapter 3). Notice the quality of content (Chapter 8) and the resume architecture (Chapter 11).

Take Aim

Customize! For maximum impact, you need to target each resume you send out to a specific employer or career field. Look for a resume pro who understands this concept. You need a resume that has "you" written all over it — *your* theme, *your* focus, and *your* measurable achievements — all matched to a career field you want. Skip over those who sell the same cookie-cutter resume over and over.

Avoid resume pros who offer assembly-line presentations, virtually indistinguishable from thousands of others created by the service. Ignore resume pros who plug your information into a fill-in-the-blanks standard form, garnished with prefab statements. Double ignore those who, even in this digital age, try to cover the sameness of their work by printing out resumes on 11-by-17-inch parchment paper and folding them into a pretentious brief. Employers use these *la-de-da* resumes for kindling.

Consider a Certified Resume Writer

Resume writers who belong to resume-certifying organizations are likely to stay current in resume effectiveness. In alphabetical order, here are selected certifying organizations. The certificate designations awarded by each organization are noted.

Career Directors International (CDI)
Certifications Awarded:
Certified Advanced Resume Writer (CARW)
Certified Expert Resume Writer (CERW)
Certified Resume Specialist (CRS+X)
Master Career Director (MCD)
Certified Employment Interview Consultant (CEIC)
Certified Internet Job Search Expert (CIJSE)
Corrections Career Transition Certified (CCTC)
Certified Military Resume Writer (CMRW)
Certified Federal Resume Writer (CFRW)
Certified Web Portfolio Practitioner (CWPP)
Certified Electronic Career Coach (CECC)
Web site: www.careerdirectors.com
Contact: Laura DeCarlo, laura@careerdirectors.com

Career Management Alliance
Certifications Awarded:
Master Resume Writer (MRW)
Credentialed Career Manager (CCM)
Web site: www.careermanagementalliance.com
Telephone: 603-924-0900 x640
Contact: Liz Sumner, liz@careermanagementalliance.com

The National Resume Writers' Association (NRWA)
Certifications Awarded:
Nationally Certified Resume Writer (NCRW)
Web site: www.nrwaweb.com
Contact: Charlotte Weeks, President; Yvette Campbell, Administrative Manager, adminmanager@thenrwa.com

Professional Association of Resume Writers & Career Coaches (PARW/CC)
Certifications Awarded:
Certified Professional Resume Writer (CPRW)
Certified Employment Interview Professional (CEIP)
Certified Professional Career Coach (CPCC)
Web site: www.parw.com
Contact: Frank Fox, parwhq@aol.com

Resume Writing Academy (RWA)
Certification Awarded:
Academy Certified Resume Writer (ACRW)
Web site: www.resumewritingacademy.com
Contact: Louise Kursmark, louise@resumewritingacademy.com

Visit the Web sites of the above organizations to locate members who are well qualified to write your resume — no matter where you live. You can reside thousands of miles away from the resume writer and still get a superb product.

Remember That Design Counts

Review pointers in Chapter 11 to recall how a top resume is supposed to look. Clunky and junky is out; distinctive professional is in. Before signing on the dotted line, ask the professional(s) whom you're considering to show you the variety of designs recommended for the type of job you hope to land.

Know That a Cheap Resume Is No Bargain

Appreciate the hidden costs of a poor resume: A hack job can cost you good job interviews.

When the finished product is in your hands, you should be able to say:

- ✔ This is an OnTarget resume. It shows that my qualifications are a great match for the job I want.

- ✔ This resume suggests that I offer the employer a good return on investment by showing how I can make or save the company more money than I cost.

- ✔ I like reading my resume; it won't put the recruiter to sleep.

Chapter 21

Your Ten-Point Resume Checklist

In This Chapter

▶ Confirming your resume is a match for job requirements

▶ Smacking down tacky resume errors

▶ Standing back for a fresh look at the impression you're making

*B*efore going public with your resume, give it a final walk-through. Give yourself a checkmark for each item only when your resume meets that OnTarget standard. Each checkmark is worth 10 points. If you don't get a score of 100, go back to your keyboard and try again.

Tit for Tat

You remember the new drive to customize resumes by matching your qualifications (skills, education) with the specific requirements of a job, or by matching your qualifications with the expected qualifications in a career field. If you write a two-page resume, you remember to customize the first page, even if you do not customize the second page. (Chapter 6 discusses the customizing requirement and why it's so important.)

Image and Focus

You don't say the equivalent of, "I thought you might have an opening I could fill," but state what you want to do for an employer and why you're qualified to do it. You consider your resume's overall impression — its look and feel. Your resume has a unifying theme: You present yourself as focused, not merely desperate to accept any job. (Refresh your recall of focus in Chapter 9 and of image in Chapter 11.)

Format and Style

You select the best format for your situation. For example, *reverse chronological* when staying in the same field, or *functional* or *hybrid* when changing fields. (Chapter 9 covers formats.)

Accomplishments and Skills

You directly relate your skills to the skills/competencies needed for the job. You cite at least one accomplishment for each skill or competency. You measure any claim you can by using numbers, percentages, or dollar amounts. (Turn to Chapter 18 for measurement tips.) You highlight results, not just a list of duties and responsibilities. Try using the PAR formula: state the *problem*, relay the *action* you took, and show your *results*.

Language and Expressions

You make the most of your word choices. You use adequate keywords (nouns) to make your resume searchable by software. You use action verbs to put vitality in your resume for human eyes. You eliminate words that don't directly support your bid for the job you want, as well as such meaningless words and phrases as "References available." You use industry jargon where appropriate, but you translate acronyms, technical jargon, or military lingo into easy-to-understand English. (Chapter 10 reviews word usage.)

Content and Omissions

Your content supports your goal. You begin with either a skills/capabilities summary, a bulleted list of accomplishments, a profile of your value, or a job objective. That is, you start off with a bang to grab a reader's attention.

Next, you state your experience that shows you can do what you claim you can do. You begin with your education only if you're a new graduate with virtually no experience, or if your target job is related to education and training. You don't list personal information that isn't related to the job you seek, such as marital status, number of children, or height. (For a refresher on content, see Chapter 8.)

Length and Common Sense

You use a length that makes sense for the amount of information you're presenting. Even though today's resumes are shorter and crisper (because most are crafted for digital distribution), certain guidelines remain. You limit your resume to one or two pages if you're lightly experienced, or two or three pages if you're substantially experienced. These page counts are only guidelines — your resume can be longer when necessary to put your qualifications in the best light. Additionally, your resume can stretch even longer when it's a professional resume or a CV (curriculum vitae), which I describe in Chapter 9.

Don't jam-pack a jumble of text on one page, making your resume way too difficult to read and way too easy to ignore.

Social Media and Other New Things

You tailored a message showing your value to an employer. Consider this criterion when you offer your resume on LinkedIn, Facebook, Twitter, another social media site, or on teeny-weeny mobile screens. Although seasoned workplace veterans come across as "with it" and youthful by using the new tools, the fact that you're up-to-date alone isn't enough to get you hired. (If you did not use one of the new platforms to convey your resume, count this criterion as a "free throw" and give yourself 10 points.)

Sticky Points and Sugarcoating

You thoughtfully handle all problem areas, such as grouping irrelevant, long-ago, part-time, and temporary jobs. You account for all the gaps in the time frame of your resume. You scour your resume for possible hidden negatives and eliminate them as described in Chapter 13.

Proofreading and More Proofreading

Your resume contains no typos, no grammar disasters — no errors of any kind. You not only use your computer's spell checker, but you double- and triple-check) your resume. You ask others to carefully read it. Typos are hot buttons to many employers — two goofs and you're gone.

Resume Power in the Brave New World of Job Chasing

In this age of now, new, and next — when a seemingly endless stream of platforms for communication engulfs us — resumes are ageless.

Resumes endure as the most important personal power tool in job-finding because the medium is not the message in your search for new employment.

No matter the delivery system employers use to receive your resume — e-mail, courier, postal mail, e-reader, tablets, smartphone, social media, Web portfolios, a company employee, or carrier pigeon — nepotism aside, employers always seek to hire people whose qualifications meet their requirements.

Employers want your message to put them in a comfort zone where they're assured that you'll make more money for them, deliver greater benefits to them, or save them more time and treasure than it costs to hire you.

That's the strategic message you must deliver in each resume. Anything less is a roll of the dice.

Plunge into writing your OnTarget core resume sooner rather than later. Accomplishing this important step right now makes it much easier to whip out customized editions as needed, bringing you leagues closer to finding the job you want.

All best wishes for your happy success,

Joyce Lain Kennedy, *Resumes For Dummies,* 6th Edition

San Diego, California

Index

• G •

• H •

• Z •

...ple & Macs

...ad For Dummies
...8-0-470-58027-1

...hone For Dummies,
... Edition
...8-0-470-87870-5

...acBook For Dummies, 3rd
...ition
...8-0-470-76918-8

...ac OS X Snow Leopard For
...mmies
...8-0-470-43543-4

...siness

...okkeeping For Dummies
...8-0-7645-9848-7

...o Interviews
...r Dummies,
...d Edition
...8-0-470-17748-8

...sumes For Dummies,
... Edition
...8-0-470-08037-5

...rting an
...line Business
...r Dummies,
... Edition
...8-0-470-60210-2

...ock Investing
...r Dummies,
...d Edition
...8-0-470-40114-9

...ccessful
...e Management
...r Dummies
...8-0-470-29034-7

Computer Hardware

BlackBerry
For Dummies,
4th Edition
978-0-470-60700-8

Computers For Seniors
For Dummies,
2nd Edition
978-0-470-53483-0

PCs For Dummies,
Windows
7 Edition
978-0-470-46542-4

Laptops For Dummies,
4th Edition
978-0-470-57829-2

Cooking & Entertaining

Cooking Basics
For Dummies,
3rd Edition
978-0-7645-7206-7

Wine For Dummies,
4th Edition
978-0-470-04579-4

Diet & Nutrition

Dieting For Dummies,
2nd Edition
978-0-7645-4149-0

Nutrition For Dummies,
4th Edition
978-0-471-79868-2

Weight Training
For Dummies,
3rd Edition
978-0-471-76845-6

Digital Photography

Digital SLR Cameras &
Photography For Dummies,
3rd Edition
978-0-470-46606-3

Photoshop Elements 8
For Dummies
978-0-470-52967-6

Gardening

Gardening Basics
For Dummies
978-0-470-03749-2

Organic Gardening
For Dummies,
2nd Edition
978-0-470-43067-5

Green/Sustainable

Raising Chickens
For Dummies
978-0-470-46544-8

Green Cleaning
For Dummies
978-0-470-39106-8

Health

Diabetes For Dummies,
3rd Edition
978-0-470-27086-8

Food Allergies
For Dummies
978-0-470-09584-3

Living Gluten-Free
For Dummies,
2nd Edition
978-0-470-58589-4

Hobbies/General

Chess For Dummies,
2nd Edition
978-0-7645-8404-6

Drawing
Cartoons & Comics
For Dummies
978-0-470-42683-8

Knitting For Dummies,
2nd Edition
978-0-470-28747-7

Organizing
For Dummies
978-0-7645-5300-4

Su Doku For Dummies
978-0-470-01892-7

Home Improvement

Home Maintenance
For Dummies,
2nd Edition
978-0-470-43063-7

Home Theater
For Dummies,
3rd Edition
978-0-470-41189-6

Living the
Country Lifestyle
All-in-One
For Dummies
978-0-470-43061-3

Solar Power Your Home
For Dummies,
2nd Edition
978-0-470-59678-4

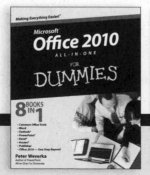

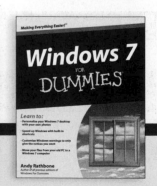

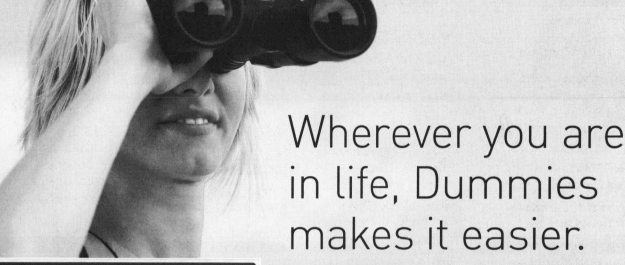

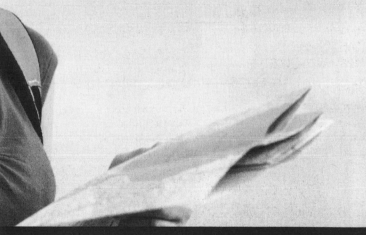

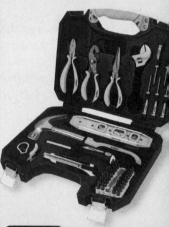